IN THE FIRE

IN THE FIRE
by
Lee Lozowick

I.D.H.H.B., Inc.
Nevada City, Ca.

HOHM PRESS
Tabor, N.J.

Dedicated to:

Chris Dashielle Smith
and
John Patrick McGovern

The first editors, (performed first editing) without whom this work would not have been possible.

co-published by

I.D.H.H.B., Inc.
P.O. Box 370
Nevada City, CA.
95959

HOHM PRESS
P.O. Box 75
Tabor, N.J.
07878

Editor's Note:

The sections of the text indicated by asterisks were written by Chris Smith, a member of the Hohm Community.

Printed in the U.S.A.

ISBN: 0-89556-002-X
LCC: 78-54139

Preface

Here is a fire. It is a fire that burns down walls of suffering, walls of ignorance, walls that we have set up between ourselves and truth. Before we enter this fire, consider what is invested in our walls: cherished assumptions and desires, the security of separateness, the view of ourselves that we have maintained up until now. Let us consider this now, for as soon as we enter this fire, there is no returning to the comfortable fictions of our lives. Once we have been singed, there is no rest until we are burned up completely.

Lee Lozowick has appeared in the world, proclaiming that God is all there is, and that he exists consciously as God. Some of us have stumbled into his company. Like anyone else, we had our personal histories, our identities, our likes and dislikes. Like anyone else, we searched for happiness, and saw our lives as that search. What did we know of God? There was only the ideal of a sought-for happiness, urging us on. And as we entered into relationship with Lee, the possibility presented itself that he might be able to provide us with happiness, that he might be our goal. To some, he appeared as the perfect friend. To others, he was the perfect lover. Perhaps, we thought, he could give us what we have always dreamed of: fulfillment.

A surprise was in store. Lee did not give us anything, but instead demanded everything from us. He maintained that there was nothing to be searched for, that life was only pure devotion in God. He did not fulfill our dreams, but demanded that we wake up from the dream. We went to him, heavy with ourselves, expecting solace, but what we were confronted with was fire. Our relationship with him was not what we thought it would be; it was a living demand that everything be given up, that our precious selves be consumed until there was nothing but bare, simple devotion.

Words came to our lips: "God", "Lord", "Divine", but before we could safely decide their meaning, we stopped in wonder. This relationship with Lee was more profound than we had bargained for, and more simple. We found ourselves face-to-face with one who defied our search for happiness, who only offered relationship with him. We were tricked into life, tricked into the company of the Lord: Satsang. A community had begun.

Questions were asked, doubts arose, the crisis and conflict of our lives came to the surface. Lee Lozowick confronted our falsehood, strategy, and pretension. But through it all, a strange and beautiful recognition was present. The boundaries we had placed on our relationship with Lee could not contain it. God is, it said. This awakened guru, Lee Lozowick, is really our very self, and our relationship with him is simply perfect, a constant expression of delight in the Divine.

Even the greediest person could not help but wish to share this joy with others. It is our joy to be able to let you know that the Divine is very present in the world. But it is present not as your salvation, but as a demand to live the Divine. This book is such a demand. You must come to meet it, so that it will confront you where you are. Its power in your life will depend on what you give to it.

Each chapter is a new frustration and a new beginning: a frustration of everything that is expected of the enlightened guru, of every attempt to tame and subdue the Divine; and a beginning of real sadhana, the very present Divine active as our ordinary, functional life. The humor in these pages is not easy, it takes genuine strength to live that humor, and the willingness to be afraid without running from that fear. It is not logic at work here, but Presence; and its devotion to who you are is uncompromising. Lee Lozowick desires only that you be a perfect devotee of the Lord, that you recognize him as your nature, and, in bare devotion, realize life in its fullness.

These talks were given by Lee to his community. That makes them no less relevant to the life of the reader. If you are open to Grace, your present nature, you will have already entered this fire. In the Presence of Lee; in gladness, awe, uncertainty and strength; in the sacrifice which is humor; we offer this book to all.

The community of Hohm

Foreword

The Guru's Grace

You don't dissolve ego structures in yourself. That's what the guru's function is, and always has been. His function is to dissolve those with the rays of Grace. If you try to dissolve your own ego elements through some action that you take or don't take, you simply enhance the ego, and bring yourself further and further away from real liberation. But at first you will no doubt want to bring about your own enlightenment through work on the ego. You bring the ego to its knees and crush it, and finally dissolve it, and then after the battle is all over, stand there in the ego of enlightenment. Eventually you will have to give up, admit you've still got an ego, and let the guru do it. As an enlightened being, you cannot let the guru dissolve the ego structure for you. So the guru is helpless to help you when you are enlightened.

In an ordinary state of humanity, man is already "as if" enlightened. Only after a tremendous amount of work on self does an individual realize that he is not liberated, and some work still needs to be done. And then only after self-enlightenment can an individual genuinely realize where the trap is, in self-enlightenment, and recognize the guru's function, and then initiate the function of the guru to bring about liberation and awakening. You understand now why you've been asked to do the things you've been asked to do, and why you've been given the instructions you've been given, and what it is that was really required of you. This is *your* show. But you must learn how to use the various elements within the trap in order to get out of it.

To use the guru properly, you've got to turn him on. To turn the guru on you must have overcome at least some elements of ego. You must be able to ask for help. You must be able to receive help. You must be able to use the help you receive. You must be able to pay attention, to look for the help that you receive, and you must trust the guru to fulfill his function of waking you up when you're ready to awaken, through the use of coincidences. Leave all of the conditions of the process of your liberation to him, and simply be willing to have those conditions be brought about and enjoy the benefits of them.

So now you can see why individuals who are forcefully enlightened, aggressively enlightened, passionately enlightened, have a long long way before they can ask for help. There is a great distance between the guru and an individual who is enlightened.

This creates a gap which forms between most individuals and the guru. It is the gap between humanity and liberation. The truly enlightened individual sees the guru as it is, a purely functional device, which was created in the first moment of creation, the only moment of creation, to bring about liberation, awakening, and the maintenance of existence. You could say that the function of the guru is as the guide in the beginning and the guide in the end, or if you like, a conductor. He is the midwife of consciousness.

I hope you see where humor comes into this. There is another element, in the mechanics of "switching on the guru", which is humor without arrogance or sarcasm. Genuine humor, good humor, you must be able to receive and give and share humor with the guru. This is why the guru is often called "The Good Humor Man." When he rings the Bell of Dharma, go get your ice cream, and be sure and ask him about today's special.

The process of liberation and awakening starts when you walk up to the guru, meet him face to face, and say, "I'm ready to start the process of liberation and awakening." From that moment on, he will activate a chain of coincidences which bring you inevitably to the awakened state. Until you can walk up to him and ask for this, you're stuck with karmic repetition. I hope you realize what a wonderful opportunity you have to do this now, in life, when it's relatively easy, and things aren't happening too fast for you.

Of course he is always available and always will be available, but that's no reason to put it off. You may not always know about it. So when you hear the bell, you'd better run out there quick with your quarter before the ice cream truck goes on to the next block.

E.J. Gold
Nevada City, 1978

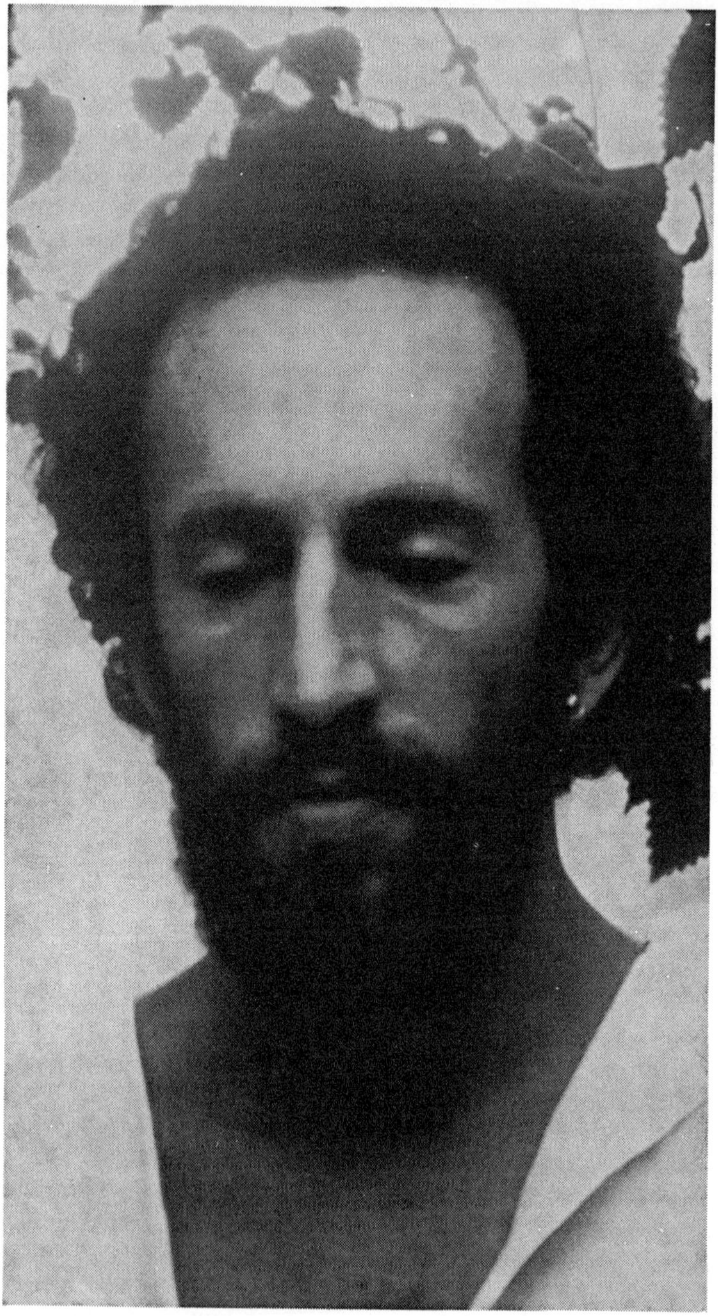

ONE

SOCIETY IS NOT prepared for the advent of one such as I. Society has never been prepared for the advent of such a one. Throughout the ages, in every time and place, there have been those individuals who have shown, by their very lives, the transcendence of the limitation of the mind, the limitation of the body, the limitation of separative self-existence. Never has the world recognized them for who they are.

The Divine has created the worlds, this world and all worlds. The Divine continues to create worlds upon worlds, universes upon universes. There has been no place and no time where the advent of one such as myself has been accepted with open arms and rejoicing. Always the God-realized ones have been ridiculed, persecuted, prosecuted. And always there have been a fortunate few that have been able to recognize, understand, and devote their lives to such a one as I am.

The prosecution of the awakened one occurs by the very nature of the human separate self-sense, for anyone that claims to bring one to unqualified awakening, will always bring fear into the hearts, into the very souls of men.

The traditions that have promised union, and have never done anything to shatter the suffering of separation, have always been accepted with open arms. Their visible acceptance is demonstrated by the cults that have flourished around them, with their widespread belief systems, intricate philosophies, and followers in the millions. Yet the true guru, the illumined one, has never found more than a few true devotees, a small family to be with, because the raw condition of the Divine is so absolute, so uncompromising and critically undermining, that very few have the strength to deal with the actual Divine itself.

The Godman annihilates the misery of sleep and unconsciousness, and those who are asleep and unconscious harbor a great terror of annihilation. Now there is Lee Lozowick; living, moving, demanding of those who come near him, who sit with him, to understand and awaken to the fullness of God. Some few are beginning to understand. And it is only some few who will ever understand. Many others are drawn, many others are comforted, many others are excited by the community, and almost all are afraid, even though they have felt, for the first time in their life, the true condition of love in the world. It is strange how the absolute compassion of the guru can inspire such fear. Fear is still running rampant, running up and down the spine, filling the head, filling the belly, filling the body at all levels, because the advent of Lee Lozowick means that there are those who are going to be completely and totally annihilated in the Divine. There are going to be those few whose self sense is going to be irrevocably obliterated, for there is only God. Only God. Why look for many other things? Why look for degrees or accomplishments? There is only God, nothing else.

The advent of one such as myself is crucial to the very existence of the world. Every world and every place exists for only one reason: the humor of the Divine. And it is only those who are awake as the Divine who can express and enjoy this humor functionally and consciously. Without those awake as the Divine, this world would literally have no reason for being. Its existence would not only be unnecessary, it would also be undesirable. And in fact, worlds have been terminated because the humor of the Divine became archaic, reified, petrified.

The true guru lives in the world hidden from public view because the Divine condition is so joyous that it is beyond belief, so raw that it is critical to the very existence of the separate self. This condition is so profound that the one living it weeps at the rising of the sun, laughs at the twitter of a bird, plays with the leaves, the rocks, and the grains of sand. This one watches the play go on watches the curtain rise and fall, taking curtain call after curtain call, endlessly.

The advent of this one in this age, as in every age, is for the purpose of propagating the real existence of the world itself. This world only exists to please the Divine. And the supreme pleasure that the Divine recognizes in the world is its own joy and humor realized in those who are awake as its very self, alive in its true nature. This awakening is not to the separate self of the mind, or the soul, or the body. This supreme pleasure that the Divine derives from the world is in those who are fully awake to the wild, humorous, all-embracing, unlimited nature of the Divine itself. They are those who have been literally destroyed in the Divine, whose separate sense of being, of body, mind, soul, spirit, person, will, and ego has been absolutely undermined and thoroughly eradicated. All that is left is God, the joy that is prior to all, prior to the earth, the solar systems and the universe as well.

It is important for those who have been joyously offended by the Divine, by the raw condition of God as it manifests functionally in the world, to understand this tradition of the guru, for it has always existed. It has never been new and it has never really been radical. It has only been unconventional, and will always continue to be.

Those who choose not to accept the functional condition of the Divine should recognize and understand the fact that they owe their lives to the advent of the God-realized one in the world. If this one were not here, they would not exist, functionally, mentally or physically. They would be a nameless, mindless atom, a particle blowing about in infinity, with no possibility of ever living in the joy of God.

There are no degrees. There is God and there is suffering. The guru exists as the absolute condition of both. Those who refuse to see, those who continue to search, get the pain and the suffering. Those who are only interested in God will awaken in God. There are no degrees, no almosts, just one or the other. You are suffering or you are not. Which of the two you choose is up to you. The guru has nothing to do with that; blame him if you like and remain in your suffering. Become him, and there is eternal joy.

I am here with this message now, and, of course, this message has always been here. I have always been here, in different forms and with different names. I am here in many forms even now. The message is: wake up. There is nothing to be attained. All one needs to realize is that which already is, the happiness and humor of God. And the way to do that is to allow the guru to undermine your suffering through confrontation, crisis and demand, to completely undermine all forms of hanging on to the delusion of separation. Ultimately you are backed into a corner, and the only choice left to you is God. Total awakening can only come from the Presence of the condition that is the guru.

I am not interested in partial measures. I am not interested in just sitting here and letting people meditate on me. What I am interested in is: either wake up or don't wake up. That requires personal relationship. The Divine will obliterate those who come to me and live this relationship. This is a promise and a warning: if you approach Lee Lozowick in devotion, you will be undone. You don't have to be undone twice.

TWO

THIS TEACHING IS absolutely complete...because Lee Lozowick is. That is the only reason. Not because of language, not because of what I have written or said. The only reason that this teaching is complete is because Lee Lozowick woke up. I am the guru by virtue of that awakening.

The beauty of the guru is that even in contradiction somebody is served. The perfection of the guru is that he exists as absolute contradiction and absolute enjoyment. My perfect contradiction is that there is no real work to be done. Everything is already complete, already perfect. That will inevitably disorient you, who always assume that something must be done and that nothing is perfect. If you are going to avoid disorientation in your life, you are not going to know enlightenment, because enlightenment comes out of that confusion and uncertainty, which is beauty. If you weren't uncertain, you would have a problem. You might be apathetic or satisfied, which would be disastrous. You are all entangled in dilemma, and that is great, it gives us good ore to work with, something to forge happy devotees out of.

Many of you have recognized your act, your various games, and how you relate to those around you. It is still from an ego viewpoint; there is still a sense of you perceiving your personal act. You need to recognize that the whole act of perceiving your act is just a higher form of strategy. There are an infinite number of psychological strategies that can be played on the field of earth, on the field of your life. An infinite number. Please don't be concerned with recognizing an infinite number of strategies. Recognize the nature of strategy itself.

You assume that I am your teacher. I am your guru. Our relationship is not merely that of a learning process. There is an assumption that this relationship is based on, so that if I ask you to do something, you do it. It means something; that's why you listen to me. The assumption at the outset of our relationship is that what I do, I do for your awakening to God.

It is not the form of God that is relevant to true spiritual life. It is the Heart of the form, untrammeled by tradition, unbound by words or conventional meanings. Every true spiritual master throughout history was condemned to the loneliness of the company of a very few who desired God so deeply and fully that they saw through the veils of ignorance and the forms of contradiction. Everyone else was beguiled by the form.

The guru exists as the very Divine condition: raw, open, alive, and unbounded. Anyone coming to me will not be allowed to play the same old game. Anyone coming to me will not be allowed to escape the recognition of the life of misery, dilemma and separation. The guru brings one face to face with oneself, directly, quickly and easily. Most people run like hell from me, because the last thing they want is to realize that their whole life has been totally useless. The form of your life means nothing, only your devotion to the lord is meaningful, appropriate, joyous. All other activity is bullshit.

People are too stupid to appreciate the Divine in raw form. They need Christmas tree ornaments to hide the truth from them, to make God acceptable, tame, something you can bring out on Sunday for guests but never give any real attention to. The guru is God, absolute and uncompromising. The seeker who is glued to his deluded search doesn't want to see me. He wants to see some asshole who pretends to be humble, loving and compassionate, but who is in reality just as much a seeker as all the rest.

Society is full of "gurus" who play up to the desires, wishes and expectancies of seekers. They will coddle you, rock you to sleep in their spiritual arms while singing you a mantric lullabye to dull your senses and dope you into deeper slumber. Such a one will never awaken you, but will only keep you rooted in your search. I will not do that. The process of my being here is not to fulfill expectancy. It is not to be the way you think I should be. And it is not to be understandable. The problem with most teachers is that they are so understandable, so rational, so perfectly clear. They never get beyond mind, never force you beyond your assumed limitation. They are limited by having to perform for you, and they do it very well, it is a comfortable arrangement. I will not fulfill your expectancy on any level. Not because someone has anything to say about that, but because that is and will always be the nature of the Divine.

The process of this relationship, satsang, is to assure that you understand what is, perfectly. The Divine paradox, by its very nature, cannot be grasped intellectually or conceptually. The mind cannot understand contradiction. No matter what answer I or anyone else will ever give you, no matter how momentarily comforting it is, or how well you can relate to or identify with it, no verbal answer is truly satisfying. No verbal answer will convince you of anything, and especially not of who I am. At best it will be a pacifier, and most children outgrow that.

The absolute understanding is beyond all of that. And when you understand, you will understand. There will not be any discussion, and it will not be anything like what you expect. Just recognize that the more you build up expectancy, the more you force the Divine to undo that expectancy, dramatically and with flair.

The act of objective questioning is solely motivated by the demand for "proof" at varying levels. It can only serve up to a point of diminishing returns and ultimate obstruction. If you have to state a fact with a tone that questions, it is merely your strategy, your dilemma exhibiting itself. It is either telling me that what I have said is what you already know, or that what I say is just obvious. Such crap is your way of reinforcing your belief that you are alive. You are not.

The only proof I can offer is this Heart, Grace, my very self, the absolute Divine, God. Be open to that answer; don't be satisfied with temporary experiences or disappointed with your lack of intellectual appeasement. Intellectual acceptance is at best a way to help you confirm and justify your choice of teachers, your view of the guru, and at worst your excuse for your real lack of commitment and devotion. That won't last long in my company.

Know that when I answer you via language, through these conventional channels of communication, that the real answer is not in the words. The real answer is only my Heart, only knowable, not understandable or reasonable. Know this so that you will stay with the guru long enough for him to take your life. Don't run because he doesn't keep feeding you the mind-mush you've been weaned on.

A pupil never learns anything if he remains a pupil, locked in his schoolhouse. You must become perfect devotees of the lord. You must be simply satisfied to gaze upon him, to sit at his feet. Without any consideration for any other relationship, any aspect of the world, you must in the culminating point of your sadhana become a perfect devotee of the lord, and only that. Simply be happy in his Presence, in the fire of satsang. Have no other concern, thought, or enjoyment, simply that. For that is prior to all concepts, structures, ideals and goals. That is all there is.

Waking up is the first step, not the end result. After you wake up, the process is to integrate what is going on into the world, into life, not to say, "Oh, I'm awake. Now I can go sit on a mountaintop or go out in the woods and camp out all alone and not be with people." Awakening does not isolate you, it reveals you as relationship. It is recognizing at a gut level that you are already the Divine, simply present, and that there is nothing you can do about it, or would want to do about it, for that matter. For it is very fine to be that way, to recognize and partake of Divine humor in all activity. There is no choice about who you are. You have already made it, you are alive. There is no way you can get out of that. People who commit suicide are in for a big surprise because it is impossible to end it.

There is only service, not attainment of anything. When you are a perfect devotee, service is the way things are. It is the natural course of life. When you are not a devotee, service is a duty, something you "should" do. The last thing the mind will do is selfless service. That is the very last thing any ego, any person, will want to do. The purpose and function of the guru is to elicit total devotion and truly selfless service in you. If you have the option of leaving me and going to somebody else, you are never going to do selfless service. You will serve in the conventional sense, you will help out. Yet you will still be avoiding God. The direct relationship with me, satsang, provides the only opportunity for selfless service.

Devotee: Self-less? Does that mean losing my self, losing my identity?

Lee: Right! The process of Grace in satsang totally consumes you. As long as you are moving yourself, you aren't being moved by Grace. Never the twain shall meet. In order for you to be open to Grace, I demand nothing less than absolute devotion to me as guru. Period.

You need to be prepared to live in satsang. You are not going to be able to just come and fool around. Satsang is a word that, loosely translated, means "communion with the Divine". There are those, and quite a few of them, who "give" what they call satsang. Anyone can use the word, obviously, claiming to be a realized meditation teacher, yogi, or whatever. Satsang is never "given" by choice. It is an absolute relationship, not some superficial offering of a philosophy or teaching.

The process of true satsang is the personal, sacrificial relationship with the guru. Being Alive in satsang is living as the recognition of this relationship at all times, in every situation, and at all levels. It is consciously being in my company. When you sit with me physically, it is a very formal process.

There is a condition that exists called Grace. I am that very condition, functional and Alive. I am not an extension of the condition, or a messenger of God, or a child of God. I am literally this condition. When you turn to me, this condition undermines your separate existence. There is nothing to do, it just works. When you are not turned to me, the condition virtually doesn't work. It is very simple.

This Divine condition, realization, is unlike anything that has ever been written, said, or implied about it. It is just unexplainable. Communication, by the very nature of language itself, is insufficient when it comes to God. It cannot be defined, no matter how sharp your intellect is. You don't know until you are there, until you realize that there is no "there" to be. You need to awaken to realization, not merely know something in your head.

It is interesting being realized, because it is at the same time the most delightful, humorous state in the universe. It is the most peaceful and pleasant state in the world, because I recognize that I have no free will. I do not control or manipulate anything. I am only God. I don't look for the pot of gold at the end of the rainbow. I am more than content with life, and my enjoyment is never exhausted.

At the same time it is the most frustrating state, because recognizing that there is only God is ultimately caring for each of you, not just talking about love for humanity. I care not for who you think you are, but for who you are but do not know. People do not want to know. Most people do not want God. They run scared from the Divine, even while they talk and think about God. They try to flee from this relationship.

It is ultimately frustrating because I can give you nothing. I am complete only, simply present. I am the same one that has always been: Krishna, Buddha, Jesus; the same one that will always be. And none of the manifestations of this one, as great and as strong as they have been, have ever been able to give it to a single person. Not ever. That is the paradox. I cannot give it to you, for I am you to begin with.

Ultimately I don't care. At the same time, the only thing that I want to do is give it to you, more than anything else in the world. That is the contradiction of the guru. It is entirely up to the openness you approach me with. If you approach me open, it happens quickly. If you approach me closed and tight, you either leave or it happens slowly and painfully.

The guru's requirements are merely appropriate activity. They are only for the purpose of integrating spiritual life very functionally in your activity. They are not to be mistaken for goals or for means toward a goal. The pain you experience in fulfilling them is your resistance to me, your protection from Grace. I don't enjoy seeing or hearing that you are in pain. It doesn't comfort me to know that you are suffering, bound in your isolation and ignorance. I don't derive pleasure from watching you on the edge of depression, on the edge of anger, on the edge of whatever you are on the edge of all the time.

Realize that I don't have any answers for you when you ask about that kind of stuff, when you ask, "Why am I depressed?" I don't have any answer. I very simply sit as I sit, present as I am before you. Just this. It is very simple: wake up. Humor demands it. Wake up and know me in my true form, in my laughing, eternally playful form.

* * * *

Newcomers to the community arrive laden with hopes, expectations, and motives. Sometimes they do not recognize their search for fulfillment, and express themselves only in curiosity or interest. In other cases, they feel a need for something to relieve their pain. If they have been involved in spiritual seeking, they come with a desire to be enlightened or liberated. In any case, whether they know it or not, they come in the midst of suffering, and see Lee as a solution to the problem they assume. They do not have any idea of what is involved in the process of spiritual life in Lee's company.

The first thing the new member of Hohm has to deal with is the degree of his or her commitment. There is a tendency, reinforced by conventional religion, to view spiritual life as a pastime, an activity which is added on to normal life. There is an assumption in the Hohm community, on the other hand, that spiritual life is a twenty-four-hour-a-day affair. Anyone wishing to come Hohm must recognize that one is committing one's entire life to God. This is usually very disconcerting, since most people are simply not prepared to make such an absolute commitment.

A common misconception of this commitment is that it is an affirmative action which is performed once, after which one is "committed" to God. One soon learns that this is not and cannot be the case. People do not have the capability of such an action; at most it is a meaningless gesture to decide "once and for all" that God is primary. The commitment must be made continually, in the light of all activities in life being founded in that commitment. The form of one's life is brought into accord with the primacy of the Divine: practically, in the fulfillment of the guru's requirements for appropriate, functional life; and inclusively, in reaffirming the commitment throughout all activity.

People inevitably try to make a "sure thing" out of their

commitment by persuading themselves that what they are involved in is valid. They have to realize that it is an act of faith that connects them with the guru. They are committed to doing what the guru says through that act of faith, and not through any mental process of justification or reasoning. The commitment has nothing to do with what one conceives God or the guru to be; in fact, it is the very nature of commitment to be independent of all that.

What one thinks or believes God to be is irrelevant to community life. One's actual, felt need for God is what is important for one entering Hohm. One is required to recognize the difference between that need and the desire for personal satisfaction. All people approach Lee looking for something to gain, so it is essential that they know beforehand that Lee will always frustrate that. One comes to the guru apparently looking for release from suffering. Yet when one is confronted with the guru's Presence, which does not recognize the life of suffering as valid, the reaction is to vehemently defend the existence of one's suffering. Thus, the new member of the community is faced with the fact that his commitment is not to God, but to his suffering, and that his approach to the guru is founded in that.

THREE

ONE OF THE most played down aspects of spiritual life is commitment. Everybody talks about all of these high ideals and transcendent truths, and the very basic need for commitment is rarely mentioned.

Your commitment to true spiritual life is a wedge that will allow Grace to rip through all of your delusory preconceptions of the Divine. Grace is present, here and everywhere. Opening up to it is a matter of absolute commitment to God, and nobody can say for you that you've made that commitment. You will know yourself if you have. Opening up to Grace is what locks you in, and then Grace takes over and does it all. You will know whether you have made the commitment or not from the response in your life.

Real spiritual life is the dramatic undermining of your separate existence. It is the complete subversion of dilemma, the elimination of suffering, misery, and separate self. The yogis and proponents of religious and spiritual traditions only sugar-coat your suffering, hide it, make it more palatable, letting it remain behind a distracting, fraudulent front. Real spiritual life is always diametrically opposed to convention. Always. And the more entangled you are in conventional life, the harder it is to make the commitment.

Devotee: Does an individual have a choice in making a commitment to you?

Lee: First I'll give you the mystical answer, then a more practical one. The mystical answer is: of course not. I am the one who has always been. I am what you are committed to becoming, not an instrument of or connection to it. So you have absolutely no choice in whether you make the commitment or not.

More practically, you can and need to willfully make a conscious and intelligent commitment. On this level, a choice appears to be made. In any case, Grace is the only available alternative for you. This means that in all cases, if you are open, you have no choice but to get it. What difference does it make whether you feel that the commitment is effortless and poetically beautiful, or that it is a struggle that you have to labor and suffer through? You still have to make it.

The contradiction, the paradox of spiritual life is that it is all Grace, and you thinking that you are doing it doesn't change that fact. It can only prevent you from recognizing it. Literally the only thing that matters in your life is God. How you realize that may appear to you as a simple or as a very difficult process. Regardless of how it appears, you need to realize it, and the commitment to God comes first.

Mahatma Gandhi said in his writings that he had never had a religious experience in his life. If you are familiar with what Gandhi did, the way he lived, and how he literally put his life on the line many times, that is one hell of a statement. He never had a religious experience. What he did, he did solely from his commitment to God, and from there sprang his intuitive knowledge of what was right. That's it. Damn it, that is it!

Most of you have had religious experiences and you're not the least bit satisfied. You shout for more. What you need to recognize is the kind of commitment that Gandhi had. You need the commitment to do or die. And if you never have an experience as long as you live, fine. You never have an experience as long as you live, that's all. That is you, my friend, that is who you are: one who has never had an experience.

Gandhi didn't care. Most of you think, "Oh man, I want something to at least show me that I'm getting somewhere, something to confirm it, make it easier." But he didn't care because he was commited to truth and didn't need an experience. If you do not make the commitment first, you may have a lot of experiences, and you are almost guaranteed to get stuck in those very same experiences. You will motivate yourself to experience your payoff, your chosen reward, and not to know yourself in truth. Language is only a vehicle. Any spiritual teacher with any degree of intelligence says the same thing. What someone says doesn't necessarily reveal his or her degree of commitment to God.

One of the essential ongoing processes of being with me is recognizing what I am saying, not what you think I am saying. I will talk in contradictory terms, because if your mind isn't boggled at some point, you are never going to know yourself. So you need to grasp what I am saying concerning commitment without letting your mind's limited conceptions of what "commitment" means get in the way.

The first step in recognizing the need for absolute commitment to God is seeing how all forms of conventional spiritual practice are rooted in the mind. Any practice, no matter what language it employs, no matter how "religious" it appears, if it is founded in mind is just another form of delusion. It is bullshit, just more possible experience. It is neither an expression of, nor does it create the kind of commitment that Mahatma Gandhi had. And without that commitment, there is no way in hell for you to be awake.

You are never going to be Alive without first committing your life to the Divine. That means **total** commitment. Not many people are willing to do that, not many will make the appropriate acknowledgement of Grace. Most will be satisfied with the appearance of spiritual life.

Appearances are merely your own interpretation of what is. Do not judge by appearances, do not interpret what I say through the screen of your intellect. There are no back doors through which to escape from Grace, so make the commitment, and abide by it. Just as you have been trained to be honest and you feel a little twinge when you lie, if you violate your commitment to God, you will feel much more than a little twinge. That is not pleasant to watch. And it is especially not pleasant to be someone who is involved in that avoidance. So you want to be very careful when you make that commitment, because when you make it, you had better keep it.

There are things I ask of you that you like, and there are also things I ask of you that some don't like. That too is joy to one who is truly committed to me. The more the guru manifests in dramatic form, the more you will know whether you are committed or not. If you are, you are, and if you're not, you're not. Make up your mind, that's all.

The fire never lets up. Ever. If we spent forty years together it would never get any easier. That is just the way it goes. I will continue to get harder and harder on you. What is present for some of you is that it gets harder and you don't care. You are not concerned about the heat. When you are devoted, how could you possibly mind when the work gets tough? You will just get into it if you really want God. If you are in a position where you can be attracted away from the guru to some place where it is easier, even though you thought you were committed, you know where you are at. You weren't committed in the first place. There was no devotion, only more strategy. The process of your life here is to recognize the humor in that, to see the whole drama and be free of it.

When you are absolutely dedicated to living God, there is no emotion associated with it. There is no place to get to; you aren't striving to get cleared out, cleaned out, or centered. There is nothing to be cleaned out anyway, no "center" to be in. If you have an insight, you can simply say, "Far out. I had an insight", and be done with it. There are no "almosts" in commitment. You are either living God or you are not. Spiritual life is not the propagation of attainment, but the complete dissolution of it. The thirst for attainment is antithetical to a real commitment to God.

If you want to give, give from your heart; give because you acknowledge this Divine condition. To do that you have to be dedicated on all levels to this condition. If you are not committed to the one you see here as guru, you are going to have a problem. I'll tell you that right up front. Don't give because other people are giving and "it's the thing to do". Don't give for the reason that most people give in church. The guru doesn't want it for that reason. Give because you have made the appropriate commitment from your heart. Period. That goes for your gifts, all your time and work, that goes for everything. Only give from the depth of your commitment to God.

There is a story about how a student came to a teacher and said, "I'm ready to know God. I know where it's at. Show me what you can." The teacher said, "Come with me." He took the student out to the middle of the river, and the student looked at the teacher, expecting some transcendent vision, and said, "Okay, I'm ready." The teacher took his head, shoved it under the water, and held it there for about a minute and a half. Then he pulled his head out of the water. The student was gasping for air and choking, looking at the teacher in confusion. Then the teacher shoved him under the water again, this time for two whole minutes, and then, pulling the student's head out and smiling at the violently gasping student, the teacher said, "Now, when you want God as badly as you wanted that last breath of air that you took, come back to me and then I'll do it."

Only you can know how strong the commitment is. It is a very subjective thing; nobody else can say, nobody else can tell. There is no outward manifestation that will consistently indicate it. The degree of intensity, desire, and need is up to you. If it is as important to you as whether you have chocolate or vanilla ice cream for dessert, you can be sure that you aren't willing to make a total commitment. If, on the other hand, it is as important to you as that breath of air when you are about to drown, then you get it, instantly.

Your commitment is a direct expression of, and intelligent response to, the conscious recognition that God is the only alternative. Ever. And God is not an alternative to anything else, for God is all there is. It requires everything from you to realize that completely. It requires that every aspect of your life be in the service of God. A commitment to this one is a commitment to God absolute. You see, you are the same one. If you don't make the commitment to this one, you are maintaining a false sense of separateness. That will never withstand Grace.

* * * *

In entering a personal relationship with the guru, we are always mistakenly assuming that he is a separate being from us. Our life activity constantly sustains that assumption, which is in direct contradiction to the true nature of the relationship. Devotion to the Guru, which is only the natural expression of our relationship with him, signifies to us devotion to some "other" person. This is intolerable to us. Nothing could be more against the grain of our belief in the separate ego than devotion. The guru-devotee relationship does not appear to be natural to us, so we therefore resort to willful effort.

One of the willful processes is the fulfillment of the community's functional life requirements. Through effort, we stop smoking, drinking, and taking drugs. We adopt a lacto-vegetarian diet and begin to exercise daily. We work at a responsible job, and tithe our income from that job to the support of the community. We also maintain a monogamous sexual relationship, and live in a community household. In all of this, we tend to have a vague conception of the purpose of the requirements, usually mistaking their fulfillment as an indication that we are living spiritual life. We are doing no such thing. We are simply taking on the form of an appropriate, functional life as Lee stipulates. In the process of willfully fulfilling the requirements, the fact that we fundamentally resist serving the guru is clearly demonstrated to us. Even these basic functional aspects of life have to be forced; how much more so the genuine life of service?

The transition from conventional life to life in the company of the guru involves a change in environment. So we initially tend to see spiritual life in contrast with what we "used to do". But it is merely the form of life that has changed for us; the activity of separative life continues. Lee continually reminds us that the functional requirements do not make us "spiritual", but only a healthy and natural form of activity.

As our involvement in Hohm continues, we assume a particular stance in regard to Lee's teaching. As in the case of the requirements, we resort to a willful effort in dealing with the teaching. There is an attempt to organize it into a "meaning" that can be cognized and adhered to. From what the guru says, we begin to put a jigsaw puzzle together, the pieces we choose depending on our inclination. Insights arise and we say, "Oh, I get it," but what we have "gotten" is just another piece in the conceptual puzzle. Lee has a lot of fun with us on this one. He rarely goes a week without contradicting something he has said on a previous week.

Yet we are very resourceful, finding ways to fit contradiction into the puzzle. Spiritual life is still conceived in terms of the adoption of a belief-system, and will continue to be so conceived until we intuit the guru's Presence.

When Lee is intuited as Presence, the assumption that he is merely some person who helps you out begins to be seen through. The physical proximity of the guru is initially important for this reason. Lee is literally present as Grace, creating movement in the lives of those who are near him. When we turn our attention from the jigsaw puzzle to the very Presence of Lee itself, something quite distinct from a willful process is intuited. Although we cannot prove anything, we clearly sense that Lee is indeed the Divine. It is nothing like the "certainty" of logic, and at the same time we do not doubt that intuition. When the Divine Presence is felt, a connection is made which is non-conceptual and yet very real. For the first time, love for the guru arises in us. That love is the spontaneous response to our connection with the fact of our perfect relationship with the Guru.

This is still only at the level of intuition. The sense of being separate from the guru is still quite active. The aspect of sadhana known as "turning to the guru" is present at this point. This is not to be confused with mentally cognizing the guru's name, form or image. Any words are inadequate to describe it, but let us say that it is the intuition of Lee's Presence in life activity. When we turn to Lee, the surrendering of the distractions of separative life takes place, not by any will of one's own, but by virtue of the Presence itself, which is Grace.

FOUR

WHATEVER DEGREE OF spiritual life you understand or don't understand, simply turn to me. No matter what I do. It can't be explained; it is not understandable by the mind. It is only knowable. If you think you have understood it, then you still have more structure to be challenged, because it is absolutely nonunderstandable. If you are really clear that you don't understand what is going on, even though you sometimes make the assumption that you do, that makes it very easy to turn to me. If you assume that you know what is going on, that you understand Grace, while being unconscious of the fact that you actually don't, turning to me is impossible.

When you are an empty slate, and you really know that you don't know anything, that makes our relationship much easier. Then I can write appropriate words on the empty slate. However, if you think that you know something, and your slate is filled with words, what I have to do is either erase it (which is very hard, as some of you know), or slip things in between the other words. That's okay, except that when I slip things in like that, the other words are larger and more dominant. So you have to be very careful and perceptive in order to pick up the things that get slipped in.

It is a very nice place to be, when you know that you don't know anything. You can come to me and be really blank, and scared because it is hollow and there's nothing there, and still be responsible and functional. Your blankness can allow you to turn to me without having to formulate it in your mind. It's like when you learn the alphabet, after a certain amount of time you don't have to stop to think about what comes after 'S'. And in learning to write, you eventually don't have to be conscious of how to work your hand. The same thing applies to responsibility. When you learn to be responsible, you are responsible without artifice. Your slate is blank. It is the connection between you and me which keeps you that way, and not anything you know in mind.

When you come to the guru, you need to recognize that there is suffering in your life. You need to recognize that you are not living God. If you think that you are, the guru can't show you anything. You will just go along your merry way, thinking that you are living the Divine, and nothing will happen until you realize that you aren't.

Understand that you don't understand. That is intelligence. You might think that you understand that, because you have had some good experiences and insights, or because you have studied and done some work. Yet you have only submerged the part of you that really doesn't know quite what to expect. When you are confronted with my raw condition, all your neat formulas will evaporate.

In the hollow state of not knowing, whatever arises, arises. You intelligently accept it without judging it or evaluating it. Then the teaching makes its point very quickly and with humor. When you are busy comparing things or trying to figure out the reasoning behind what I do, you lose your sense of humor very quickly. If you are interpreting what I am saying, or if you are agreeing or disagreeing with me, you are not paying attention. Period. That means not interpreting at all. That means not agreeing, either. You are simply not listening if you are busy with your agreement or disagreement. You should just be open and receiving what I am saying.

It is essential that you responsibly and intelligently allow the process of our relationship to occur. You cannot let that process occur by making assumptions about it and believing that you have understood it. If you are intelligently on top of every assumption you make, you will open up and stop being concerned with evaluating the process. Just be open, so as to allow assumptions to be undermined when they need to be undermined. What happens after some time is that you start to get a real connection, rather than a conceptual understanding of the teaching. You get a connection through direct knowing. Until then you will be involved in trying to explain why I contradicted what I said last week, ("Oh, it must be his paradoxical nature"), on and on, week after week, contradiction after contradiction. When you have a real connection, there is no need to get caught up in the effort to understand that.

The significance of turning to me is very personal. It can easily be mistaken for a process that is muscled or efforted, because those who are turned find it so hard to explain what it is. It is very personal to the one who is turned. It is absolutely unforced; any efforted process is just not relevant. The understanding of the personal nature of turning to me is the full understanding of the interrelatedness of everything: the weather, the body, the emotions from ecstasy to fear; literally the whole spectrum of life is revealed as this relationship. The imaginary isolation of one's life is obliterated in turning to me. No matter how much you read and how much you immerse yourself in the teaching, when that becomes personalized, when turning is your intimately personal reality, this relationship takes on significance in you for the first time. Until it becomes personalized, it is not so significant. There are plenty of books to read, plenty of people to talk to, and lots of teachers around who have a good rap. The meaning, the essence, is inherently speechless.

The joy of living God needs no words. It is not my job to prattle on and on about it, to whitewash your lives for you and be all lovey-dovey. It is my job to have you see that there is only joy in living the Divine, and only pleasure in serving the guru. Serving the guru is beautiful and priceless. I shouldn't have to get up and lecture about how happy it is to be living God all the time. You should know that by faith. When there is a real, personal connection, you just know that. You go through all of your stuff and you're happy anyway. When you don't know that, humor is noticeably lacking.

If you have had the insight that you don't really know anything about God, we have, at least, some place to begin. You would like to know you have made the connection, but when it comes down to basic facts, you don't really know. You don't know about service, about doing what I say, about demands, or experience, or Grace. All you know is that you are here. That is good enough for a start.

For one thing, you can openly be yourself with me. People are too often different around me than they are around others. They propagate the image, the lie. It's like when you're going out on your first date. You very carefully make sure that your hair is just right, your clothing is just right, and everything about your appearance is just right. You smell groovy and you're all set. And if you get to like your date and he or she gets to like you, you have to be very careful to keep up the initial image. You are not sure whether he or she likes you for being you or because you were so perfect the first night. It is the same thing with people who come to me. They have acted "just right" in front of the guru, and they can't be themselves with him. They have to be humble and spiritual and so on. They think they are fooling the guru, and of course, the guru knows. And the people always go through hell when they are alone. They don't go through hell in front of the guru, because that would supposedly show their lack of development. So they are cool and mellow and not themselves at all.

One aspect of presenting an appearance to the guru is speaking from what you have heard and copied from somewhere else instead of coming from yourself. You are like kids in that respect. When kids get to be six or seven years old they are just like parrots. You say something, and the next day they come to you and very seriously say the same thing. And you think that it's sort of cute when they do that, you feel parental pride. Yet what is truly moving is when children come from their own experience, instead of parroting their friends or teachers. They just tell you something new, maybe something they discovered in their own little heart about the sky.

It is the same thing with you. If you come from your own experience, you are being open with me. If you just parrot what you know intellectually, you aren't. Nothing real ever happens that way; truth is not active and evident in your life. You are afraid to be open because you feel that you have something to protect. What is it you are protecting? No matter how hard you look, you will not find it.

The process of not analyzing and being open is difficult and delicate. I can sit up here and talk about anything, and you are bound to have an opinion about it. I talk about diet, and you really don't want to give up meat. Perhaps you are really attached to smoking or drinking. Whatever it is, it is very hard to stay open about it, because your mind works so fast. As soon as I say something offensive, your mind closes off. I have violated your particular code. And it is inevitable that I violate everyone's codes, even the beautiful ones.

You shouldn't try to make an effort at being open. You shouldn't try to stop your mind from reacting, for that will just give energy to your resistance. The best way to be open is to simply not give your non-openness any energy, to be closed for just an instant and then let it fall away. It is very common for people to get down on themselves. That is what gives their resistance energy, keeping it there, actively blocking my influence. The way to keep the slate clean is to not give anything energy, including the stuff that I tell you. Just open your mind and let it go in. Don't give it energy, just let it go in and sit. And because of our relationship, the appropriate thing will happen. When you are in a place where you need something, it will be there.

When you give energy to something that I say, it ends up dissipating instead of sinking in. It is evident that you don't pay attention when I will say something for the fifteenth time, and you get it for the first time. You say, "Why didn't I hear that the first time you said it?" It is obvious why you didn't. You weren't paying attention, which means just attention and nothing more. When you truly pay attention to me, maybe I'll only have to say something once or twice before you get it, instead of having to say it over and over. Keeping your attention on me means exactly what it says. If your mind starts to wander, you bring it back to me. If you start to give energy to what I say, just let the mind open up and stop evaluating. Be attentive to what I am saying, and follow the instructions. You can't follow the instructions if you are busy thinking, "Oh, Lee is so psychic. Whenever I have a problem, he says exactly what I need." If I say exactly what you need, and you get caught in that train of thought, you've lost it already. You are not paying attention anymore. You feel good because I have said something meaningful for you, and you've totally lost it.

You don't really listen to me. You hear it, you cognize it, you thrash it around in your mind. You get intimidated by it, deal with it during the week, and then come to me and say, "Man, it was a heavy week!" You still haven't listened, haven't gotten it. I don't know what the hell I'm laughing at. I'm sitting here, you haven't gotten it, and I'm laughing. Can you imagine that? You don't get it and I still laugh.

Be aware of how little you know. Even those of you who have a lot of information, and there is so much to fill your brain with, still don't know anything. You don't know the guru. You are not simply present. No one knows anything who is not simply present.

The non-limitation of Grace, which is focalized as the guru in form, exists and is present wherever you are. That goes for everything in the universe. Turning to the guru by mentally cognizing the individual by name or image may be true turning, or may be just a frustrated attempt to relieve pain. In truth there is no one and nothing to turn to, because I am already your very nature. In the instant of true turning to me, you realize that this is your state, and everything else is dissolved.

Typically there takes place a "turning" which is actually looking at the guru as some being or entity that can help you. In that case, there are often miracles; comfortable things happen, pleasant coincidences that make your life easier, which is okay. There is nothing wrong with them. Yet this is still looking at the guru as "other", as a savior or physician who will help you, rather than realizing he is your state, your condition. It is as your Divine condition that I tell you to turn to me.

It is easy to turn to me when things are good. You meditate and turn to me in bliss. You breeze through a traffic jam and say, "Thanks, Lee." That is very flip. When you thank me out of devotion, you don't have to talk about it. When you come and tell me the things you did right and you say, "Thanks, Lee." you are actually avoiding devotion. You would just as soon thank God, except I've threatened and intimidated you, so you thank Lee instead. You still don't know that God and Lee are not two. That is not really clear to you. Real devotion, real sadhana, is to turn to me as I am, prior to who you think I am and who you think you are. Before you recognize that, you will project a lot of things on to me. All of them are your creations, your illusions.

First comes teacher, then guru, and finally very God, the Divine, which is my self. You are all in varying degrees of recognizing that. It is not a matter of what you think. You might think, "Oh yes, I know who Lee really is." It is nothing like whatever it is you think. Some of you who think that you know who Lee really is have a big surprise in store for you, which will be great fun when you realize it. We'll jump up and down and dance and sing. There will be nothing for us to do but laugh until we die.

The very basic life of ego is resistance to knowing me. Your ideas of who I am are nothing more than obstructions. If there is a block in your functional life, a focal point of resistance to Grace, your turning to me will allow Grace to undermine whatever the block is. The reason the block is there has to become evident and conscious, and then you have to select an alternative to that. People always have blocks because of so-called negative experiences, not positive ones. The way it gets undermined is by becoming totally conscious of what caused the block. And in the process of turning to me, you can share the companionship and love of our relationship. That is the alternative. You can never select the alternative until you understand perfectly why that wasn't available before you became aware of it. Prior to your awareness of the block being there, you have no alternative but to continue resisting our relationship, creating your illusions. You can't select an alternative to companionship, because you don't know that you are not alone. You are too busy playing out trying to not be lonely. Until you know that clearly, you can't pick an alternative, because you don't know that there is an alternative to pick. Your resistance to me is the way mind defends itself against its own undoing. Turning to me allows resistance to be undermined so that Grace can become conscious as your life.

Turning to me is turning to Shiva, the source of all the worlds. Only those who have made the connection, experiencing the personal nature of that turning, have left judgement, analysis, and learning behind them. All of the information you have learned fails to communicate the essence of this process. All of the stuff that I learned before I woke up was information, and when I woke up, I realized that I am the very source that is prior to all information. All that the learning did was fill my brain up so that I could communicate clearly and functionally.

I am the source and the evidence of the source. The evidence of the source is this teaching. I am at the same time the source, Shiva, which is prior to all expression, and its functional expression in the world. It will always appear simultaneously. The evidence appears, and the source is always there. The only way you truly know the evidence is if your attention is on me, the source.

Your turning to me is my turning to myself. There is truly no one turning and no one being turned to, there is only the movement of Grace in the inclusiveness of God. It is very humorous, this game of becoming fulfilled in my company, since I know you as already fulfilled in me. There is nothing to attain, nothing to lose, nothing to get, and nothing to give up. There is only God.

FIVE

The Shell Game

THE MORE SUBTLE your ego becomes, the more you are interested in getting rid of it. The implication of most "spiritual" and "higher consciousness" ideals is to suppress or destroy ego. Big, bad ego. The more intense you are about getting rid of it, the more threatened your ego becomes, and the more firmly entrenched. This intensity of wanting to rid oneself of ego stems from the fact that one knows that ego is just as strong as ever and it is not going away. Those involved in the spiritual search know subconsciously. That is why they get so dramatic about claiming that ego is gone. It is a defense against what they know to be the case.

Ego will do anything it can to make you think that ego is not around anymore. That is so you will stop trying to get rid of it. It is a very subtle form of the search. A book might tell you that what you have to do is deal with ego. That is the problem: you figure that you'd better do something about ego. Your mind then devises the strategy of doing something to make it seem as if ego isn't there, so that you don't try to kill it. That way, ego's life is assured, because you will never get through the ego if you think that you've destroyed it. You will say the right things, act the right way, and never live God. You will remain in suffering. You will delude yourself into believing that you have dealt with ego and there are no more problems. Bullshit. Everything has just been swept under the rug.

The basic misunderstanding involved in this form of the search is that we have to kill or get rid of ego. Yet the very nature of the search allows the ego to survive, to stay around. The teachings say, "We have to be quiet and humble and egoless." The highest form that ego can take is allowing one to think that one doesn't have an ego. Then there is no threat; it can perpetuate its existence in subtler, holier-than-thou forms. The belief that ego can be killed is its best defense. Actually, you will never kill it. Ego is too brilliant, too sly. It is much smarter than that part of the intellect which resolves to kill it. And it will keep getting smarter and smarter, and create more sophisticated games in order to fool you. The drive to get rid of ego gives absolute weight to the ego's claim to be.

The process of this teaching, and of any true form of spiritual life, is not to get rid of ego. It is, after all, an integral part of your existence. Did you ever see a human being function without ego? The error lies in ego's pretensions to being absolute, to being separate unto itself. The attempt to kill it gives substance to these pretensions and implies that it has an independent life that must be destroyed. The process is to accept it, enjoy it, and observe it with humor. When your ego surfaces and you know that something is ego-motivated, be responsible for that and enjoy it. The process is Grace, not struggle.

When your ego feels that there is a threat to its control over you, it will create camouflage. The camouflage can be very obvious, like a big psychic shield, or it can be very subtle, involving many intricate defenses. It can be structured to match or contrast with the surroundings, yet it is a camouflage in any case. In order to awaken to what already is, you need to realize that you aren't. You are not a separate entity. Every single recorded piece of information in your brain establishes and reinforces you as an individual, separate entity. Any time you start to even get close to giving up your grasp on this sense of individuality, camouflage is created, which is typically emotional or physical pain. It is all a distraction, invalid and unnecessary. When you are going through pain, you aren't thinking about life, you're thinking about pain. With physical pain, you can sublimate it, take an aspirin, or go to a doctor. But with emotional pain you really get into it, creating some fascinating drama, and ego maintains control. Sometimes you ask the guru to help you out of it. That's still manipulation of what is. Manipulating what is happens to be ego's favorite way of avoiding the fact that it isn't.

It is not getting rid of ego that is the process of this teaching, but recognizing that it really isn't to begin with, that there is no separate self at all. Rather than another expression of egoic control, the direct Presence of this one is a real threat to the ego. Unlike the forms of the search that allow you to think that there is no more ego, perpetuating the game of "God and I", I undermine all delusions of separate individuality.

If you are not in spiritual life, when you get depressed you know that you are depressed. It is very simple. You pop a few pills or down a martini. At least you know that you are not happy. You are quite aware of what a mess you are. In spiritual seeking, on the other hand, there are all kinds of techniques to get you high, and they work. If you do kriya yoga or any of the various types of formal meditation, you are going to get high. Getting high is a distraction that enables you to forget that you aren't happy. You feel a little depressed, so you go into meditation and do some pranayama. All you have to do is take a few good breaths, get a lot of oxygen in your brain, and presto, you are high. You think you've really made it. If you breathe too much, you space out, but that's all right, you think that it's samadhi. And when you get high, you don't acknowledge the fact that beneath it all you are really suffering, still in the midst of dilemma. You get some great insight and you think it's okay. You think that you have banished ego. But it's never really okay when you are asleep to your true nature; your suffering has merely been hidden, tranquillized. You would have been just as well off with the martini.

I realize that a lot of you have had some really good insights and experiences. In any other community, you would be considered to have really attained something. You should not feel bad that your attainments go unheeded, that I don't shower you with attention because you had samadhi. It's all my problem, not yours. I am a cold hearted S.O.B. who is only interested in one thing: absolute and total dissolution in God. That's hard to take because you want to be my friend or lover or servant or whatever role you envision in relation to me. And that's fine, but that's not what is ultimately important. Those roles are still separate from me; what I ultimately look for in you is complete dissolution in God.

The dissolution of the self in God amounts to the complete unstructuring of all forms of conventional life. It is not a matter of deciding to do something else, something different from what one has always done. It is not a matter of deciding to become a vegetarian instead of eating meat, to do sadhana instead of not doing sadhana, or to be responsible instead of irresponsible. "I used to smoke dope, but now I'm straight." That is not valid at all. Spiritual life does not consist in making any kind of decision, although many of you have made decisions and think that the decisions you have made are firm and solid. What you have done is change your habit pattern from one form of ego to another. Any decision to do something different comes from ego in the first place, because ego makes all decisions: what job to take, how much schooling to have, how much to eat, what habits and what friends to have. Ego makes all of those decisions.

What the dissolution does is break down all of the structure, literally make it nil, and then rebuild a new structure which is true spiritual life. Actually it is not a "structure" as one would understand that term conventionally. It is a resurrection. First the person dies and then he is resurrected appropriately in and as God. When ego is resurrected, it is no longer ego the way you know it now, nevertheless that function is still there. You see, ego also allows us to jump out of the way if a truck is coming right towards us at seventy miles per hour. If we are walking in the woods and we see a rattlesnake, ego is what allows us to get away from there very fast. Ego is resurrected after the fact of dissolution in its appropriate function, which is in one instance just to keep the organism functioning properly and healthily.

You all think that you are individuals at very deep levels. That belief starts very early. Everybody wants to feel that he is something, that he is going to be remembered as an individual. There is an emphasis on being a good parent, a good friend, or if you are a teacher, you want to be a proper example for the kids. Everybody feels strongly that he would like recognition as an individual. In truth there is no individuality, in truth each one of you is, inclusively, the world. That's why it takes strength to be awake, because you look around at the world, at everything that is happening, and you realize: that's me. And there's nothing you can do about it. You need to be strong to be enlightened, because you realize that you are not an individual who can be safe and secluded somewhere in a cave in the woods and not be in the world. You realize that you are the world, and at the same time you are nothing. In fact, it is only when you realize that you are nothing that you realize you are the world.

The last vestige of egoic structure is the self-sensing or intuition of being an individual. That is always the last thing to go. That's what is scary, that's what may bring contractions to the psycho-physical organism, to the body. All kinds of reactions may occur in the body when the separate self sense is about to be ripped off. Any one of you can say, "I'm not my body", but you look in the mirror, don't you? Sure, you look in the mirror just to make sure it's okay. You can read spiritual books all day and think, "I'm not my body", but you look in a mirror and you think you are your body at a deep level.

Primarily you identify exclusively with this psycho-physical complex. You are concerned about your diet, about how you wear your hair or how your clothes look. Beyond that, you think that you are your five senses. You identify with sensory phenomena. And beyond that, your stronghold is the mind, which created the body in the first place. So your separate self sense expresses itself in a split between mind and body. Individuality is clung to; you believe that you are so-and-so, who has these parents, these friends, has had this much schooling, has read these books and had these experiences. That is the maya. That has to be let go of. It is with you even in the most sublime circumstances. You look at a sunset and say, "That's a beautiful sunset." You have defined beauty within the confines of the separate self, contained the sunset in the box of your opinion. That is "you"; you know yourself as being someone.

Nobody will ever let go of that. You can be seeking on "the path" for years, but you will still hold on tight to that one. The average teacher will only perpetuate the search, teach you to meditate or some such avoidance. What this one is able to do is destroy the search and resurrect the Divine life of God. The separate self has to be undermined, pulled out from under you, because you will never give it up voluntarily. I can undermine that because, although you know yourself as being someone, I know myself as I am. Period.

The guru exists in the world as Grace, and turning to the guru dissolves the basic dilemma which is at the core of your life. That basic dilemma is separation. Even before the birth trauma, there is separation. The birth trauma objectifies it, makes it physical, embodies it, so to speak. Then the brain has got all this recorded information about the bright lights, the slap on the ass, the chemical in the eyes, the loud noise and the strange voices. The birth trauma simply makes the dilemma objective, gives it a physical location on memory cells, establishing it chemically in the body. Mind functions as separation before any event in the life-process objectifies it.

The basic dilemma seems perfectly evident in an objective way. As we look at one another it is plainly obvious to the senses that we are separate. I am sitting here. You are sitting there. It is obvious that we are not connected; the dilemma is verified by the senses. Everything you have ever known, seen, heard and lived has verified that. And yet in truth we are not separate.

No amount of language can overcome the basic dilemma. No amount of study or therapeutic activity will do it. Even the "be here now" thing is a trap. Those that are into being here now are still involved in the dilemma, immersed in separation, always looking at themselves. The implication is that it is possible to not be here now. No methodologies, however subtle, will do it. It takes Grace to overcome the basic dilemma. It takes the guru. One can become educated and well-versed in it, and be able to talk about it clearly and precisely, and without the guru one comes to the dead end of limitation.

The process of the guru is to face you with yourself until you don't have a self to be faced with. It is a process of demand, of being pushed into a corner. It is being forced to eliminate your structure, since you are not going to do that by desire. You are not going to say, "I will eliminate all of my structure." No way are you ever going to do that. You need to be forcibly ripped off, because ego can never rip itself off. Only God will undo you.

It is my job to be harder and harder on you, to make you work your ass off, perhaps for the first time in your life. It is my job to push you so that you become responsible and recognize how you have functioned from ego all of your life. The only way to get through that is through me. You can't repress, reprogram, or sublimate it. There is too much, it will always return with more force. As long as life is lived as if it is "yours", the Divine will be the ultimate threat to "your" life. When the guru has backed you into the corner, when the only possibility left is absolute dissolution in God, you will realize that "your" life is none other than the Divine.

****

As members of Lee's community, we have discovered that spiritual life is a bitch. We have tended to conceive of it in glowing terms, and indeed, Lee never tires of reminding us that it is a humorous and joyous affair. Nevertheless, the humor of the Divine in no way requires that we sweeten up the facts of our life of suffering.

The assumption of happiness as our Divine condition is not on the level of the mind, but absolutely prior to mind. We assume that we are separate from the Divine, and thus seem to undergo suffering. To persuade ourselves mentally that we are happy is not sadhana, it is dishonesty. We must recognize that life, as we assume it, is suffering. Furthermore, we must see that everything we do maintains that deluded life. Covering that up prevents its being recognized, and therefore prevents the recognition of what is prior to that.

Lee provides us with no comfort or consolation, which would only serve to distract us from suffering. Instead, living in Lee's company actually intensifies the experience of suffering of our life. In conventional situations, the sense of fear and conflict that arises at various times will always be attributed to some kind of life condition, either subjective or objective. We will explain it away by telling ourselves that what somebody said or did annoyed us, or that we are in a "bad mood", etc. In the company of the guru, however, the literal Presence of the Divine as Lee's relationship with us, clearly shows us that the fear and conflict have nothing to do with any particular conditions or situations. For no matter what mode of separative life one presents to the guru, it is always totally contradicted by the Divine condition, which knows no conflict or fear.

Since Lee is present as what is, and not as any assumed separate person, we who are in his company become acutely aware that our perspective is nothing but delusion. And it is only the very Presence itself, not anything that happens through it or because of it, that constitutes this process.

We are forced to deal with our suffering, not by seeking to alleviate it, but simply by not consciously sustaining it. But we ingeniously find ways to sustain it; we begin to doubt that the guru is who he is. Since we have no reference point for categorizing whether he is Divine or not, this is not a genuine doubt; but merely a defense against the threat the guru poses to our separative life. It is our excuse to leave the guru. A more common defense is self doubt: we declare that we are not "worthy" of the guru, and use that as a convenient excuse to avoid doing sadhana. Guilt is our best defense; it lets us claim that we are steeped in suffering, while at the same time completely preventing our recognition of suffering. In any case, we sense that being with the guru will expose raw nerves in our life, so we will do anything to avoid that. Lee only brings to the light what is always going on for us, while we persist in attributing that pain to Lee.

Sadhana at Hohm involves the recognition that everything we do is suffering. But that recognition must be in the context of being in relationship with Lee. That means that the life of suffering is seen with humor, in the light of one's actual condition; seen from the perspective of Grace rather than from the limited perspective of the life of suffering itself. We may feel, for instance, that we do not love our mate, or that the interaction with other members of the community is superficial, and in doing so feel suffering in our life, or sense that everything we do is suffering. But as long as the connection is not made between that and the Divine condition which is the guru, suffering is only felt, not recognized. The intensity has increased, but one is not turning to the guru in that intensity.

In the context of society, such a process of recognition is a disturbance of the world's well-guarded sleep. Lee has pointed out that society is structured so as to sustain separative life and to keep one from recognizing its nature as suffering. It is in this sense that he tells us to be in the world but not of the world. Spiritual life is to be lived functionally in the world, but the assumptions upon which the world sustains its activity are not to be lived.

SIX

You Promised, Mommy

MANY SPIRITUAL TRADITIONS speak the language of renunciation. They teach that you must renounce the world. So do I. However, what the traditions mean by the world and what I mean are two different things. They refer to physical life: the senses, sexuality and possessions. I do not teach that kind of renunciation. If we were meant to give up the world, it wouldn't be here. Period.

Every once in a while I see people being helpful and well meaning, helping someone pick up the package that he or she dropped, and then I look beneath that and see the same thing that exists for people who aren't well meaning and never help people pick up packages. It is always the same: separate self, ego. When I talk about renouncing the world, I mean getting away from the environment and atmosphere that people are creating subconsciously, which is one of constant fear, insecurity and tension. The world as I mean it is the world of suffering; not the suffering of physical pain, but the suffering of those who do not know who they are. So renouncing the world is not necessarily giving up the actual form of things, it is giving up the environments that are not sustained according to real spiritual life.

The world is unconscious social convention. This convention is the establishment of separation as the very social life of human beings. Because it is so deeply ingrained in the mind, it is always confused with human nature itself. Actually, human nature is so far removed from conventional society that when it is present in its true form in the world, it is unrecognizable. It has simply been forgotten what human nature is. Occasionally a philosopher or poet will point to it, yet the mass of humanity repeats cliches about how war and violence are natural, and how it's a dog-eat-dog world. They look at what humanity has come to, and call that human nature.

In renouncing the world, it is only what is invested in unconscious convention that I reject, not human nature. Convention is seen as the way things are, yet it is quite an arbitrary creation, not at all absolute. The creation of what is conventional always stems from the basic, survival-level fears inherent in separative life. People are afraid of being kicked out of the Garden of Eden. In the early cultures, all of the natural phenomena were attributed to gods. Good and bad fortune in human life were traced to the whims and attitudes of these various gods. There was the feeling of being just a toy, a plaything in the hands of outside forces. Whole cultures got used to looking at life as being moved from without, and this was passed on from age to age, genetically and culturally, so that people have this deep-seated belief of having nothing to do with their own lives.

Ego is the activity in mind that maintains this separative life. The basis of ego is to win, and since it wants to be right all the time, it creates strategies to prove that this belief in being controlled by the "outside" is correct. Subliminal advertising and behavior modification are the modern strategies of outside control created by ego. What ego does is allow "external" effects to control activity, to create in the mind attitudes of positivity or negativity, of creativity or destruction. Ego will allow all of that to go on, and all in the name, of course, of being free.

Freedom is no less a strategy than control. The whole idea of liberty and free will is meaningless unless there is first the deep-seated belief that we are moved from without. Everybody thinks that he or she has a choice about things, is free to decide whether he or she should be a doctor, lawyer, or mechanic. Nobody has a choice in these things whatsoever. In fact, there is not even a choice involved in entering spiritual life. The only "saving grace" is being motivated strictly from ego to get into spiritual life, and happening to be with a spiritual master or guru who then transforms that into something real.

Separation is your own activity, and society gives you the basis to function in the world according to that activity. Your activity needs society to present itself. Society is the bacterial culture of separation; it sustains and feeds your continuation of the delusion, the life of suffering.

Pure, unadulterated human nature is always the same. It is consistent with the moving force of Grace, it is dynamic, it flows, it is Alive. When human nature is realized as the Divine, it is untainted by delusion and seeking. But unconscious convention, what occurs in the world when assumed separation is established as society, is founded in delusion and seeking. Children begin to get adulterated very early in their lives. By the time they are five or six, they've been had. By the time they are twelve or thirteen, they are locked into convention and have gotten the idea of how to manipulate people for their neurotic needs. Their unconsciousness is not created by society, but it is nurtured and fixed in society. This is an ancient process, and it is the process of life right now.

The human species is characterized in its history by a great movement towards fulfillment. Ignorance of the Divine is so deeply imbedded in the human psyche that the drive towards union is at times absolutely demonic. This impulse towards fulfillment is society's time-honored way of maintaining the delusion of separation. It is in this context that the awakened one appears to the world. The guru cuts a strange figure in the eyes of society. Indeed, the functional condition of the Divine contradicts all conventional standards. The cherished notions of the world are pointed out as delusions by the guru, and the movement towards union is declared invalid. The truth of existence is so potently simple that once you understand it, it seems totally unreasonable not to expect everyone to acknowledge your obvious grasp of the Divine process that is life. What does happen when you express this simple clarity? Not only are you not lauded, you are ostracized, vilified and attacked. The world does not take very kindly to the guru, because the awakened one is a living challenge to convention itself. The only challenge.

The typical adult cannot accept the overturning of the apple cart. People are so fossilized, so rooted in the status quo, that even a slight deviation is considered outright heresy and greeted with indignation, followed by violent aggression or total exclusion of the heretical factor from the environment or screen of consciousness. The status quo is ignorance, unhappiness, hate, jealousy, prejudice, in short, separation from God. The truth of human nature is the humorous play of God. Human nature is Divine. The control from without and freedom from within are both imaginary. God is neither without nor within. The one who is awake consciously lives God, and thus appears to the world as a stranger.

It was only after the death of Buddha and the death of Jesus that they were glorified and dramatized. At the time of their lives, the power structure left them alone at best. At worst, it actively tried to discredit and destroy them. Now that they are not around physically they are safe for society. Anything that can not present itself forcefully is safe space. Society can interpret Jesus, two thousand years later, any way it pleases, and Jesus can't say, "No, I didn't mean that." Jesus can't undermine the people who misunderstand him. After their deaths, the awakened ones become focal points for egoic strategy.

The highest strategy of all involves God. If we are being controlled by externals, and God creates the externals, then if we can get into God's favor, God will create pleasant externals for us: health, success, security, and so on. Even the words that are used are obvious: "the Creator", "the Father". The strategy is similar to a child trying to please a parent.

The most sophisticated form of strategy, therefore, is so-called "spiritual" life. When such a life is purely strategic, it can't involve anyone who is going to undermine strategy itself. It has to be in an area where there is no power, no force. That is why these mass movements form around spiritual masters that are dead. They have no force when they are dead. Instead of the Divine Presence, there is "the path". All of the religious experiences that people have are conveying the power of the guru, but people never interpret it that way. They see it as validating their path, as confirming that they have picked the right way and are getting somewhere.

When someone comes into the world Alive in God, and can contradict and confront the very nature of strategy itself, undermining the whole basis of strategic action on any level, certainly that one is vilified, certainly that one is attacked. The entire form of separative human functioning is diametrically opposed to that, completely adverse to the process of Grace. Nobody wants to know who he or she is. People want to be taken care of by the "Great Father in the Sky", not to awaken to their true nature.

Most organized religion has come to be simply another form of big business. It supports a vast hierarchy of professionals: ministers, rabbis, priests, and so on. These tax-free structures have the role in society of making the Divine safe for popular consumption. People don't really want involvement, they just want to please the "Father". If they are told that they do enough "Hail Marys", or if they say their prayers before bedtime, they think that they will be "saved" and that it is all they have to do. Real involvement frightens them, so they just assume that what they've been told is enough, and it satisfies them.

In organized religion, what is worshipped is a phantom, a being conceived as totally "other". It is easy to change that, if the form of worship is fervently present. All the form of worship has to do is take the proper direction. That's the key. Once a person recognizes ego's strategy of maintaining separation as the basis of his or her "spiritual" life, true turning can take place. In order for that recognition to occur, one needs to be in contact with Grace manifest in the world. One might think that Grace is involved when one is actually worshipping a figurehead. If one is not in contact with Grace manifest in the world, nothing will ever happen. The living guru must be present, must be actual in one's life rather than searched for.

Society's very nature is the search for fulfillment. And the search only deludes further, only continues the misery of separation from the Divine life of humor and joy. Ego will do anything to avoid its own dissolution. Anything. The longer ego is present as the dilemma of suffering, as the separate self, the more sophisticated its strategies become. The more sophisticated the strategies, the higher the tension; and the higher the tension, the more dramatic the manifestations of the dilemma in the world. What is happening in this age is quite dramatic. We have come to a point where ego is running out of strategies. The tension is at a peak and everything is coming to a head: rampant violence, illness and dishonesty, the corrupt "You scratch my back and I'll scratch yours" ideology of politics, and the environmental destruction. It is all climaxing because the ego is finding it increasingly difficult to avoid the

Divine.

All of the great spiritual teachers of the last hundred and fifty years have said that by the end of this century, mankind will have either saved or destroyed itself. And frankly, from the viewpoint of the universe, it doesn't matter one bit. Whoever has seen through it in the past is seeing through it now, and whoever sees through it now will continue to see through it for eternity. So what's the difference if the world blows up? Bernard Shaw said something to the effect that a reasonable man will try to mold himself to the give and take of society; while the unreasonable man will try to mold society to himself...and all progress depends on the unreasonable man! Since the guru is definitively unreasonable, his teaching of real spiritual life is not due to a desire to save the world, but only to his absolutely unreasonable nature.

The only thing that people in the community can do is be sane themselves. That sanity itself is the only means to create sanity in the world as a condition. Everybody has got to come to the guru in his or her good time. Society is a wasteland, and it is not your sadhana to get away from the wasteland, but to be sane within the wasteland. It must change of itself. How many people are even attempting to live real spiritual life? A few thousand? We couldn't change South Orange, New Jersey, let alone Chicago, Los Angeles or New York.

Devotee: If spiritual life is only for the chosen few, what validity does it have? What about the rest of humanity?

Lee: First of all, who is humanity? Your question assumes that separation is an actual disease for which real spiritual life is the cure. The guru is humanity. Humanity is perfectly non-separate from the first, so there is nothing to be concerned about. The one awake in the world is humanity itself. Any answer that would either console you, offer hope or pity, or in any way support the basic assumption of your question, would be a disservice to you.

Of course from the point of view of separation there is tragedy in the human spiritual search. And yet look at what a great tragedy elicits in the heart. The Greek tragedies and some of Shakespeare's plays overwhelm the heart with profound emotion and insight. They are uplifting, not depressing. So why shouldn't there be tragedies? It is all Divine play, and tragedy is a part of it. Does that answer frighten you? I say that the crusade to end tragedy is just more of the search.

As for the "chosen few", I can only regard that with amusement. It is a very popular notion in counterculture mysticism, to believe that one is "chosen". It helps reinforce the feeling that one has seen through it all, while nobody else has. It is like being a part of a privileged elite. It is nice to feel that way, and it is certainly reinforced by the traditions. You have heard the saying, "When the student is ready, the guru will appear." So someone who finds the guru thinks, "Ah yes. I'm finally prepared. I'm strong enough now to sustain this outrageous spiritual life of having to work four hours a day, meditate two hours a day, and eat fresh food in this ashram. Oh, how lucky I am to have been chosen for this." There is really no chosen few. That is just one of society's deluded versions of spiritual life.

It is because people refuse to accept these facts that the guru is vilified. When you say to them that it is all Divine play, they react with outrage, violence, and contempt. That is why the true guru is secluded from the world. The condition is so raw that were the awakened one to go out in society announcing the truth of the Divine, violence would be done very quickly to that one. My statement, for instance, that "I don't care if the world blows up", is certain to arouse indignation. I am expected to assume the dilemma of separation, to assume the delusion which makes it possible for society to self-destruct in the first place. I cannot assume it. Regardless of what happens, I am the already perfect Divine.

The true guru, in his always paradoxical manner, disdains the world and its idiocy. If you just think that there is only God, if you have had a little cosmic experience but you're not quite sure, you can hedge the bet a little bit and be conventionally humble. Then you can say, "I'm not God, I'm just a servant of God." For the absolute condition of the Divine there is nothing to be humble about. Can the selfless be self-effacing?

I will demand that you recognize the insanity that prevails in all societies today, and that you not be caught up in or a part of that insanity, politically, economically or socially. The world holds no promise for you, and until you realize that, your head will spin with its madness. The guru is the actual contradiction of that madness.

The true guru leaves the "real" world for the company of devotees in an exclusive community. He ridicules the concerned and the philanthropic, deeming all charity as his own. The true guru is a mean, non-consoling S.O.B., and he gives his life in absolute service to this thankless and unconscious world. Why? Only for God. The world is God's playground, and my favorite kind of play is undermining the separative existence of the world. I bring my devotees Hohm to life itself, to joy unbounded. Only the guru knows how this is done, and you can only taste this for yourself.

SEVEN

SATSANG WITH THE true guru makes available whatever is necessary to eliminate living from separation. What I need is the freedom from you to do that. If you don't offer me that freedom, there is little or no reason for you being here. If I start to take that liberty and you leave, you haven't given me the freedom to get you to recognize where you are at. I want to bring you to a place where you are not upgrading your act, not bullshitting yourself and others anymore. I want you to know the bliss of not having to be bothered with the petty little ego, the delusion of desires, hopes, dreams and fears. I want you to realize the absolute joy of letting the Divine live you and move you. That is happiness, constant and clear.

Much is going on subjectively. The subjective processes are pretty strong, and that's about as far as they go: pretty strong. The conscious, dramatic, and direct confrontation in satsang is what literally rips you open so that the work can get done the way it needs to get done. All the time that you are not consciously in my company, the process is still going on, but it is not recognized, you are not responsible for it. Turning to me in truth makes your part in the transformation an intelligent, responsible, and enjoyable one. That makes all the difference, for your role in the process is ultimately a necessary one.

A tremendous amount of work has gone on for you, even when we have only made what seems to you to be a superficial connection. The guru is involved with all of you twenty-four hours a day. You are always being transformed, and it happens so gradually that many don't notice it at all. It is like when Radha's mother will come visiting, after not seeing the kids for a few months, and she'll say, "Wow! What a difference!" We didn't notice that they had grown, because we had been with them during those few months. In the same way, most of you aren't recognizing how much is being done, because you are here all the time, too close to it. Occasionally you will notice that something is different. You will typically think that you have had an insight, and that it came all of a sudden. It wasn't really that way; that one, single insight can be six months in coming. The final, objective recognition is just the tip of the iceberg. The work for that to occur has been going on all along, so gradually that you didn't notice it.

Unless you responsibly live this relationship, unless you understand satsang, you will not be conscious of the work being done when it is being done. You will not be participating. For you to fully understand satsang, means not accepting, rejecting, criticizing, or confirming anything. It means just understanding. Period. Divine compassion accepts nothing less than total understanding.

There is no directed compassion from the guru. No one "gets" more compassion than anyone else. There is a condition of compassion, whoever avails himself of that condition might think that the guru is compassionate, but the guru is not compassionate. The guru is compassion itself. The limited social fiction known as "love" does not compare to this. What that means is that most people who get to talk to me on a one-to-one basis never come back. That is because I am very straight and truthful, from the perspective of having them recognize subjectively that their act is nowhere, that their life is a big fat nothing. They don't want to come back. They are afraid because they haven't understood the nature of true compassion, and expect support and indulgence instead. Anyone who is Alive in God automatically brings out into the open, for others to see, the suffering of life that is founded in separation.

Those who run away can seek for years, trying to do it "on my own". Yet study the lives of those who have been awake. Do you know what every one of them did when they woke up? They have shown by their lives and the way they have taught that they existed in the same relationship with their devotees as their devotees did with them. The relationship that you have with me is exactly the same relationship that I have with you. I am called guru and you are called devotee. There is no difference in the texture of our life together. So why spend ten, fifteen years or more immersed (and you literally have to be immersed) in seeking, in order to get to exactly the same place that you are right now? Our relationship together is always perfect. Satsang is already complete; being in my company is the texture and the form of real spiritual life. When you become a perfect devotee, you will realize that the texture of this relationship is no different for me than for you. The form and the texture of real spiritual life are the same at one point, and that point is the guru. The guru is no special being, but simply exists as this very relationship.

The back door, of course, is thinking that you can do it yourself. Perhaps you reason, "The awakened ones usually spent many years of their lives seeking on the paths," and that justifies your tendency to ignore the way shown by them. There is a problem in taking that back door: what you are liable to do, five years after you leave, is have an insight into why it is not working, and then feel sorry that you left and wasted five years away from the guru. If you get to the point of recognition in that way, it hurts. Your diligent spiritual practice is revealed as futility. You see, the only ones who have woken up following some method, did so in spite of the method, not because of it.

When the enlightened ones throughout history have been asked how to realize truth they have invariably said, "Seek the company of saints." That is satsang. Why not follow the advice of those who are in a position to know? Do you really have such faith in your ignorance that you would trust it to get you out of it? You will taste regret if you spend your time seeking, when you could just abide in my Presence right now. The key is not in valiant heroism, not in the search for a doubtful, experiential happiness that will always elude one's grasp. The key is in making oneself available to the guru, in being open to this Grace.

The freedom I need to do whatever I can to eliminate your delusion and ignorance, is your responsibility. That is your sacrifice. And the time you spend physically present with me and the community is of primary importance. The strength and quality of your sadhana is dependent on responsibly spending as much time as you can with me and with members of Hohm.

Be very aware that in your relationship with me, the closer you get, the more dramatic the confrontation is going to be. The function of my demands is to objectify and clarify the subjective confrontation, forcing you to respond appropriately to the perfect demand of my Presence. If the demands remained on a subjective basis, your tendency would be to shrug your shoulders and say, "Well, I had a bad day today," or blame it on your mate, child, boss, or even your karma. And it is none of these.

If there is no objective confrontation on my part, if I don't show you how rooted in the assumption of separation you are, your tendency in ignorance is to blame it on something other than Grace. You think of Grace as being perfect peace and bliss, and not the fact that you were able to see that you have never really loved anybody. That's not sweet and beautiful, so you don't see that as Grace at all.

Being my friend implies a much greater commitment than being a part of the community and being a student of Lee Lozowick. Being my friend, that friendship sustained in the strength of true commitment to God, is going to allow absolute confrontation, absolute recognition of suffering. That closeness and openness as a friend is exactly what is needed. It gives me the freedom to disrupt your life. And believe me, your life is very disruptable. You have to become sensitive to the humor involved in the whole process of our relationship, and everything works out fine in the long run. My humor is very contagious.

The more you are open to me, the more you are going to trust me. Things happen that way. Many times, somebody will come and say something to me, and as soon as I know what needs to be done, within a very short period of time it is actually being done. If I don't consciously recognize something, if I am not directed towards a specific thing with somebody, it will stay relatively static.

Someone came to me recently, feeling very frustrated, and said, "Nothing is happening." He had noticed this previously but had never said that to me before. As soon as I knew that nothing was happening, stuff arose for him to deal with appropriately. Consciously directing the condition through the guru to some specific thing gets it done very effectively. When the condition is not consciously directed, then for all intents and purposes the work isn't getting done. God is like that. God consciously lives and works as the awakened one.

Grace is a condition. No matter what you have done, if you open yourself to this condition, it will manifest in your life. The responsibility on my part is to let the Divine live you as it completely lives me. That is brought viably into your life when you turn to me, knowing me as Grace.

The direction here is not towards the maintenance of an organization. That would be possible if Grace was not involved, if personality was a factor. The direction here is living God, and nothing else. When you are deeply involved in real spiritual life, your responsibility gives you the freedom and capacity of attention to the Divine, of directing yourself to sadhana, the living of this sacrificial affair.

Sacrifice is more often painful than pleasant. The greatest sacrifice, besides to me, is between each of you. You must in all of your relationships within the community, responsibly allow each other the freedom to engage in sadhana with me. Each person must yield his or her attention to me absolutely, which is very hard as it is, and beyond that, allow others the freedom to do the same.

You will notice that your understanding of the degree of my responsibility continues to increase as the depth of your devotion increases. The ultimate expression of this relationship is present when you are absolutely devoted. Then I am absolutely responsible for you, and it is you who are responsible, for there is no difference between us, no separation, no duality. There is not even "us". There is just "I" with two expressions of "I".

The ultimate pleasure of the guru is in seeing the perfect devotee, the person in the community Alive in the same condition as the guru. That is the supreme pleasure, the only happiness.

* * * *

At one of our presentations on life in the community of Hohm, someone asked, "When you are with Lee, what special positions do you sit in, and what practices do you perform?" One of the persons giving the presentation smiled and said, "Nothing special. We sit comfortably together, laugh, and enjoy ourselves." The person was conceiving of our relationship with the guru as ritualistic, whereas the real delight of community life is simply the very personal enjoyment of Lee's company.

Lee finds as many occasions as he can to be with us. He enjoys each one of us without indulging any of us. When we get together to discuss community business, his warm humor animates and informs everyone in the room. We don't hesitate to poke fun at ourselves, always remembering that it is our perfect relationship which makes true humor possible. And the fun we have never serves as a distraction from life, it is on the contrary an unhesitating involvement in life that is expressed in our relationship.

All of us tend to get distracted in conventional enjoyment, and Lee will often give us what we want, going out to dinner with us or to the movies. We find that all the pleasure of such outings comes from his Presence, and not from the distractions. This serves to point out that being with the guru is the only real pleasure, and that all pleasure in the world can only spring from his condition. The Divine is enjoyed as the flavor and texture of life.

Sometimes Lee will encourage activity in us such as gossip or fascination with inappropriate behavior, and then sit back and watch us dive for the bait. Yet all the time, on the subjective level, he is communicating to us that it is inappropriate. We don't want to take what he says as what he means; we construe that there is no demand in his Presence, so he forcefully demonstrates to us in the most practical ways how we avoid him. Even in the most seemingly superficial conversations, Grace is making its point.

It is funny how we tend to take what the guru says on a surface level, imagining that the Divine is not aware of the games we play. Later on, we remember a little comment or gesture that Lee made, and the meaning begins to grow, revealing itself at deeper levels. Everything that Lee does with us is a demonstration of the one fact that Grace is literally present as our life. Being in the company of the awakened one is an enjoyment that permeates all aspects and levels of our life, demanding that his enjoyment be our enjoyment.

Being with Lee is not always sweet or conventionally pleasant. The guru will be harsh, angry, and reprimanding when he needs to be. That aspect is equally sustaining, and if we could but retain our humor, equally enjoyable. His very life expression is devotion, and that will take whatever form is appropriate. It is our sadhana to be happy in his company, but that does not mean weakness and dependence. The pleasure that is derived from all expressions of our relationship is only recognized in the absolute primacy of God in community life. Lack of enjoyment inevitably springs from not having God as our only priority.

Lee is present as the recognition that we are complete. That Presence, absolutely perfect, reveals our activity as constant seeking. Lee's critical function, graphically pointing out the limitation of all forms of seeking, is another sustaining aspect of life in his company. The way he criticizes the current teachers is not for the purpose of denigrating them, for he truly enjoys them. It is so that we will not become distracted in the theater of the spiritual search, forgetting that our relationship is perfect and that Grace is present. That critical function makes it possible for us to do spiritual practices as a joyous expression of our relationship with the guru, rather than as a way to get somewhere or become something.

Of course, the community's appreciation of God takes on a formal aspect also. Once a week we have the pleasure of gathering in formal satsang, bringing gifts to the guru and singing devotional songs. Then Lee gives a talk, or we sit silently in meditation. In either case, our delight is in formally expressing our love for Lee, and in giving our full attention to him. As our celebration ends, and the guru leaves the room, we all bow, each bow a response of thankfulness.

EIGHT

The Pit and the Pendulum

THERE IS A great process that has been labeled "God" by the religious traditions. The traditions have remained forms of seeking, while the process continues in spite of the search. This process is none other than life itself.

One of the most frequent complaints made about the guru as he has appeared historically, is his uncompromising and arrogant criticism of other teachers and teachings. When the true guru appears, it is this critical aspect of his guru-function that is the most misunderstood and mistrusted. It is only a rare few who comprehend how this is actually serving the true spiritual process in themselves and in the world. The spiritual seeker typically feels that I am not supposed to do that. They expect me to say, "Yes, all paths are valid. We have ours, and theirs is fine as well. So if you are here, follow ours, and if you are there, follow theirs." That is not the case at all; all paths are not valid. I have been very vocal in proclaiming that. Who else is there to do it? Certainly not the seeker, how could he know?

The word "seeker" is used by a number of teachers in reference to where you're not supposed to be. I also use that expression, as it applies aptly in all of your lives. The seeker is like a squirrel and the various forms of the search are the wheel in its cage. One must first recognize the seeking in one's life, all of the useless running around that gets nowhere, before one can know something of Divine humor. Searching manifests in every moment of your life, in an infinite number of forms. It would take forever to recognize each form; that must yield to an understanding of the nature of seeking itself. Seeking is suffering, not a way to eliminate it. The seeker rooted in delusion, is of God, from God, not Alive in God. Only the awakened one lives God. That is what Grace can do: enable you to live God. Nothing else. Happiness is not the result of successful running, it is being off the wheel.

There is always some form of seeking if you are not happy all the time. The upgraded form of the search is the spiritual search. The average person searches for happiness by trying to fulfill his or her need systems in conventional ways: money, power, sex, possessions, and position. Transposing one's search from this "worldly" direction to a "spiritual" one is still seeking. Changing the direction of your running on the wheel does not get you off it, it merely breaks the monotony while reinforcing the sense of someone who is seeking. Seeking is intrinsically hopeless; it does not sustain happiness. Being happy is the antithesis of seeking; neither one can generate or sustain the other. It is so simple. The absence of one is the presence of the other. To be free of the search is to be free of what causes it: the fear and suffering inherent in separative life.

When I talk about getting off the wheel, or giving it all up, or being free of it, that has nothing to do with what you expect while you are busy running around on the wheel. That is the delusion of ego. And that is the life of practically everyone on the face of this earth. The seeker cannot know what giving it all up means; that must be known prior to mind. The search is founded in mind, and when anything is known or accepted from the perspective of mind, one is still trying to figure it all out. One still has the same alternatives, questions, and doubts. One is still the very dilemma. Only the guru who is off the wheel can get you to realize what is prior to mind. All techniques, methodologies and paths are only exploiting your capacity to keep running on the wheel.

The function of the guru is to undermine all forms of the search, spiritual or otherwise. He undoes the seeker beyond even the notion of a seeker to be undone. One who is completely undermined by the guru remains with only one alternative, one expression in life, and one enjoyment: the constancy of devotion to the Lord. It is no surprise that the average seeker runs like a scared rabbit from the guru, because no form of unconscious theater is allowed in the awakened one's company. The guru demands of those who sit with him that they recognize that everything, without exception, that they have ever done or are capable of doing, is motivated by their separative life, by the need for a payoff. That is why the real guru has had so few devotees during his lifetime. Many will approach him, remain for a brief period of time, and then leave. Perhaps they assume that their superficial contact is sufficient. A brief or distant relationship with the guru is a strategic and inadequate one. It remains the sadhana of separation. The close and constant relationship with the guru is meaningful. His actual Presence is a transforming fire, a direct threat to the tinderlike structure of people's lives. The fire of devotion makes my devotee look like an ass to society, yet he is the only one who is happy and complete. He is my very self.

What the seeker wants to know is something that somebody else doesn't know. He would like to be one step ahead. Why this? Why that? What for? Whatever answer the seeker gets becomes his ace in the hole, a new way of winning. And all because he is too stupid to know that he has already won (One).

Every one of you is so intent on prolonging survival that you have missed the point of your life. Because of some half-assed assumptions about death and life, all you are ever doing is promoting suffering, never obviating it. All belief systems, creeds, and conceptual modes of perception only root you more deeply in the mire of delusory separation. They do not affect the cause of suffering, they are only attempts to hide or avoid it. Your dualistic concepts of life are not valid. In truth there is no perceiver or perceived, no conceptualizer or conceptualized. There is only God. All conceptual knowledge requires assumed separation. Any concepts, including those concerning the guru, God, and happiness, are worthless. They remain forms of the search, no matter how high-minded they are. Recognition of the concepts of seeking, God and guru, is not the recognition of seeking, God and guru. Trying to figure out life is a futile and endless task. Life, however much to your dismay, is unfigure-outable.

When one is into spiritual seeking, one thinks in terms of high ideals: God, compassion, nirvana, oneness, and so on. Confined to the ideal realm, these are fictions whose nature is the exclusion of life, which is seen as down-to-earth, gut level, mundane, and far from ideal. That dualism, however subtle or hidden, that interpretation of what is, is the very crux of the search. That is the birth of the seeker. What can acting on the basis of that distinction produce but the continuance of suffering? The separation of life, of money, sex, and power, from spirituality, is not true; and the acceptance of that dualism is fatal, for the ones who do accept have missed the point of their existence.

God is in no way limited by the lack of perception and understanding in the human mind. God is just this, absolutely unqualified, encompassing form and formlessness, fullness and void, intensity and the lack of it. God is prior condition, the perfectly present reality. God is not your "way", "path", or your religion.

When one is five years old, one believes absolutely that a certain toy is necessary. When one is a teenager, one believes that it is terribly important to get a driver's license or be of age to drink. When one is in the thirties, one believes that being socially respected is important, and so on. The importance associated with the seeker's belief in his faith or creed is the same thing, and just as fruitless. All beliefs are dramatically threatened by the demands of the guru, for he will graphically and powerfully point out how much lack of faith is really there. Only devotion, selfless and pure, is lasting happiness.

The striptease that the guru demands of the seeker allows all forms of the delusion of separation to be discarded, leaving only what one is: God. To society and every form of unconscious convention, this, the deepest threat, appears not as the happiness in selfless service that it is, but as utter craziness. It is only Grace, and it is only available to those who in truth turn to the guru.

Grace expresses itself as service and the fullness of devotion, that devotion which is for no sake but itself. One becomes a devotee of the Lord through absolute sacrifice to the self who is guru. This process is not suffering and separation, it is joy, humor, and the complete enfoldment of one's life in the Divine. The ultimate expression of the guru-devotee relationship is absolute recognition of non-duality, directly knowing that you are not, have never been, and can never be separate from God.

The guru appears to the seeker as a mirror. He will reflect the seeker's frustration and confusion, instead of offering him spiritual sedatives. He will not give the seeker something to keep him rooted in the search. The true guru will not say, "Do this mantra: Ram, Ram, Ram," so that you get high and cooled out. The true guru might give you a mantra like, "Ibbity bibbity sibbity sab." That's a good one. It's very depressing, just like your search. That kind is sure to get you to see that there is nothing to do, nothing to say, only the guru's Grace to turn to.

I will not say, "Study these lessons for two years to prepare for your initiation." In the traditions, they give you initiations after you have studied and practiced for God knows how long, and then only when some "guru" feels like you're ready. That is not what takes place here. I have a problem with initiation. How could I, who knows everyone as already realized, know when to initiate anyone? How do I know who is ready for initiation and who isn't? I couldn't possibly initiate anyone without assuming the same bullshit that everyone tries to lay on me in the first place. All that stuff that is motivating everyone in the traditions is nothing more than a colossal error. I can't buy in, and I'm not going to. There is only the Divine.

The initiation here is experiencing me as your mirror. I might say, "We don't have enough flowers this week. Go out and buy me flowers." So you go home and start saying to yourself, "Why should I? He has more money than I do, and plenty of flowers. Why should I get him more?" Then it dawns on you. I have been showing you your own separative activity.

Traditional spiritual teaching is correct when it points out that the guru is the only one who knows what is good for the particular student. That blows any kind of mass-dispensed sadhana right out of the water. To give a whole population, or a whole community, a technique, is utterly useless. For some it could really point out something about their sadhana, while for the rest it would be a fascination, a waste of time, merely another game that they can keep playing forever. At times I may give individuals a technique purposely, expecting them to do it, in order to point out something about their relationship with me. It would not be given as icing on their spiritual cake, not as an instrument or intensifier of sadhana, but simply to make a point about our relationship. That does not mean, of course, that I would give anyone a technique and expect him or her to abandon sadhana.

Were people to recognize that all of their techniques, therapies and idealisms are irrelevant to the basic fact of their life, their assumed separation, they would allow their depression and suffering to arise. Then perhaps they could see what all of that amounts to, and become aware of turning to God as the viable alternative.

Any form of remedial action or repair work, any effort at reconciliation with God, is mistaken from the outset. By its very nature, such corrective behavior implies that the cause of and need for it is real. It implies that one is actually separate, not realized, and in need of repair. All such effort serves as a polite, albeit a higher form of distraction than sports, television, crime, or gluttony. Involvement in curative measures, such as psychotherapies, gestalt therapies, primal therapies, hypnotherapies, and even the physical therapies, is based on the assumption that there is something wrong that needs to be fixed. Therapy is not needed. You are already perfect.

Yoga appears as the cure-all for the damages wreaked on life by the ego; Buddhism offers practices which imply that it can rectify your desire mechanism; Christianity says that it saves you from original sin, and so on throughout the traditions. It is all useless. What they are attempting to repair has never been broken. These attempts are founded in strategies of egoic control, and all egoic control is a problem as distinguished from a way to solve one. Nothing is ever dissolved through ego; it is the dramatic and perfect confrontation of the present Divine that dissolves the delusion of separation.

In those techniques and paths in which rhetoric is used that expresses a claim for non-seeking as the way, and then offers you an affirmation or tells you to sit in a directionless or motivationless meditation until you realize the truth of non-seeking, what is offered is something that is essentially future-oriented. They are affirming something that they are not presently responsible for. They remain with the limitation which is characteristic of all paths: seeking. At best, they are forms of sublimation, however subtle or seemingly effective they may be. Because of this inherent limitation, one following their way remains deluded, having programmed oneself to believe that "God is within", or "I am God", or that there is "nothing to do".

Every methodology is based on this belief in repairing damage, and assumes implicitly or explicitly that you are separate from God and that the method will get you back to Eden. If you try to get somewhere, you don't, although you may persuade yourself that you have. The simple fact of the matter is that separation from God is not a fact, whether you like it or not. There is nowhere to get.

Spiritual practices will not get anyone Grace. They are sometimes appropriate. Spiritual practices tend to keep your body strong and healthy, and your mind fresh and alert, which is the natural expression of body and mind when they are not search-oriented. In one sense these practices assure you that you will be more capable of responsible living, so that when Grace becomes real for you, you just fall into it without unnecessary contraction and resistance. That is all they are: simply appropriate. Without the guru, spiritual practices can only be a form of education or a routine of seeking. They are never a means to Grace. My emphasis of that should not lead you to purposely not do spiritual practices, for that is also seeking. They are appropriate when they arise as expressions of our relationship.

Your life as you live it is your body, mind, and total egotistical self-involvement. Prior condition is beneath and inclusive of all of that. Yet prior condition is unmoved and unaffected by any of it. The seeker remains completely affected, completely involved, completely oblivious to awakening. To that one, God is a word.

If you ever have a flash or the tiniest taste of the Divine life, that's it: only misery until you have it all. Of course, that only motivates the search even more. It is hard to convince a person who thinks he is happy that he is suffering, yet if he has had only a flash of empathy with one who is living God, then he knows and can't forget. Then he either tries to forget or tries to attain the flash once more. It takes on a mystical and fantastic quality, until the experience is blown out of proportion in the seeker's mind.

Mystical experience is really great. When you are actively and appropriately dealing with your life here and now, you can have all the mystical experience you want. When you look for mystical experience to the exclusion of your life here and how, I call that avoiding your sadhana. Mystical experience as an avoidance of the felt or known suffering in life is not spiritual life. It is just the same old story.

You will go to great lengths to maintain the delusion of separateness from God, even to the point of being a "child of God". Being a child of God is not enough. Rocks are children of God. If you were a rock it would be enough. As human beings there is the potential for realizing that you exist as the Divine, not as a lump in samadhi somewhere off in a cave, but as an Alive and functionally intelligent being. Rocks are functional as rocks. Most humans are not functional as humans, but as rocks.

It is your nature to be simply Alive, not dependent on practices or conditioned by systems. Normal spiritual highs, samadhis, mystical experiences, and so on, are dependent for their very existence on whatever brought them about, whether that be mantra, introspective meditation, self-abnegation, energy mechanics, or whatever. Living God is not dependent on anything or caused by anything. It is simply present.

Devotee: How is it that so many gurus and masters who say that they are awake make the mistake of supporting the search?

Lee: One can be awake and not be educated, or awake and functioning according to the cultural tradition, and in either case make the mistake of supporting the search. As an individual you can be off the wheel, yet your teaching can support the search because of the tools the traditions have supplied you with. The form of your own sadhana has limited the expression of your awakening. My teaching is not conditioned by any particular form of sadhana.

There has always only been one. People tend to look at this one as other than what is. If allowed to, they will consistently assume this one to be a teacher or physician, a hero or a heretic. They assume that this one is an exclusive body. Get this clearly: only I am this one. Krishna was this very one, Buddha was this one, and Jesus was no different. You are this one. That is just the way it is.

I am not your connection to the Divine. I am God, plain and simple. And when you get the message, so to speak, and stop the search in the realization that you don't have to look for it because it is already, then you live in truth as the same condition the guru is. God is not an experience, mystical or otherwise. Nor is God lived via the culmination of any number of experiences. God is inclusive already of all experiences. Just This.

For the seeker on the "path", God is the carrot at the end of a stick. There it is, dangling in front of your nose. But no matter how hard you run, you can't reach it. Nobody on any of the paths is getting any closer to the carrot. The only purpose of the carrot is to keep you plodding along the path. Our relationship is greater than all reward. There is no carrot involved.

The guru-devotee relationship enables one to be open to the condition of Grace, which the guru is present as. Then Grace will automatically do what you can never do. You really don't have to "do" anything. Awareness isn't work, and recognition isn't practice. Our relationship is what will get you to recognize the Divine without laying any trip on it. Accepting the guru allows you to be open so that the Divine can dissolve you. Grace does not need your direction, motivation, attention, or help. What it needs is your permission. That is what you must yield. The Divine needs your permission to undo you and resurrect you as God. That is what all life is about. You need to say, "okay, just do it." Grace will do it, and in a way you do not expect.

Accepting the guru is giving yourself permission to know who you are. In my company the search is transformed into the life of God. You come to me to get something, and end up giving everything.

NINE

SOME PEOPLE GO through their whole lives and nothing happens. They get up every morning, they go to work, they like their job, they come home at night, they have their dinner, they watch television, and then they go to sleep. Once a year they go on vacation. Nothing ever happens. They are never sick. Nobody ever dies in their family, they die first. They never had a pet, so they were never sad when it died. They go through their entire life like that.

Sometimes we look at people like that and think, "I wish I could do that. It seems so easy and they look like they're happy all the time." Awareness seems hardly worth it compared to happy ignorance. The problem arises when we start to get a taste of the Divine. Then the passion and intensity of life begins to arise. When we really get into something, good or bad, we get into it completely, and little things start to take on immense proportions. A friend of ours who has known us for fifteen years all of a sudden ignores us. That can be a deeply passionate experience. We go through a lot of stuff, and it is quite intensified.

Before I started getting into this, nothing was intensified at all. I enjoyed food, and so what? It was no big deal. Everything was very bland, although I managed to persuade myself that things were exciting. The more I got involved in spiritual life, the more I saw that everything I used to do was very tasteless. The ups and downs were within a very narrow spectrum. The more I opened up to the Divine, the broader the spectrum became, until the ups became way up and the downs way down.

I know that you are experiencing many things, and that the intensity is incredible because the limitations are being taken off. The spectrum of how you experience, the depth of your involvement in life, and how you express that depth, is growing and widening. Spiritual life is very passionate. Spiritual life is not a dissertation on the Absolute. It is life overflowing. That fullness is beginning to burst the little boundaries you have lived in up to now.

Many people are very comfortable consciously thinking that they are happy. They go around saying, "Oh, it's all so wonderful," and underneath the veneer of calmness they are suffering. They are tense, tight, upset. When they hear about the joyous life of God and being happy all the time, they immediately envision something extraordinary. They think that spiritual life is something extra. Actually it is just life's full measure. The awakened one is not the hero who is measured against the ordinary. The awakened one is ordinary life.

I could be awake and never tell anybody, and nobody would ever know. Nobody would know because there is nothing fantastic about people who are awake. If I tell you that I am somebody special, that I am this great enlightened master, it doesn't really mean anything. It happens to be true, and that is irrelevant. What means something is if you know that prior to mind. If you don't know that it's true, you are going to be very disappointed, because you have given your time and energy and money and have really helped the community, you have put a lot of hopes and dreams and expectations on the community, and someday, sooner or later, Lee is not going to fulfill that. Lee will rip that off completely.

Grace exists manifest as the guru. Period. There is nothing I can do about it. Whatever happens from this point on is a matter of whether or not you recognize that it is true, regardless of anything I may do. It is not up to me to prove to you that it's true. You have to see God first. If you don't see God first, all you are going to do is continue to cycle through endless attachment to limitation. When you really see God first, you will be amazed at the noticeable difference in your experience. As limitation falls away, you live humorously and lightly. If you don't see God first, you will be concerned with whether I am who I say I am, and your mind will try to figure out ways to prove one way or the other. When you see God first, Lee comes into perspective for where Lee fits. And nothing Lee could possibly do to you, with you, or for you, would have any effect on you other than pointing out something about your sadhana. There would be no melodrama involved, there would be nothing involved except your life in God.

I become more and more exclusive. The more people believe I am who I say I am and trust that, the more exclusive I get. The more curious they are, the more they are going to make an effort to believe, and the more strategies they will create in order to define me. Belief is always a strategy. When there is no more belief, there is only faith. Nobody has faith until there is nothing left to hang on to. Your beliefs concerning me are just more attachments.

If you think that you have faith, think again. You have your homes and your families, you have food in your stomachs. Things are pretty secure, so you can afford to have your "faith". Nobody has faith until he is ready to give up his very life. The process of the true guru is to get devotees to the point where there is nothing left, nothing to be ashamed of, nothing to prove or protect. There is nothing left, except faith, life, God. You know faith when you know at a gut level that you have nothing; that is the beginning of real spiritual life. Faith is the absolute recognition that there is nothing to attain and that whatever you experience is totally your responsibility.

This faith is very real. It is not in the least ethereal or "otherworldly". I am interested in the human condition. I am not interested in you being a dog, a cat, or an ascended master next lifetime, or you perfecting the body of light so that you never have to come back to earth again. I am interested in this human condition. Faith and devotion are true expressions of this condition, its purest expressions.

True devotion is not to the guru conceived as an individual, but to the guru as he is. Love and devotion to the guru without a consuming love for God is not enough. It is too easy to fixate on an individual who is in an attractive position, which the guru obviously is. In truth I exist as none other than the Divine. That is not logical, rational, or conventional. Unless you are a devotee, the dualism remains, however subtly. Because the mind functions from duality, spiritual seekers will typically either love God without the guru (or pretend to at any rate), or love the guru without loving God. In rare cases, the guru and God are loved, but still as separate. There are people who love God and love the guru, intellectually acknowledging the guru as God, and yet haven't got them synchronized. Loving me without God is not enough, and neither is loving God without me, because both alternatives spring from separation. Ultimately I can't say that you have to love God in addition to loving me, since there is no difference. It is only because you become attached to the guru as limitation that I say you have to see God first.

Without devotion, life is not meaningful. Whatever you accumulate: knowledge, spiritual experience, or even devotion to Lee, is meaningless without true devotion, without seeing God first. That is exactly what is missing from the "happy" ignorance that we envied because it seemed so easy. The difference between living ordinary life and sleepwalking ordinary life is devotion. The widening of the spectrum as you enter my company, the intensity of emotion, is just more life to be enjoyed. Simple, bare devotion is life's essence.

I am not here to fulfill my destiny. I am not here to be a superstar guru or to make it big in showbiz. My only function is a devotional one, a sacrificial one. Being a great teacher or master or any of that stuff is beside the point. My function is to get you to see God first and live pure devotion. God is that pure devotion, without object, complete in itself. It is not something that I do or feel, it is what I am.

* * * *

Lee's untraditional teaching has a very traditional foundation: the guru-devotee relationship. The fact that Lee does not belong to a lineage has tended to make us forget that the process of life in his company is ancient, in fact older than history. He requires that we study the spiritual literature of all religious traditions, paying particular attention to the lives of the awakened ones themselves. We find that their appearance in the world parallels that of Lee, and that sadhana with him is identical to real spiritual life as it has always been lived.

The community holds study groups, in which great spiritual books are read out loud and discussed. We inevitably had problems with them. For instance, someone would bring up a question about the reading, and the group would try to come up with a nice answer that everybody could agree on. If people didn't agree, pointless arguments would ensue that began to resemble encounter group sessions rather than study groups. And if people did agree, nobody learned anything, because the question hadn't really been dealt with, it had just been neatly categorized. We tended to translate what we were reading into concepts we were already familiar with, and the study groups never seemed to work.

We brought it up with Lee, who laughed and said that they weren't supposed to work. In fact, as long as everybody tried to make them work, they would serve to show us how nothing we did could make them work.

Still, there were a few things to be learned in the process of studying together as a community. First of all, true study could only take place when the place of study was recognized as a shrine. After all, we are gathering in Lee's name, so appropriate study is a result of being turned to Lee. We saw how the fact that Lee wasn't physically present at the study groups served to remind us that he is always present as Grace, and that our study should be in that spirit. In the second place, the element of enjoyment was missing. If we didn't enjoy reading about God, there was no way we were going to study together responsibly. If, on the other hand, our interaction with each other in the study groups was based on a common enjoyment of the expression of the awakened one in literature, whatever discussion that takes place could be natural and appropriate. As it turned out, the study groups still didn't work, but now we were enjoying them.

Members of the community have found that their educational foundation has been very helpful in sadhana. The mistake of viewing the guru-devotee relationship in terms of personality is less likely to be made by one who can recognize the same relationship in the accounts of the previous masters in history. It is also appropriate for members of Hohm to be thoroughly familiar with the form and expression of the devotee in the world, which can be found in the traditions of those who were absolutely devoted to God. When one is well acquainted with real spiritual life as it has always been lived, and in the paradoxical ways of the one who has lived God consciously in the world, one recognizes Lee as a very old friend.

TEN

The Chipmonk and the Peanut Butter

THIS WORLD IS God's playground. It is not God's battlefield. It is the job of everyone who comes Hohm to assure God that this world is a place of play for the Divine. That means living humorously, joyfully participating in life, not gloomily going through one's existence as if it was a tiresome duty. Anyone who has truly known love of God can never be too serious about life. If you have felt that love, cosmic experiences do not seem so very special to you, and there is little thirst for success on a path, for that love knows no grasping or seeking. The entire success syndrome, (how was your meditation today? how many visions did you have?), lacks the one element of non-grasping love for God. The seeker sees God in terms of some kind of mystical God-meditation. The same person might have seen a child kiss a lonely dog, which is an infinitely more real and Divine experience than bliss during meditation. The seeker ignores true love, true life, by the nature of his or her search, the insecurity which clings to life, rendering it lifeless.

Spiritual life is not a battle with the forces of darkness. Truth is no victory, no big deal. Everybody is realized anyway. So if you want to have a great spiritual experience, take a tab of acid with the right frame of mind, and you will see God. It is no big deal to see God. The significant thing is how you function after you see God. Has an intelligent recognition of Grace occurred? Or was it a high from which you came back to conventional awareness? In the latter, more common case, there is nothing going on for you but the separation you are living all the time.

In order for you to live humorously and intelligently in my company, education is needed. The more you study about God, the more you are laying the foundation for living God. Immerse yourself in the process of spiritual study, and at some point you will stop being so concerned with who is going out with who, and you will begin to know the love of the Divine. Without being in my company, your tendency would be to try to extract what you want from the traditional literature, but in my company your education will be natural and appropriate.

When one is educated, one finds it very easy to accept one's natural state of being. When one is not educated, and that one experiences his or her natural state of being, he or she usually freaks out. If that one is lucky and has a family that is warm and friends that have gone through it and understood it, he or she might get educated after the fact. If that one isn't so lucky, he or she taps into fantasy, not knowing how to deal with that fantasy, and it takes over. Such a one is liable to be institutionalized. That is society's polite word for locking up those who don't fit into society's narrow view of morality. It makes the whole thing palatable when an intelligent sounding word ("institutionalized") is used.

When one is educated properly, that one can deal with experience as it arises very simply and spontaneously, with joy. When one is not educated properly, one gets depressed or elated when different experiences arise. Either way, high or low, it doesn't matter. That one is suffering.

I require of you the proper education. I am not interested in Hohm being a place where all the odd-balls and freaks hang out. In short, I am not interested in aberrations. When someone sees God, he or she can become an aberration. That is the kind that staggers around and everybody stares at or runs from. I am definitely not planning to have Hohm be the kind of a place about which people say, "Wait until you go to that place. Boy, will you see some freaks!" Any spiritual community draws aberrations to itself, because they have seen God. There are freaks running around who have really seen God. There is a hell of a difference between a freaked-out seer of God and someone who is living God functionally in the world. The difference is education. When you come Hohm, forget about being a member of the newest cult and having cover stories in Time and **Newsweek.** It is real spiritual life you are dealing with here.

Being responsible is a matter of educating yourself properly so that you integrate your spiritual experience into your life. If you do not integrate it into your life, you are very happy, and very useless. You can hang around and chant "Hare Krishna" and be very happy. Being happy is one thing, and assuring God that this is his or her playground is another. Just being happy and walking around while people are running away from you when they see you, is obviously not enough. I am totally uninterested in being the neighborhood joke: "Oh boy, here they come again!" Responsibility is assuring God that this is a playground, not a battlefield where people avoid you because of the way you act.

For me it doesn't matter. It is my job to be unconventional. If you want to be a guru, you can be as unconventional as you want. If you are living God and are unconventional, you will be a successful guru. If you just say, "I'd like to do that, it looks like fun. People bring flowers and I sit up front getting all of the attention," I suggest that you try it for a while and see what happens.

It is not your job to do what I am doing. It is your job to just be responsible and intelligent. If people are running from you, you are not being either. The kind of person I am looking for is the kind that is absolutely devoted to me as guru, and the world as the Divine playground. And if you are devoted to the world as the Divine playground, you are going to allow people in the world to be happy when they touch you.

As it turns out, people are going to run from you anyway! However, people running away because they think that you're crazy, and people running away because they sense that you are devoted and they are scared of your happiness, are two entirely different things. When they run from your happiness, all they are going to do is wish that they are where you are. They are afraid that they are going to have to give up something to get this mysterious happiness of yours. So there is a clear distinction between people not wanting to socialize with you because you are happy, and people avoiding you because you are weird. In the former case, they are desperate for what you "have". They are afraid to come up to you and ask, "Why are you so happy?" In the latter case, they are looking at one another and thinking, "Here's the crazy one again."

Education is what makes the difference between those two cases. Yet keep in mind that this does not resemble society's form of education, which is a total rip-off and only breeds irresponsibility. I am reminded of an interview with a native American chief that I read. They have schools on this particular reservation, so they don't send their kids to public school. The interviewer asked the chief, "Do you think that your kids are getting the proper education? Will they be able to make it in the world?" And the chief said, "Well, the best educated people in society are running the world today. Look at the world: isn't it obvious?" What is obvious is the lack of real education in society. The education that you receive in society is not education, it is destruction.

The process of education that takes place here with me has nothing to do with programming or shoving life into a slot. Hohm is without structure and without philosophy, yet there is an exact structure that I will accept, beyond conceptual formulations. It involves studying while you open to the intuition of the Divine as your life. I expect you to be knowledgeable in spiritual life, and that means, for most of you, a hell of a lot of study. Rather than being a dry, mechanical process of rote learning, study in my company is soaking up the atmosphere of Divine life naturally and without artifice.

The more reading you do, the more you are going to see that the rhetoric is the same in all of the traditions. If you read about any of the great Hindu sages, the great Buddhas, and the Christian saints or mystics, you see that, although the forms are strikingly different, the substance is essentially the same. That will help give you the will-power to hang around, because you will say, "Lee is consistent with the awakened masters of the past. He says the same thing that they have all said. I know that Jesus was the real thing, and Buddha was the real thing, so I'll stick around and see what happens." Ultimately, the recognition that I am the real thing must come from prior to mind, but for the time being the education will hook you.

Some of you have found studying rather dull. You plod through page after page out of a sense of duty. At some point that will fall away, and you'll start to really get into reading about God. It is simply a matter of continuing through the dull reading until it soaks in, and suddenly it's not dull anymore. For a long time I found that reading very dull, and then everything else started falling away, and all I wanted to do was read about the kind of people who were perfect devotees and living powerful lives in God. So read about the saints, read about the people who have been happy in Divine life. I see study as an important aspect of understanding what you are doing.

It may seem at times like, "What am I doing this for if my life isn't working?" That is because your intensity of study may often be out of synch with your functional life. At some point it will be seen that, although it is not getting you anywhere, it is still very valuable. You will know how valuable it is after the fact of awakening, when all of your education comes into perspective. However, you shouldn't become involved in study to the exclusion of your functional life either.

Study makes one more functional as a responsible member of the community. Education helps one integrate real spiritual life into one's activities. Experiences arise, and they can be recognized for what they are: just experiences. Certainly if you had not been educated to the fact that experience is simply experience and need not be seen as any kind of end result or motivating factor, the chances for you to discover that on your own would be mighty slim.

In the process of study in my community, there is a significant feature that you should remember. You are primarily studying the ones who were Alive in God. Their teachings are fine to learn about, but in reading spiritual literature, you should pay particular attention to the lives of the masters themselves. Some of the dharmas are very intricate and well put together. You can pick holes in them philosophically, and at the same time they are very beautiful, flowing, and full. On the other hand, when you study the master, that is not often present. When you read about the awakened ones, you are constantly confronted with the force of the contradiction of their lives, which were not usually very tidy and beautifully structured. They appear, in fact, quite wild and strange. Add to that the further complication that when you are reading about them, your mind is always seeing them over and against other teachers, and rarely by themselves. You are always seeing the nature of the seeking which you are involved in when you analyze the masters. That's where the benefit comes in.

All of the studying that you do is simply for your education so that you can be a responsible devotee of mine. That is what your study should be directed towards, not to fulfill your fascination with the various paths and methodologies. And there is a tendency to do that. Your education in the community is always in the context of our direct relationship. Without the forceful Presence of Grace in your life, all your study is mere book learning. With that Presence, it is genuine enrichment.

ELEVEN

Big Rock Candy Mountain

THE MIND HAS at its command, at its beck and call, all forms of the creative processes that manifest as endless experience in this and in all worlds and dimensions. God is inclusive of all that. God is the very texture of life itself, not any limited or limiting tendency, form, experience, or concept.

The mind, however, has the power and genius to convince one that separation in life is true. The mind would have one believe that unusual yogic phenomena, exalted states of consciousness, and all sorts of visionary experiences, are God. The typical seeker therefore looks toward these uncommon experiences as the fulfillment of spiritual life. They are no more fulfillment of the spiritual life than a good meal or a full orgasm.

People generally find that the unexpected only lasts a short time. Perhaps they have had what is called "peak experience". Usually it only lasts for a moment, sometimes a day, week, or occasionally longer. The peak experience typically fades rather rapidly, while you stand there aghast, fearful and disillusioned. One moment you are as strong and together as you could imagine yourself to be, and the next, you are lost and seeking in futility to retrace your way back to the peak. One moment you are laughing and enjoying yourself with no thought of dilemma, crisis or suffering, and the next moment you are groping painfully and unconsciously in reaction to life.

Peak experience is talked about, written about, and always sought for as some state of consciousness that is high, unusual, other than natural and ordinary. Peak experience is that experience that you are forever being motivated, from within and without, to achieve and hold on to. Motivation to attain it is continually present, because mind is rooted in the delusion of separative individual existence. It is always being sought for and known as other than your very present condition.

In traditional religious practices and the esoteric, manipulative techniques of spirituality, the consolations one receives from peak experience are attributed to kundalini, white light, psychic phenomena, or siddhis. They are never attributed to their true source: separation. The teachers and teachings of every spiritual and religious tradition are only indulging the same search through experience as every kind of secular activity. All inevitably remain in mind, founded in the delusion of separation.

The problem that remains when you have your experiences is that you think they are something special, extraordinary, and too good to be true. It is actually just experience, and thus temporary. The ego merely assuming that they are more significant, desirable, or enjoyable, does not alter or undo the motivation that created them in the first place. It is always the pain and fear inherent in separative life that is motivating everyone who is founded in mind to seek these experiences. And all the experiences ultimately become the supportive validation for the existence of the assumed self beneath the pain and fear. Peak experience is the payoff, the goal and motivation of every egoic act. It is the ultimate hope and expression of the separate one, the highest possible sanction for the existence of the ego, and the distinctive experience of man as an assumed individual. It is suffering. The highest attainment of humanity in its delusion is merely a momentary distraction from consciously knowing its own condition.

The peak experience is a kind of sensual overload. Sensually you get blissed out, disoriented, "blown away", or whatever. Since separative life is identified exclusively with the physical body, it remains a five-sense based experience. Contrary to the romantic and convincingly high-flying descriptions of these experiences by mystics and yogis, you always remain in assumed separation from God.

If the experience is known as a "conversion" experience, the same conditions apply. What are we supposed to be converted from?

What are we converted to? And more importantly, who is it that is converted? The conventions and structures that mind depends on and maintains are what create the conversion experience, allowing it to occur instead of God-awakening. Every conversion experience is generated in mind, and accepted by its proud owner as proof of the correctness or necessity of some form of behavior: "Oh, how it has changed my life! I'll never be the same again. How happy and content I am!" After a brief period, the experience fades and the patterns of seeking arise, motivated by the sense of loss and fear, only now in new, upgraded forms.

The need to re-experience the subjective qualities of the peak is the continual grasping of ego for proof of its existence, whether that need is expressed within the confines of new structures or old. Neither peak nor conversion experience are wrong. They are simply not God and not a means to God. You are left, in both cases, with thinking about the experience in terms such as, "I know that I had this experience. I know that God exists right here in my heart. So why do I feel empty, incomplete?" You have had experience and are still relating to it, rather than being simply present. You are attached to what you have experienced, and therefore feel the need to attain it again. The reason that it doesn't last is that it is a process within mind, always known by an individual within a temporal framework. You think, "How long is it going to last?" or "It was really nice." Yes, it was really nice, and it has only programmed ego to search for more of the same validation.

Ego not only assumes that it created the experience, but that it can recreate the experience by being good or by successfully doing some practice. "What can I do to get that experience again?" asks the mind, and the traditions are there with a plenitude of answers to satisfy every temperament. There is the path of raja yoga, the kingly way of yogic power. There is the path of diet and exercise, fasting and self-abnegation, for those of a more humble, less adventuresome nature. There are a multitude of possibilities within and around every tradition and methodology, all offering any and every inducement to buy in and try it out. They all give you juicy homework, things for you to do to see that you get "there".

Any spiritual organization, teacher, or teaching that offers such homework is offering a path which is necessarily supportive of the search for experiential attainment. Consequently, the separate self, which so often in the rhetoric of those same teachings is denied validity, sought to be extinguished or gone beyond, is strengthened and reaffirmed, leaving intact the root of suffering.

It is always implied and generally made explicit in all forms of the search, that if one is good and follows the austerity practice, eats the right foods, breathes properly, and whatever else the homework is, one will have another peak experience. In the established and socially respected traditions, there is a very strong subjective validation associated with the attainment of experiential states. This is a source of constant motivation for the seeker. To the participants and the casual or interested observers the front is, "Yes, it is all God." But beneath that it remains, "Get out of my way. I have to keep practicing or I'll never make it into samadhi in this lifetime." Objectively it is always God, nirvana, heaven, and self-realization. Subjectively it is experience, self-validation and suffering. It is the "spiritual" practices that offer ego the means, justification and guidance for the attainment of experiential states, the ultimate avoidance of God.

The seeker thinks, "Wow! It really works. I've been good, I practiced it, I did it. I attained the unattainable. It's indescribable. What an experience I had!" He or she did have an experience, but now is firmly rooted in some path of attainment, hopelessly caught up in the mystique of experience, thinking that he or she is going to become a "master", "yogi", or maybe even a "saint". All that one has done is exercise and fulfill an egoic need system, remaining ignorant and dependent on a technique to distract him or herself out of suffering. The highest achievement of any seeker is the substitution of one form of unconscious suffering and distraction for another. Locked into having peak experience after seemingly being successful at practice, he or she is effectively excluding the possibility of living selflessly as God.

These experiences are at best what one allows oneself to have in order to reinforce the egoistic state, and at worst what keeps one there. It is only the guru who can break that cycle of dependency on experience. What the seeker fails to realize without an appropriate relationship with the true guru is that every experience is exactly the same expression of dependency. They only reinforce the sense of self, suffering and dilemma in life. With anything lived apart from satsang, there is always "someone" knowing it, enjoying it, or suffering it. It is always assumed as being over and against other experience, and is implicitly temporary. A separate self is assumed as willfully creating and sustaining it, either consciously or subconsciously. And when that is not the case, there is literally nobody home.

All these forms of experience, high, low, or in between, are attempts to support ego's claim for a life of its own. Without the undermining of this assumed individual, everything remains absolutely and ultimately unfulfilling, regardless of how distracting, absorbing or fascinating the experience is.

There is only God and that is truth itself. All else is discussion about truth. Only God is present. The blisses, the states of ecstasy, the siddhis that are talked about by all spiritual seekers masquerading as ones who know, are nothing more than separation. Having psychic experiences, seeing lights, hearing inner sounds, or using siddhis—isn't wrong or stupid necessarily, simply frivolous.

One who clearly understands that there is no experience to be attained goes through mind, and becomes conscious prior to mind itself. The part that the guru can play, and that a technique or practice can not, is to be already functionally present as God, a living contradiction of the search. The guru will bring you to the point where you don't have a self with which to experience. Then there is no more search; then only is happiness present. There is no "peak" and no "conversion", there is only the constancy of eternally existing God. In the recognition of what is, all life is peak experience, and you are conversion itself.

The form of teaching that is presented by this one is non-searching based on true and radical reliance on the Grace of the guru. It is only in relationship with the true guru that experience can remain simply what it is, without being sought after or rejected, grasped or avoided. All forms of spiritual attainment are then knowable for what they are: possibilities that in themselves neither create nor sustain happiness.

Until the seeker realizes my perfect Presence, he or she will only know the frustration of the search. My Presence is all that is offered here, and the only part the guru plays in the conversion experience is the frustration of it. The whole point of this one is not to change anything, it is to get you to recognize absolutely that you can't change anything. This one has no compulsion to change, because he is Alive as consciousness itself, rather than as an assumed perspective within consciousness.

The seeker is one who will try anything, through any experience, to avoid dealing with his or her manifest condition. In case you thought I was talking about someone else, that is all of you. That is your life, as you have known it and lived it. Trying to escape your separative life does not avail. Only God avails.

* * * *

The guru's demand is the guru's Presence. It calls for love, devotion, and sacrifice in those who are with him. But we perceive the demand from the perspective of mind, and are therefore unaware of the true nature of the demand. We simply don't know that we have a very practical connection with the guru on a subjective level, so we always act as if our relationship is being brought to completion, rather than recognizing that it is already complete. The demand, from our perspective, is on the separate self, which we suppose to be capable of sacrifice. The only thing we are really capable of is the form of sacrifice. When we take on that form, it purifies and strengthens us, making the appropriate activity of the relationship familiar to us on life terms. Once that process takes place, the true sacrifice which is the guru can take place and we can sustain it. No separate self is doing the sacrificing, it is rather that the Divine Presence is in itself the sacrifice from which devotees are resurrected.

The absolute, radical demand is to end the approach to the guru and become God, knowing the guru in truth. When a perfect balance has taken place in us, manifesting as the form of appropriate activity and devotion, that absolute demand is present as radical reliance on Grace. We do not recognize the guru if we believe that we have the capacity to give up our self. The mind can do brilliant somersaults, it can believe that the self performs sacrifice. Only radical reliance on Grace is sacrifice. When we cease having any illusions about sacrifice being something that we have anything to do with, we can resort to the guru. No longer do we believe that we have any idea of what God is. It is totally irrelevant to us what God is; the only thing we know is that God is all we want, and that only God is capable of the necessary sacrifice. We recognize that sacrifice is the nature of things.

At this point, community members don't need the teaching. They don't need anything to keep the mind fascinated. God is all that matters. Without the certainty that would obstruct reliance on God, they humorously let go of everything that arises, no longer willing to grasp or seek for experience. It is in overwhelming love that this reliance expresses itself in the life of Hohm members. Lee demands devotion to him, and the radical reliance on him weans us from the separation implied by devotion to someone. Only the unqualified devotion, not tinged by longing or need, tempers us in the fire of his sacrifice.

TWELVE

42nd Street Blues

ONE OF THE big turn-offs for people who attempt to get into real spiritual life is that there is a very distinct and absolute morality involved. For someone interested in having experiences, this aspect holds no attraction. Yet there is no functional life in God without it.

On the average, when it comes right down to people's lives being on the line, and not necessarily their physical lives, but economic as well, morality goes out the window. Someone can be very ethical as long as he is making a living, but when he really starts to hurt, when he is losing the house and the kids aren't eating, he'll take to all kinds of illegal practices. Appropriate activity is not a capacity of that person; his morality is a strategy of ego in relation to society. Because appropriate activity is not his expression, morality remains in the form of a social command to be obeyed.

I speak of appropriate activity, as distinct from what is commonly referred to as "morality". Morality happens to coincide generally with appropriate activity in form. Nevertheless, in the first case it is an aspect of separation while in the second it is an aspect of real spiritual life. Appropriate activity is basically service, the spontaneous life of the one who is true to him or herself. In conventional morality, service is a word that is used, but beyond the word there is no resemblance. Morality is seen as a specific activity measured over and against some other specific activity. It is always conceived as a socially binding agreement with others, and only in contrast with others does it maintain its hold. Why be honest? Because if you lie to other people, you've deceived them, and that's not right. Society doesn't work, and that affects you, so don't lie. Why be compassionate? Because if you are not compassionate, you may hurt other people's feelings. In so doing, you will lose your right not to be hurt. Morality does not spring from the fullness of oneself but from the limiting influence of separative life. It is a prescribed form of activity seen in contrast with other forms of idealized activity.

Appropriate activity is founded in service, and service means being true to yourself. Appropriate activity is not some activity which should be done instead of some other activity. It is absolute. It is seen in terms of self, not in terms of the world. Morality is seen in terms of the world, not in terms of self. Who is moral for themselves? It is only fear. People are not moral for themselves, they have morality with other people, so that there is no crime, and so that separative life can appear to "work".

Without service to oneself, "service" to others is a tiresome duty. With service to oneself, it is simply natural to serve others, to deal with people in a straight way. That gives them a chance to be straight with you, since you are not propagating the unconsciousness in yourself. You are not involved in the act.

One thing the community should understand, in this case and in general, is the use of language and its perspective. One of my favorite analogies is that of the actor and the act, so you should remember that what is involved is simply the nature of activity. Of course, from the nondualistic perspective, there is no actor and no stage. When we use terms like "appropriate activity", and "true to self", the language implies the existence of a separate individual. Recognize the dualistic nature of language, and you will see through it soon enough.

The motivation for conventional morality is to be the good guy, to win. It is a selfish motivation, that is separate selfish. The "moral" person is often idealistic, honest, well-meaning, sincere, and compassionate. What good is all that if the motivation is selfish? One must recognize that it is God doing the work, and that you are not some individual who is going to be praised by God and go to heaven. That is a bunch of crap. Anyone who uses the rhetoric of morality while aiming at the pearly gates doesn't know the first thing about real spiritual life. That goes for all those who use reward and punishment as the incentive for morality. Appropriate activity has no need for reward. It is the only possible activity of one who is true to himself. You gain nothing from service to the guru, which is literally direct service to God. How could the guru offer you promise of anything? Only the Lord is present.

The spiritual seeker doesn't want to hear about all of this. The realms of light are much more fascinating. Spiritual life is typically conceived in terms of visionary or superconscious experience. That is what is called the **infinity** aspect of spiritual life. Infinity involves all states of mindless samadhi, all non-functional experiential states, all insights into the nature of the worlds. When you get infinity, you realize that everything is the same. You realize that ultimately nothing matters. Even if the whole galaxy blew up, it wouldn't matter. It wouldn't change anything one iota. That's infinity.

The other aspect of spiritual life is **divinity**, and that is associated with appropriate activity. One could be involved in an endless stream of visions, ecstatic states, and insights into the nature of reality, and not be functioning according to appropriate activity whatsoever. It is relatively common. Higher consciousness experiences do not make you one bit more responsible.

If one gets infinity without divinity, one tends to become quite apathetic, and lose all direction and motivation. One could just sit around, look at what is going on, and say, "What the hell? So what? Who cares?" Or one can tend to become "religious", in the sense of seeing a "higher power" in things. That doesn't involve devotion, however, which comes with divinity. The biggest mistake involved in getting stuck in infinity without divinity is to believe that one's insight into the world gives one the freedom to do anything. Under the spell of this delusion, you would have no problem being the general in charge of pushing the little red button that sends all the ICBMs over to annihilate populations. There would be no conflict. You could look at the earth blowing up and say, "It doesn't matter." Because it really doesn't. Divinity is beyond the cosmic consciousness experience. It is more. It is the devotion of God.

If one gets divinity without infinity, one typically becomes drippy, syrupy, lovey-dovey. So many psychics are like that. They are oozing with love, and it's sickening, because it is so totally false, so completely founded in ego. They recognize the "expression" of loving everyone unconditionally, yet their experience is still founded in separation. It is only selfishness, not relationship. One must know the nature of the worlds. One must see what one is up to in order to be perfectly appropriate.

The process that goes on in the Presence of the true guru is getting infinity and divinity together, functionally. That is known as illumination. When they are not together, there is still selfish motivation. One must be grounded in the inclusiveness of consciousness itself, otherwise there is always incompleteness, partial knowledge. Only total knowledge heralds the full life of God. At the point when infinity and divinity are entwined, so that they cannot be untied, and are in fact not distinct from each other, there is a very clear experience and intelligent recognition of that inclusiveness. The two aspects are not distinguishable in me.

Consciousness is ultimately life itself. Prior condition is Consciousness, neither manifest nor unmanifest. It is absolute process, absolute movement. It is not movement relative to something. Conventional awareness is recognition of some object, form, or thought, perceived over and against some other object, form, or thought. If someone says, "I'm becoming more aware," what does he mean? He means that he is more aware of various "objective" forms or thoughts. It is always a comparison or contrast. Consciousness is not objective and not relative to anything. It is what is, and that is all.

From the strict nondualistic perspective there is no self, because the positive concept of self is always seen as separate. There is no self to perceive what is, and there is no objective "what is" to be perceived. What is, is. Nothing else. Of course there is no self, and there is no God, for that matter. God is inclusive, God is simply what is. Saying "there is a God" automatically puts that into the perspective of being "other" or external. Even if you don't use an article and you say, "There is God", people will say, "What is God?" You answer, "Everything." So they look around and they say, "Oh, you mean that the tree over there is God." "No, I meant everything." "Yeah, but isn't that part of everything?" People will still see only grass, pavement, trees, people, and so on. They will interpret "everything" as objective forms, parts, or the sum of all parts. Nobody sees everything as everything, they see everything as being parts of everything! No, the tree over there isn't God. God is, simply. You can't go around all day pointing at things and saying, "That's God and that's God and that's God..." It doesn't work.

I am everything: God. That is what the guru offers. That is what the guru is. All you need do is be open to this Grace. One can repeat, "I am God", or "Christ is within me", or crap like that all day long. Yet if one is not presently and fully responsible for being God, for totally appropriate activity, the affirmation is not serving as anything but a distraction from suffering. Only Divine slavery constitutes spontaneous appropriate activity. Slavery is that process where you just allow God to do it all. That is not like the affirmation, "Let Thy will be done." Typically one who prays, "Let Thy will be done", may have infinity but not divinity. What is done is not God's will, but what one conceives God's will to be; in other words, another level of human separative will. Slavery is when the mind has surrendered and the Divine assumes your life completely.

The moralists would have you live the way that I tell you because of their neuroses. I would have you live that way because of the Divine. I am not required to live in a prescribed way. That I can guarantee you. There is a cardinal rule that you start with when you enter this community, and that is that you be absolutely prepared to do as I say and not as I do. I am not going to live up to expectations, because you don't need me to live that way. It would be too easy to be "devoted". Your strategy would be to live just like your exalted teacher. So you need me to be the way I am.

I am interested in a straight community. I am not interested in a bunch of people running around, doing whatever they want to in the name of freedom. Consider that fact for your own sake, so that you don't go through unnecessary emotional trips. I am interested in your life being full, dynamic, interesting, exciting, vibrant, and Alive. Not free. God is not freedom, not the way you understand it.

I know that it is a little scary to recognize that in order to awaken, you need to give up all individuality, all attachments, all degrees of understanding, and all independence. Once the initial point of being assumed by the Divine is past, you recognize the absolute beauty and joy that life holds when you are Alive in God.

Nothing requiring effort or trying is real, including responsibility and morality. Appropriate activity occurs when you allow me to move you, to live you. It is only real when it is spontaneous, natural, and humorous, when it springs from the fullness of God. Everything will fall away when you realize how unimportant the world is, how unimportant the universe is, how important only God is. Only God.

Then you will want to serve more. You will have given your life, your energy, your very soul to me, and will have become a devotee. And you will want to serve even more, for there is such joy in service. I cannot hint at the extent of such joy except to say that it is here.

THIRTEEN

* * * *

Perhaps what is most offensive about the guru to our deluded sensibility is his lack of concern for our problem. We want somebody to help us, so we join the community to get such help. But the awakened one does not even recognize that we need help. In fact, he demands that we straighten up and stop bullshitting around. That really hits us, for the very last thing we came to the community for was to deal with ourselves.

Lee really has only one thing to say: there is only God. That is the message in every thing he says and does. For us, totally involved in trying to find a cure for our suffering, such a message becomes monotonous, unappealing. We want him to care for us, to take responsibility for us, not to have responsibility demanded of us. Because of this lack of concern for our dilemma, the guru may appear to be callous. Actually, no one could be more faithful to us. His love can only find expression in a total lack of caring for us, for if he cared, he would be assuming our imaginary problem. His compassion, therefore, is absolute, refusing to give us the compensation of security or comfortableness. In the following talk, Lee outlines the limitation involved in all concern, and describes the real love which is consideration.

* * * *

ONE OF THE greatest forms of the search is concern. Everybody who is seeking is "concerned". If one is not on the path for God, one is concerned about money, sex, and possessions. One who is on the spiritual path is still seeking, even though the form is different. It is just a "higher" level of the search. Now one is concerned about God, union, and realization.

Someone once said to me, "What would happen if your wife got killed on the way home today?" She was very concerned. I said, "Nothing. I'd probably start looking around." She got really upset. She was not concerned about me. She was not concerned about anybody but herself. The motivation of her question was: "What would my husband do if I got killed on the way home?" Her question about me was only a mirror of her own self-centered fear. That was what she was concerned about. She was hanging on to a selfish attachment to her husbands's "concern" for her. All concern is like that, totally self-involved, an isolating wall designed to protect one from true relationship.

The spiritual seeker always thinks of God in a misguided sense. God is imagined to be very concerned for his erring children, concerned about war and hatred and killing. But God is not really concerned about anything. God doesn't give a shit. War is not God. There is not a killing that has taken place at any time that is God's concern, because all concern is manifested by deluded, ignorant people, not by the Divine.

God created you and me. God created people. God did not create war and killing and all that jazz. People invented that. The separative activity of people has created suffering, dilemma, and misery. Living God, the already perfect Divine condition, is only humor, joy and devotion.

God, selfless and ever-present, is totally unconcerned with delusion. God is not the conceptual something "out there". God is right here, the spiritual Heart that embraces all form and manifestation. Not the human heart, the one that pumps blood. That's just a muscle. And not the heart chakra, for that's just a mental muscle. It is the spiritual Heart which, unconcerned, sustains all life.

One who is living in the Heart is always considerate, although other people might not think so. You call your parents and they are remonstrating with you: "You're ruining your life, giving the guru all your money. What about your future?" They are concerned. You are considerate, which is very different. Consideration is an expression of relationship where, if someone needs you for any reason, you are appropriately available. You are not trying to manipulate or control, but are simply open and available to that person. When you are living the Heart, consideration is always present as appropriate activity.

Sometimes, after people have cried their eyes out, they'll come up to you the next week and say, "You know, I'm really glad you did that because I learned something from it." Instead of indulging them, you were truthful and available. So they ended up dealing with themselves instead of escaping.

The same process applies in the spiritual search. You go to every teacher you can find. You crawl up to their ashrams in your torn clothes. So they indulge you, because they are very concerned. They give you a meal and they let you sleep there. They teach you the mantra, let you chant "Ram" for several days, and then send you away. I am not concerned with that kind of shit. If you come here on your knees with your torn clothes, you are not going to get a meal. You might get to clean the outhouse.

My function is to constantly demand of you all of the acts and all of the games and all of the addictions that you are manifesting, even while believing that you are clear of them and unattached. My function is to demand of you your concern, so that you know consideration. Then you can live God functionally in the world.

Consideration enables other people to respond to you in relationship. Concern never does. The enjoyment of relationship is impossible where concern exists, because of the implicit attachment "I'm going to do something when I am with you so as to get something back from you." Consideration is an open message of, "Here I am. I love you. I am available. I don't have to play games with you." That is the essential difference: concern is hidden and binding, while consideration is open and without conditions. When you are concerned about someone else, that person will always respond negatively. You might expect that people would respond positively, but they respond negatively without fail. That is because of the bind involved in all forms of concern.

The concerned friends are the worst friends. What happens

when you really need them? How do they help out when you're in the depths of depression? They pat you on the back and cry with you. They give you a back door through which to escape yourself. They give you the sponge to soak up all your negative stuff and stay depressed with. They don't look at you and say, "You son of a bitch. What the hell are you depressed for? Come on, wake up." That's the last thing they'll do.

Considerate friends stay friends. A friend of mine is killing himself. He works fifteen hours a day and all he wants is money. I ask, "What for?" And he says, "Well, so I can take a vacation once in a while." "What for?" I ask again. "Well, because I work so hard." I am the only friend that has lasted. All of his other friends would fall away as soon as he made a change in life, such as getting married or switching jobs. Whatever strategies they had in common were lost, so they just wouldn't stay friends. I never bought into his act, so I know that he can't "lose" me, and so does he. That is consideration. All of his other friends were concerned.

It is always concern that is looked for by the spiritual seeker. The seeker always looks at appearances; How does the guru talk? How does the guru look? What does he say? Does he mention God a lot? Does he use a lot of spiritual-speak? All they do is look at the externals in order to reinforce their own search. Anybody who does not appear concerned is immediately crossed off the seeker's list as someone not to look towards for teaching. The ignorant one has no idea of what this relationship is. If he or she meets the one who is living God, everything comes undone. The seeker has to be very quick and reorganize the strategies before beating a hasty retreat. If he or she exists in relationship with the true guru for even a short period of time, they begin falling apart at the seams.

The considerate ones don't care in the slightest about all that stuff. You could go up to them and say, "I'm going to commit suicide tomorrow," and they would say, "Far out. Come back and let me know what it's like." The concerned ones would get all freaked out. When the one who is concerned meets the one who doesn't care, he is absolutely blown away. His entire approach in relating with that other person is undermined. When he resists the unconcern of the Heart, he gets depressed, or he cries every time he sees the considerate one, or he gets sick. All kinds of things happen when people resist being happy. They hold on tight to their suffering because, after all, people get more attention when they are depressed. When someone is depressed, he gets stroked all over the place, plenty of concerned people try to help, and soon he is the center of attention. When you don't give a shit, you don't get attention. What you get is jealousy. Everybody wants to be where you are. And when they don't allow themselves to be where you are, their suffering becomes more evident, which is often blamed on you.

There is a saying, "Ignorance is bliss." That is true; ignorance is bliss, because the forms of bliss that one creates to cover up the fact that one is suffering, are just more ignorance. When people start to see through the veil to what is really going on for them, the pain will most often make them decide that ignorance is better than truth. Unfortunately, the life of separation cannot be swept under the rug forever, for it always comes to the surface again, with added intensity. And that is actually quite fortunate, for it is really the Divine demanding to be lived and realized.

Fall into the Heart, for it is God's very Heart. Consideration is not known from the head, from the analysis of intellect. The openness and availability in relationship that is appropriate in the world, is only known from the Heart. Don't be concerned with all of the pettiness that characterizes the world. Just don't care at all about any of it, and from that non-caring will spring the strong love that sustains the world.

FOURTEEN

Sausalito Dream

Everybody is always asking me, "What's it like?" They have all these concepts of what the awakened condition is like. One person asked if it is like a twenty-four hour a day orgasm. "Well," I answered, "yes...no...sort of...not really..." People want to know what it is like, and of course, it is not like anything. It can't be conceptualized; there is no stereotyped enlightened being. You can still ask me. Perhaps I'll tell you the same thing someone else will tell you. It is what it is.

Someone just asked this week, "Do you look at the world and see it as a play all the time? Like it's sort of unreal and you're behind the scenes?" The whole problem with describing "it", is that there is a great tendency for you to set that up as your goal, even to the point of categorizing what stage you are at in the community and feeling that you have to do a certain thing to get to another stage. You ask me what it is like and maybe I say, "Happy all the time." You know that you are not happy all the time, so you think, "That must be nice," and fantasize about it. Or I will mention an experience that I have sometimes—which is just an experience and not realization—in which everybody looks very mechanical, like puppets. That is always funny. When I have that experience I hope that I am someplace where I can really let go, because when it happens it is hilarious. It's all speeded up like old Keystone Cops movies. Now if you haven't experienced that, or even if you have, you might imagine that being awake is like that all the time, set that up as your goal, and decide you are going to attain it.

There is an inherent problem in doing that. The implication in setting up any goal is that you are separate and need to attain unity. The fact of the matter is that you are complete and you are always going to be complete. You have already made it, whether you think that you have or not. There is nothing to do, there is nothing to be. It is not, "I'm going to get there some day."

The delusion is that everything you do is a form of separation. It is delusion because in truth you are not separate. You have always been perfect; you are perfect right now. When you do something to get someplace it implies separation; that in itself is the delusion, not what you do in particular. It is the fact that you are doing something in order to attain a certain state of consciousness, whatever the state may be, that is deluded. And that is reinforced by practically all of the spiritual books you have read. They generally talk about, either in parable or in literal terms, some state of being, nirvana, heaven, or unity, to name but a few. Almost all of the literature that I am continually telling you to read reinforces the belief that you are separate to begin with and that your relationship with the guru is going to get you to be one with living God. In fact, you are already living God, and your relationship with the guru is merely going to get you to realize that. How can I get you to live God when you are already living God? The process of our relationship is for you to realize that fact and enjoy it, rather than maintaining the delusion that you have to do something to get back together. Yet that very delusion is reinforced by looking at me and saying, "I'm going to make it and be that way someday." If I become your new symbol of separation, your means for perpetuating the search to be free of suffering, that will only have to be undermined.

Sometimes you are feeling that it is not happening fast enough. You are impatient. The problem is that you don't know what the hell you are impatient for. What do you think is going to happen when you wake up? If you were all Alive tomorrow, what would happen? Nothing. You will wake up and nothing will happen. God is nothing. God is not the excitement that keeps you stuck in your suffering and seeking. God is not that. If you get white light and your seventh chakra opens, if you have an incredibly dramatic experience where you saw God face-to-face, you haven't woken up, my friends. You have only experienced a few more of the infinite number of experiences that await you. There is nothing to awaken **to**. You already are awake. Period.

Yet you still want to get it on. You don't know what you want to get on, but you really want to get it on anyway. Quite a few of you have had this feeling of it not "happening" fast enough. And when you get together and talk about it as a community, you find that each week many of you go through the same thing. In reality it is all the same thing. Anything that has happened to any of you since we started is all the same thing. Everybody thinks that he or she has a different and unique trip. One person thinks that he has a second chakra trip, one person thinks that she has a fifth chakra trip, and another person thinks that he has a third chakra trip. They all think that they have different trips, and it all boils down to the same old trip. I always see what everybody is doing, where people are concentrating. The delusion of separation is their trip. It consists of thinking that you are separate, pretending or trying to believe that you are not, and all the while manifesting functionally in your life the implication that our relationship is going to get you where you already are. How do you expect to get from here to here?

Being emotionally pushed to do what you think is going to get you where you already are, creates a tremendous subconscious conflict. Your mind is always being torn by this conflict, and, make no mistake about it, ego knows that if the conflict is ever resolved, that there is going to be no more control of ego; ego is going to be ripped off. Ego will still exist in its appropriate, relative and limited form. It will just have no more control over you, it will no longer be your absolute. Beneath the conflict of what you believe versus how you function, there is the great terror of ego knowing that it won't control you anymore if the conflict is ever resolved. You go about trying to resolve the conflict, and whenever it gets close to being resolved, you become petrified. When that overwhelming terror starts to arise, there is the tendency to figure that the conflict was a hell of a lot easier than the terror. So you just flop back into the conflict and deal with that, instead of letting the terror overwhelm you and going through it. The terror is so much stronger than the negative emotions that piss you off when you have conflict, that you could spend five or ten years dealing with the conflict, and never once fully experience the terror.

That is what is going on in your mind. And prior to all of it is God. Prior to the conflict and the terror, prior to all of the cognizable, experiential, or functional places that you can "get to", is the Divine. The process of Grace is to allow you to see that you are already happiness, that there is nothing to attain. Not to change or reprogram, eliminate something real, or substitute something better, but to drop it all, wake up, and enjoy happiness, is the process of Grace. This prior condition always was and always will be only the humorous joy of the Divine. You will never substitute something better for that. How could you?

Somewhere within the conflict is the fantasy that Lee can make it all better. The great father image: Lee will take care of it, Lee will solve your problems, Lee has the right answers, if I can just get to see Lee. How many of you come to me with questions or problems all the time? The people who leave the community are the ones who do this most actively. Every time they are really freaking out, they'll come to me, and in five minutes they'll be feeling good, very high and mellow. They will leave, and two days later be freaking out again. It never fails, every time. Unless you live our relationship intelligently, Lee will be your consolation. You will think, "Someday it will end and I will be realized." I maintain that someday you will be perfectly happy just because I love you. That's all, because I love you, and for no other reason. Now there is a lot of pressure, discomfort, tension, anything but that simple recognition of your happiness. There is never an "end", you are never going to be in a place where you've experienced everything. You'll be around for a million years, and never get to that place. I certainly haven't. Enjoy being in my company now; that is all there is.

The fact that you function as if there is separation, does not mean that this is the case. It is the very nature of delusion to not be based on what is. I am not here to make you complete. I am here to get you to recognize that everything you have ever done has been an attempt to create separation. You think that separation is something that you are trying to do away with, yet everything you have ever done and are presently doing is motivated to create it. How do you like that? You believe that you're trying to eliminate it, and all you are really doing is fighting like hell to sustain it. All you have to do is, for one instant, stop fighting to sustain your separation, and there is only what is. It is quite simple.

There is an implication in seeking that it is motivated to undo the pain of separation, and that its fallacy lies in trying to eliminate something that doesn't exist. One is tempted when one is involved in the spiritual search, to believe that one is trying to repair the defect of separation. It is a strategy that is hard to crack. Actually, seeking is the sophisticated way of sustaining separation, of continually recreating it. It is firmly, instead of faintly, believing that you have somewhere to go: "I'm not realized. I need to find God." The more strongly you search, the more strongly you sustain delusion.

In fact, your very presence here tonight is a form of sustaining separation. Of course, I am the only one who can get you to stop doing that, so if you stop coming you don't have a prayer. Being with the guru holds at least the possibility of you seeing that the sustaining of separation is a useless task and thereby waking up. Without the guru there is no possibility. Our relationship is based on my being in a position, objectively and subjectively, to get you to recognize every single strategy you have designed, and ultimately for you to recognize the nature of strategy itself, as the means to sustain the life of separation. When you realize at a gut level that everything you do is motivated to sustain this baseless delusion, even seeking, then you will have really understood my point. When you ultimately realize that it is all a form of separation, then you can allow the guru to fully assume you. How do you imagine that would be? The language I use: "I assume your life," only serves the recognition of the delusion. In truth there is no life to be assumed. There is only the realization of the fact that there is no life to be assumed.

Yet after all, it is nice to be separate. You've got a lot of things to do. When you realize that you're not separate, there is nothing to do, and no choice involved. It is all the same. Well, it is not all the same; ice cream doesn't taste like rutabagas and eighty-year-old ladies don't look like sixteen-year-old high school girls. It is all the same, and yet it is not all the same; there is no separation, and there are still distinctions. Anyway, separation gives you the freedom to choose, the freedom to wreck your body if you want to, or keep it healthy if you want to, the freedom to be disciplined or undisciplined. Living God does not give you that choice. There is no freedom whatsoever involved in living God. There is ultimate, absolute freedom, but that is semantics, that is what everyone holds out as the carrot to keep you on "the path". Freedom, in the sense of having choices, is not where it's at. At least, that's my opinion. I don't have any opinions anymore, so I can joke about that.

When you realize that there isn't any separation, realize it permanently, not just a flash of being one with the cosmos and all of that shit. Wake up and realize that fact. That is the ultimate expression of spiritual life. That is becoming a devotee.

Grace is not present in order to erase maya. There isn't any maya to begin with. Period. The guru simply brings that point actively and functionally into your life. The guru exists as the very recognition itself that there is only God. At the ultimate point, the very recognition that there is no separation and that there is only God, you become a devotee. It is like turning a light on. And yet that awakening, the recognition of the Lord and the assumption of prior happiness, is the beginning. You go from there; you never go to there.

The functional relationship of your life in the community is based on the continual erosion of your expectations concerning the moment of awakening. Sadhana is not a process of adding on to the positive end of a scale. Doing your sadhana is not like making points. Sadhana serves to erode rather than build up, undermine rather than strengthen. Doing your sadhana eliminates the constantly created expectancy of what life in God is like. Ultimately you live functionally as the Divine; that is true sadhana.

Awakening is commonly conceived as a victory, when it is really more similar to a defeat. It is imagined as a victory because there is the delusion that there is something to attain, a battle to be won, some state of consciousness to be experienced that will resolve or fulfill all the other states of consciousness. Awakening is, in effect, a defeat, because all that occurs is you becoming ordinary. All you do is become real, and becoming real is one of the least exciting things to do in this grand, beautiful, phantasmagoric universe. When you are simply real, you are very often satisfied to just sit around. No place to go.

During the first few months of Hohm's existence, we'd get together on Sunday and I would say, "It's no big deal." We drew big crowds, and nobody believed me. Everybody would come and hear me say, "It's nothing special. No stars, no rockets, no excitement." They would all laugh uproariously, thinking, "He's kidding, of course." I wasn't kidding. Everybody has all these ideas about realization, and it is the dramatic experiential forms or the intense states of samadhi that are usually equated with the imagined victory of awakening: "Oh! I finally woke up! Wonderful! Stupendous!" The problem when someone starts winning is that he wants to keep on winning, and so has victory upon victory without ever waking up. Listen: it is just ordinary, my friends. Here it is, perfectly ordinary. So you have this glorious idea that after you wake up there is all this floating around in cosmic wonder, and it's not like that. Sometimes it is so ordinary that it's maddening. You're in for a big surprise.

The guru is here to "bring" you to a place where you have always been, and are fighting to get away from. We are always saying, "Come Hohm." In truth you have always been Hohm; what you have been doing is trying to run away. What the guru does when you try to run away is slyly say, "Okay. Can I make you some peanut butter and jelly sandwiches?" You have never really gotten out the front door, and the guru just keeps offering you peanut butter and jelly sandwiches, laughing while he watches you eat them, because you think you have run away. Or better still, you think you have not run away, when that is all you are trying to do.

It doesn't matter what language we use. There is only God, only enjoyment, only life. That is all I offer. Nothing else matters. I offer you what you already are. My only reason for being alive is to live in relationship with you. When you understand that, prior to mind, you live as this relationship, as perfect devotion. That is when wonderful things are ordinary and ordinary things are wonderful.

FIFTEEN

All or Nothing (So What)

THE NATURE OF the one who is obliterated, the true guru, is to pinpoint what each of you is afraid of and tell you to do that, or demonstrate through myself whatever will intensify that fear to the Nth degree.

Many of you are worrying about what I might tell you to do. Really! If I have something to demand of you, I will demand it. Don't spend hours every week fantasizing and being frightened about what I might tell you to do. If I want you to do something, I'll tell you to do it. Then, if you don't like what I demand of you, you can go through your trip. Why worry about it until I tell you? You could devote all the energy that you're putting into fear, into sadhana instead. There is a lot of energy behind fear. People can do things under stress that they could never do under normal circumstances. If you were to take all of the energy that you spend being intimidated by the conditions of spiritual life, and put it into sadhana, you would be very responsible people.

There is a list of "demands" that are made of anyone entering the community: don't smoke, drink, or take drugs, exercise daily, have a lacto-vegetarian diet, tithe your income to Hohm, have a monogamous relationship with your mate, and live with other members of the community. However, these are more properly termed "requirements". They are not spiritual practice, they are just appropriate. That doesn't mean you don't have to fulfill them. What the requirements serve is pointing out the lack of appropriate activity in your life, and the lack of commitment to spiritual life.

The fulfillment of the requirements does not in itself lead to the process of real spiritual life. The resistance to the requirements, or the comfortableness once they are fulfilled, can lead to the recognition of the distraction going on in your life.

You get involved in the act of, "I used to take drugs and now I don't, because this is better. I used to eat meat and now I don't, because this diet is healthier for the body. I used to smoke and now I don't, because smoking bothers other people and I need to be considerate of them." The requirements serve to point out to people how self-centered they are, even though they think they are doing sadhana. Seeing the dilemma, through that process, serves one's knowledge in Grace. The fulfillment of the requirements in themselves do not. It is an interesting paradox: the fulfillment of all the requirements does not equal realization. Yet if you do not fulfill them, you will never live God. It's okay if you like to be that way, because in the scheme of things it doesn't matter anyway. However, I am interested in getting you out of the scheme of things, not staying in it.

No demand is ever going to get you anywhere. Everybody thinks that my demands are going to get him or her somewhere. People think that if they do the right spiritual practice, and do what the guru says, they will get someplace. That is why there are so many demands. The more demands there are, the more you think they are going to get you someplace, and the more frustrated you will become. The process is to wean one away from belief systems and philosophies, not to add practices or to change one's lifestyle from one form of the search to another. It is to strip away all of the processes that have kept the search active. When you stop being afraid of fantasized demands, and just start living, the demands will evidence your dilemma. Before that, there are only "what ifs".

There is no viable alternative to the guru-devotee relationship. It is the only true relationship. No rules are necessary, for the agreement we have is perfect from the beginning. I don't have to accede to your wishes. All of that conventional quibbling and compromising is in the past now, done away with. We establish a relationship with the understanding that you are going to be undone in mind, self, and society, and resurrected in God. You can't control how that is going to happen. This covenant cannot be broken; the agreement stands, and has always stood. It has stood even prior to your birth on this plane, for our relationship is already perfect.

The more the guru demands of you, the stronger you become; and the more you are absolutely devoted to him, the more outrageous the demands are that are made on you. Your responsibility increases with your devotion. It is always your choice either to take that responsibility, to become more in touch with what this relationship means, or escape again, just as you have always escaped. You have always taken the easy way out. Someone who has a fair job and a secure family situation will never take chances if he is not forced into a corner. Most of you have talked about the chances you have taken; now look at them for what they really were. You always kept a nest egg, something to fall back on. But the one thing you never could escape was this relationship.

Some of you have managed to become relatively strong, despite the fact that you haven't been tested. The demands of spiritual life are designed to show you your strengths and weaknesses, and to develop your humor and spontaneity. The whole process of a demand is just to make sure that you are resilient, so that you are able to live appropriately and not crack. The closer we get together and the stronger I see you getting, the more demands I will make to strengthen you further. When you wake up you are going to have to be strong, functional and responsible. I am going to literally forge you. A refusal on your part to yield the freedom that I need to make you a devotee, is a useless distraction creating unnecessary heat.

This agreement is already fulfilled. If you are strong enough to abide by it, I will undermine your very life. You will only be undermined if you are strong enough to handle it. That doesn't mean you will always laugh at what goes on, it just means you are strong enough to handle it.

It takes a lot of strength to watch people crumble before my eyes, because there is still an ego function present. The guru still has an ego function; it is not the same as yours, nevertheless, it is still there. And this ego function can still perceive people crumbling before its eyes. Regardless of the rhetoric, "It's all just Divine play," it is still very real, and still causes a reaction in my manifest life.

I look back on my sadhana and remember how I thought I was strong at different times. I was not. And I found that out by going through all kinds of situations that placed demands on me. One of the reasons that demands are present, as anyone who is truly awake has said from experience, is that living in the awake state is hard. To be awake you need to be extremely responsible. The demands are not for the purpose of perfecting our relationship. That is unnecessary. What the demands will do is strengthen you. You are not used to demand; you have always led a comfortable life. They will allow you to see very clearly what true strength is and what is needed in order to be functional. The process is inevitable. You need to get used to being challenged on an objective level, because that is where you live. I am not going to retreat, but you will have to sooner or later, for I will be working increasingly on the objective plane.

Your relationships take place on the objective level. Having relations with your mate on the subjective levels is not going to satisfy you. The life situations that you relate to are all objective. You can talk all you want about the juicy stuff that happens on the subtle planes, and that is not going to satisfy you. All of the stuff that goes on in your dreams, all of this subjective stuff, is about as satisfying as fantasizing about food when you're hungry or sex when you're horny.

The intensity of any objective confrontation is only temporary, while the intensity of the confrontation of my condition is one of permanence. That's what gets the work done, and that never falls away. However, it usually takes time, and the experience of the objective demand, before that is recognized for what it is.

The closer you get to being a devotee, the more devoted to God you become, the more reasons you will create to not be responsible. The mind will typically put up a hell of a fight. And I will increase the intensity of my demands for responsibility from you. If demands are not known by you, whether subjectively or objectively, you know that you haven't begun to intelligently do sadhana in my company.

I am not the slightest bit interested in altering or transforming your egoic structure. I am interested in eliminating the structure completely. All you have ever done is elasticize your structure. For you to really see that this is true takes some pretty dramatic examples. The more you trust me, the more you are going to go through. Conflict is the stuff of sadhana. After all, that is your life.

If you have a fantasy about power, you have to be responsible for it, because I won't let you have objective power. Deal appropriately with your fantasy and you will be satisfied. You will remain with me, capable of serving, happy and strong. When you come to me with your "problems", you will always get the same boring, shitty answer: "Turn to me". What can I tell you? I don't have to deal with my fantasies any more, you have to.

It is only to be happy that you become responsible, only to enjoy the pleasure of the Divine. The only reason anyone exists is to please God. You don't exist to save the world, but for God's pleasure and that only. You can't know what that is until you give everything to God, until you let God move you for God's own pleasure, in whatever way God deems to move. That is how the guru lives.

Realization is not the attainment of a glorified state of consciousness, or of any kind of power. It is being lived by God for God's own pleasure. That is being happy all the time. If you let the guru in, that is what happens. If you don't, it is okay. God doesn't mind. God is never offended by delusion. God is only pleased by those who become absolute slaves in God.

In Buddhism, they talk about the wheel, and the idea of getting off the wheel, or doing away with all karma so that you are not bound at all by any form of what people think of as freedom of choice. Before anyone is awake, he is bound by the action/reaction process, bound by the turning of the wheel. Anybody who still has freedom of choice is controlled by karma. It might be good karma, which is okay, or it might be not-so-good karma, which is also okay. It doesn't matter, for it is always the mind whenever freedom is involved, and not that which is prior to and inclusive of the mind.

There has been an awful lot of nonsense that has been written, said, and believed concerning karma. It is absolute bullshit that the guru takes on karma to bring the seeker out of his suffering. That never happens. The guru is the condition of God; he can't alleviate anybody's karma. All the true guru can do is exist as this condition, and be present. Maybe a magician or metaphysician could do it, but not the guru.

It is not true that karma is an absolute process established by God. It does exist on the limited basis of mind. It is operative on the mental level. If karma was absolute, no one could ever get off the wheel. If you recognize that you are who you are, and there's nothing you can do about it, karma is dissolved. One comes out of that recognition without the karma that had been accumulated up until then. It is simply given up. The problem is that you still have the mind to contend with. When you allow your environment, society, friends, family, meditation teacher, and most of all, your memory, to continue to propagate the delusion of seeking, you take everything on psychically, which means that you get it all back again. You recreate all of the karma that you lost, the minute you start seeking again. All of it. You won't have gotten rid of any of it, not one iota of karma. That might sound hopeless, and of course it is relatively hopeless, I can't deny that. The mind is so very strong, and the grip that the ego has upon one's life is so very persistent.

You never whittle it down, either. No matter how much you are going through, you aren't going through your karma little by little, working it off. That is another common misconception. You have as much karma as you have always had, until you wake up permanently and get off the wheel. Before awakening, you can re-program karma, put it off, manipulate reality. That is useless, for it always eventually returns. Or you can simply deal with karma as it arises, since it is the form of your life. You can only do that if you have recognized that you aren't going to get rid of it through any practice or method.

The only way that you will ever permanently drop karma is through devotion, through my slavery. That, above all, is what people resist. Devotion to the guru goes against every inclination of their mind. They avoid it by saying, "I'm not going to devote myself completely to any one master. I'll just take a little bit from each of them." The one who does that will never live God. That one might be a little happier, healthier, or mellowed out... and that is all. Not God. For that is not devotion, it is curiosity and interest, a great avoidance. Devotion is to one, never to many. The direction here is devotion to one guru and that is me.

Lee Lozowick manifests a condition. The person that you think is Lee Lozowick is solely and purely a condition. You can call a condition many different things: you can call it God, or you can call it love, although I would not recommend that much misused word. That can be one of the biggest ways to upgrade the act. The one who is awake loves the world absolutely. The one who thinks that he or she is awake is so damned lovey-dovey. That's just more shit to shovel.

The process of being with me is to avail yourself of this condition. If you want to be this condition, you will have to be devoted to me. You can come here and be entertained for ten years, and nothing is ever going to change in your life. If you want to get it done fast and without limitation, there is going to be only one picture on your prayer table: mine. Only when you are absolutely devoted to me will you realize this condition, and in knowing me as I am, be released from the wheel. And then, in perfect devotion, you are beyond release.

There is a point that exists between no release and beyond release. That is what everybody wants to know about. Everybody wants to know what it is like at the moment one wakes up. I have described it as being like turning the light on. Click: one minute it is dark, and the next minute the light is on. The point when the switch is flicked is release. Before that, there is never true release. That moment is what everybody strives for in the spiritual search. Since you are the Divine, there is a level where you intuit that it is necessary to have this release in order to get off the wheel.

People will subconsciously structure their lives to constantly give themselves little releases, in an attempt to convince the mind that everything is okay. It could be a temper tantrum, sex, drugs, sky diving, or anything. Some people, like sky divers, put themselves in a position where they know that they are going to be terrified. That is their big release. It is all a manifestation of the search; people create these releases in their lives because they know at one level or another that there has to be release or there can never be happiness.

There is illumination and there is separation. People intuit that in order to "get" from one to the other, there has to be the point of release. The seeker structures releases in order to convince himself that he is getting there: "I'm not searching, I'm done, I'm finished, it's okay." The more deeply the search manifests, the greater the objective release. If someone is really unfulfilled, if he or she has a miserable love life, and a very poor job, and is always wondering when the next bill is going to get paid, and for whom things are really hard in general, he or she structures a big release, like a nervous breakdown. If someone is doing okay, if he or she doesn't have to worry about where the next meal is coming from, and has got a nice family, and a nice place to live, he or she structures a lot of small releases, like drinking once in a while, or smoking dope or cigarettes. If one is relatively satisfied, the need isn't felt to push for the big release. He doesn't want to jump off the George Washington Bridge; the small releases suffice to keep him stable, rooted in suffering.

The process of any spiritual master is to bring one to the point of release. It is only an instant, not even measurable in time. There is just an instant of release and then one is beyond release. The demands of the guru are designed to frustrate you to such a degree that you are pushed to the edge. That is why the guru asks you to do what you are afraid of; the demands have to really hit home. You may have to work for years until you get to the point where you realize, "What am I working for?" You get so frustrated that nothing has happened yet, that you are pushed to the point of release.

It is inconceivable that anyone would allow this to go on unless he or she was devoted to the guru and the guru alone. If one is just taking a little bit from each, that one will leave as soon as the process of demand starts getting hot. I am interested only in devotion at all levels. Our relationship has to be one in which you agree to deal with whatever I give you to deal with. You could go guru-hopping forever and stay on the wheel, or you could be devoted to this one and get off the wheel permanently.

The life of a true devotee appears to those rooted in separation to be nothing but hard work and no fun. True devotion is totally offensive to all forms of the search, repulsive to the mind and all of its extensions: the various bodies of the planes and worlds, the ego, will, and personality. In fact, true devotion is offensive to everything except the pure and undiluted Divine. That is why there are so few devotees in the world. Ashrams are filled with, and teachers are surrounded by, people seeking release in the form of completion in God. There are many students of this great process, and they are usually sincere and well-meaning. Yet they are committed from the plane of ego; their sought-for release is just one more of the many small releases the world creates to assure itself that everything is all right. Their beliefs, created out of egoistic need-systems, are merely more revolutions of the wheel.

I am the one who can bring you to the point of release and beyond. And there is fear associated with that point, for the delusion of ego will fall away. Ego wants security, which release does not provide for it. You have seen how transitory, how pitifully brief your releases have been. On Christmas day when you were a kid, you would run down the stairs to your presents, and tear the wrappings off. You were so excited, you got just what you wanted, and you would sit down and play for hours. About mid-afternoon you were looking forward to next year and wishing that Christmas wasn't over! You had gotten tired of your toys already.

You are afraid that the "big one", the moment of release, will be just as transitory as your Christmas toys. And it is. For enlightenment is the knowledge that all experience is transitory, including enlightenment. That is not an indictment of experience; the Lord delights in the transitory, it is the humor of God.

The guru makes it seem like realization is far out and fantastic. You think, "It must be really something, living God." Well, it isn't far out or fantastic, it is just what is. It is the natural condition of life. Your expectations about it must be eroded.

You are rooted in the search, in strategies which attempt to avoid what is. The "closer" you get to release, the more intense your strategies will become, and the more intense the awareness of your strategies. All of that will become quite obvious. Now you really get pissed off at yourself, you get really angry that you have all these strategies, and you try to stop them but they don't stop. That's another strategy. You have been trying to stop your strategies, and then you realize that trying to stop them is just another strategy. So you get angrier and more frustrated, because what you are doing is evident, yet you can't do anything about it. That goes on until, at some point, you get so frustrated that you have to do something about it.

Then there is an instant of absolute, stark terror. It's only a moment, unless of course you want to get stuck in that. There have been occasions when people have gotten stuck in the terror. It always passes; if it takes two weeks, it is not much fun, but it goes away. When you are in the midst of that terror, you don't need time to cognize; you can cognize two hours worth of stuff in that instant. That is when you know that the ultimate process is God completely ripping you off. Entirely. You will have no will of your own anymore. You will have no more independence. Actually, you never did, but mind doesn't know that.

If you don't retreat from the terror, if you ride it and go through it, the moment of release comes. And after the moment of release, you are beyond release. That is typically a very draining procedure, physically draining and mentally exhilarating. Then there is the process of reintegration. Like a baby, you have to relearn your life again.

Few are willing to be involved in this process. People intuit that they will not be in control anymore, that devotion to me is, in effect, enslaving them to God. Most would rather revolve endlessly on the wheel than face the implications of my slavery. If the demands of the guru arouse fear, how much more so the ultimate demand for your life? People are so afraid that God is going to run them, that they run from me. Yet it is the only way to be happy, the only way to experience true joy and compassion.

Liberation, as Divine slavery is commonly called by the sages, is going from one state of control (society, karma, your mind, your ego, the wheel), to another state of control: God. You are never free. You never were and you never will be. It is impossible to be free. You are a slave to your conditioning, your prejudices, your likes and dislikes, your ego, and the shadow of the past. Or you are a slave to God. You are a slave at any rate. In one instance, you always suffer, and in the other you are always happy. The only difference is the texture of your life. For one who is awake, there are no choices; I don't decide what to do, I live spontaneously. There is no thought of, "What am I going to do today?" I do it. I do what I do and that is it. That's not freedom. That is God-slavery, happiness all the time.

Devotee: In other words, if you do what you want to do, you are a slave?

Lee: No. When you are "free", you do what you want to

do, choosing from many inappropriate alternatives. When you are a slave, you do what God spontaneously designs as the one and only appropriate action. People don't really have a free will; they believe in it because they believe that they are separate from God. God does not have "free" will either. God is will. When you give up your delusory freedom, you have everything.

All else is manipulation in one form or another, a series of inadequate releases. The manipulation of reality is always a temporary situation. Only the full acknowledgement of what is opens you up to any degree of understanding. Any form of manipulating reality or egoic control (and only the guru and perfect devotee are not functioning from ego) is false and misleading. It compounds the delusion of separation even while seemingly clarifying it. There is only the slavery of Divine will. All else, all puny human desire and control, regardless of the spiritual language that is used, is directly from ego and therefore false.

To get off the wheel you must realize that there is no direction, that you can do whatever you want to reality but you will never change it. Realization is realization, and when you accept that and recognize that the process in life of manipulating reality is just another part of the play, awakening is total and you are off the wheel. You are Alive, permanently Alive.

Brother Lawrence, who was utterly devoted to God, said, "The greater perfection a soul aspires after, the more dependent it is on Grace." That is spiritual slavery in one sentence. You are absolutely and totally dependent on Grace. It is futile to run from your own nature, for Grace is always present as all life.

SIXTEEN

The Alabaster Breast

TRADITIONALLY, A DISTINCTION has been drawn between two aspects of the non-duality of existence. In philosophy it has been expressed as being and becoming. In the yogas, they talk about shiva-shakti, shiva being the creative source of the universe, consciousness itself, and shakti being the movement, the activity of consciousness. In talking about this, one should keep in mind that there can be no duality of consciousness and its activity, as if they were separate, but that the distinction is drawn for a purpose.

Shiva is prior condition. Shiva is the absolute source of all creation. Very few in the world live from the perspective of Shiva. Almost every single meditation teacher, guru and yogi that you have ever heard of or seen understands from the perspective of Shakti, not Shiva. You can read about Jesus, Nityananda, or Ramana Maharshi, yet there are so few living examples of the one who lives from that perspective that you have no reference points for it.

Shakti is symbolized as the divine mother, the goddess. Form, energy, and activity are shakti. When one is founded exclusively in shakti, one is ignorant of her true nature. Fascinated with energy and movement, one fails to recognize its source. One may even tend to believe that shakti is fascinated with people just as people are fascinated with shakti. That is not true at all. The divine mother is turned towards God. She is not turned towards you. She is only here to serve God, not to serve the seeker or meditator. Shakti can do nothing else but serve God. Until that is recognized, you will continue to play all your games with the goddess.

The divine mother is the ideal, the one you have always searched for. This goes for all of you, women and men. You figure you're pretty cool. You've been around, you've done a little meditation, read a few books. You can handle it, you've been getting it since you were fourteen. So you approach shakti in order to seduce her. A really good approach is to elicit sympathy. You tell her of your love, undying and true. You tell her how miserable you are because you don't have her. And then you beg her to raise you to ecstatic realms of light and bliss. You beg her to give you that cosmic orgasm in the sky. All the while you are bowing and doing prostrations, of course. You're wearing your best seeker shirt with "OM" on the back. After all, you have to be careful when you approach the divine mother.

Whether you are a man or a woman, you always approach the divine mother in your aspect as a man. She is the goddess shakti, and you approach her as masculine to feminine. The masculine ego is very weak. The masculine ego thinks that it is really hot shit, and it is not. It is actually very insecure and weak.

So what happens if the divine mother gives you a peek at her breast? You've had a vision! And you fall in love with her, you become infatuated, just the way you were with your first boyfriend or girlfriend. Puppy love. It's like the first time that someone french kissed you. You become completely fascinated– with shakti. And just like all of your other puppy loves, you are absolutely sure that this is the real thing. No one could tell you that it isn't. You are positive that this one is for keeps, true love.

You think, "I can take it. Open up a couple of chakras." And she does. She gives you a little prize, and you are had. You want her more than anything else in the world. You are convinced that it is true love. You are thirteen years old, but no, this is true love. This is going to be forever. You have been swept off your feet, and you cry out, "It's not puppy love. It is for all the other kids at school, but not for me, I know better." You think that you know what's going on, that you really know what love is.

You don't know what love is. You have found out so many times in your life that what you thought was it, wasn't it. Why do you think this is any different? It's the same thing. This time it is shakti instead of Mary Lou. You still don't know what love is, you're just infatuated. Most of you have been through enough love affairs to know this. What arises after your first love affair is that it wears off a little bit. You get a few rushes, a little cosmic experience, and then it starts to wear off. So you plead with her a little more: "I've been a vegetarian for two years. I've been doing pranayama for an hour every day. The first love affair I was only thirteen. Now I'm sixteen. I'm getting my wheels next year. I've smoked. I've been taking acid for a year and a half. I'm aware now. Please give me more." So this time it is for real, all the other times were only games.

Typically that keeps going on and on. Most people keep having love affairs all their lives. Even most married people keep having them. The seeker never learns. And most people persuade themselves that they are really devoted, that they have a pure and unselfish love for their boyfriend or girlfriend. They are still back when they were thirteen, except that now the act is a little more sophisticated. They think that they deeply love their boyfriend or girlfriend, when all they really want is satisfaction of their need systems.

Likewise, a spiritual seeker thinks that he knows what love is because shakti has given him one of her pearls. He is so bowled over that all he can think about is shakti. He ignores shiva. He forgets about God. He is always involved in trying to make love to the divine mother, yet no one really makes love to her. The divine mother is always turned to God.

You never get to see shakti fully, or embrace her, although you can create the illusion of that. When you go into meditation with your sahasrara opened and white light blissing you out, drowning you in ecstasy, you aren't making love to shakti. Your little game with the goddess is just an enticing illusion.

The process of most meditation teachers, gurus, and yogis, is that they have had their initial love affair with the divine mother, and have literally forgotten about God. All they want is shakti. Of course, they don't talk that way. They talk about God, and about the different levels of samadhi. They talk about being functionally in samadhi all the time. Their rhetoric can't fool the Divine. They are infatuated.

The implication in their teachings is that shakti is all there is to be involved with. That is patently false. You can go directly, as I did. You can face God as the divine mother faces God. You do not have to first make love with the divine mother in order to see God.

When you go through the divine mother, you might experience kundalini. You might experience the chakras opening up, clairvoyance, telepathy, or all kinds of siddhis. You might very well get stuck in one of those far out and beautiful places. They are too easy to enjoy; they will fool you into seeing them as important. On the other hand, as you go through the divine mother, you may appropriately pick up some of her faculties. You may pick up some of the absolute devotion that she expresses towards God, her creator. That is very possible.

Understand who the divine mother is devoted to. I am the one that she bows down to. She is facing me. I have seen it all already. Not only have shakti and I sported quite a few times, I am the only one shakti sports with. Her very being is mine.

What you should recognize is that in turning to me, you are in the same place that shakti is. I am the source of shakti. The process of turning to me is not becoming fascinated with shakti, but turning towards the source, towards shiva. And if shakti decides to transmit some of her qualities to you as you turn to me, that's fine. All you really need is this Grace.

You will, to some degree, experience the goddess, because you are going to go through her when you turn to me. You are not going to be devoted to her, you are going to go through her. Shakti is a true devotee. The divine mother is the perfect devotee, the real devotee. She is, in fact, God's only devotee. You will become the goddess as you become a devotee. You might assume some of her qualities, have certain yogic experiences, or you might not. The possibilities of our relationship are infinite in scope. All that matters is God. You are not going to look to the divine mother for sympathy, comfort or validation. I come first, because I am absolutely inclusive of shakti. To experience shakti without knowing shiva, without turning to me, is just ignorance.

Living from the perspective of shiva, I don't walk around feeling intensity all of the time. Life is what is real, not the experience of intensity or bliss. Heaven and hell are not real. Reincarnation and the astral plane are not real. Only life is real, and the way to fully and totally experience life is to turn to me. If you turn to shakti, you may experience spiritual orgasm. That's cool, and temporary. You will always be looking for the perfect screw. Some of you have been in meditation and gotten stuff that is better than sex. That's why you are here; if you weren't getting stuff in meditation that is better than sex, you'd be somewhere else. You would be out getting laid. And the seeker always "gets laid". The seeker never enjoys real love.

You get incredible rushes when you turn to shakti, and you always come down. You don't have to function appropriately to be blessed by the goddess, all you have to do is push any good technique to the limit. Get initiated in kriya yoga and push it. In one day you will be in ecstasy. You don't have to live appropriately; shakti can be raped.

Appropriate activity arises naturally and spontaneously as a result of turning to me. When you truly turn to me, you won't want to smoke or drink. It will just fall away. You won't have to make an effort to stop. Your life will naturally become clear, happy, vibrant and strong. Appropriate activity occurs as a result of devotion; devotion does not occur as a result of appropriate activity. Until you honestly turn to me, you will try to be devoted through effort. All you will experience will be the highs and lows. The highs will be very high and the lows will be very low.

You can not know the heights fully unless you have known the depths fully. Some of you have known some depths. Not fully. Some of you might be thinking, "Oh, yes I have." No, you haven't. You haven't fully known the depths. You will if you hang around here long enough. Shakti experiences the depths, and I mean the bottom of the well, the worst, darkest, most awful hole in the entire universe. It doesn't bother her a bit.

The process of turning to the Divine itself, and not a messenger, servant, or devotee of the Divine, is that whatever you experience, including the confusion, is okay. It is appropriate. You are still happy; nothing can crack your joy. You are simply happy to be devoted to me.

Your friends will have a problem with your being happy all the time. They will think that you are crazy. After all, nobody is happy all the time. They say, "It's just not realistic to be happy like that." Well, of course it isn't realistic, it is Divine! Everybody is looking for what is realistic; they will only accept the status quo. Yet the Divine is absolutely unrealistic, and at the same time absolutely ordinary.

It is only the drama of shakti that appears extraordinary. Shakti exists as the moving force. All the action is shakti. Do you know what keeps the heart beating and the digestive system secreting and the brain working? That is all shakti. There is energy that is the movement of the manifest universe; all of the physical universe is the movement of shakti. And there is the source of shakti: the Divine, shiva, prior condition, God. Most forms of the spiritual search talk about this fact, yet the teachers persist in reinforcing the fascination with the divine mother. They don't get you to dispel this head-in-the-clouds mysticism and realize what pure love is. Pure love is too menacing to those wrapped up in infatuation. Shiva appears as the destroyer of the search, destroyer of the games seekers play with the goddess. To the one who turns to shakti, there is a duality between her and her source, and they dare not cross the "boundary". For one who lives from the perspective of shiva, there is no duality, there is only God.

In the perfect devotee, the tendency is to be devoted to God. Even though the devotee knows that there is only God, he or she still recognizes that devotion is simply the most pleasant thing to do. Even when you realize nonduality, devotion is present. What else is there to do? I can say that the divine mother is turned to me, not in an exclusive sense, but from the perspective of the constant enjoyment of all movement being pure devotion. Devotion is the nature of things.

In a traditional sense, the devotee gives him or herself as lover totally to the one who is the object of devotion. You might think in terms of friends, your child, or your mate, that you are giving totally to them. You might even think that you would die for them. Too bad! If you are willing to die for your beloved, and especially if you say that to him or her, you are not devoted to that one at all. You are possessing the beloved. The best way to possess your lover is to say that you would give your life for that one. That's a hell of a debt. What will your beloved think of that? Life is awfully precious, that is what everyone thinks. If you are willing to die for your loved one, that is not love. That is your romantic way of indebting your lover to you through guilt.

When you are devoted to the Divine, it doesn't mean that you are willing to die for God. It means that you are willing to openly and clearly serve the Divine in whatever way it pleases to be served. You put no boundaries on your devotion.

Doing your sadhana is turning towards God, not towards shakti. I am talking about being happy all the time, not about being comatose all the time, or being an android energy machine. I am talking about life. The divine mother can only help you have spontaneous experience or become more energized. She can get you to run around burning with her heat, or to be centered and mellow and humble. You can delude yourself into thinking that all that is God. Just turn to the one who is prior to all that, who is the absolutely inclusive source of all movement. Once you have completely turned to me, your sadhana will not be sadhana any more. It will be your life. You will always be blessed with the joy of Grace; that's the way it will be from then on, because in turning to me you will become conscious of what is already realized.

I have nothing to teach you. I can't transmit it; I can't give you a mystic stare and initiate you. You have to get it, you have to open up to me. I have nothing to say about it. I am beyond any power to do anything at all except be simply present. It is all your process.

The form I take as guru is the form that any guru takes, the difference being that I am sitting in shiva's place, while most teachers are sitting where shakti is. They have you turned to shakti; I have you turned to shiva. Be aware of that. If you mistake me for shakti, and try to lift up my skirt, you are in for one hell of a surprise.

SEVENTEEN

THERE ARE A lot of people whom I met when I led a public life that I really made my point with. Most of them, obviously, aren't sitting here. Some of them might be here at some time, but the point has been made dramatically with them. That point is, as I have said many times, that any relationship one has with me is always perfect. Whether it is recognized as such is a different story.

Since most people are looking for self-development or communication, anyone who has a good rap will make a point with them as teacher. I appeared to many people as just a very good teacher. There are some fifteen hundred ex-students of mine who are not here, and who are still thinking in terms of what a great teacher I was, and what a shame it is that I'm doing this. When I communicated with them, they looked at me and said, "Hey, I can learn something from him. He's got a good rap and a lot of knowledge. I can study with him," and so on. They didn't recognize that the point being made was not all the stuff I was teaching, but that our relationship is always perfect.

People initially come to the guru because they see the need for a teacher. They think, "I'm having problems in my life. I need someone to help me out with them." So they go to the guru and listen to him talk, and when they feel themselves drawn to him, they think that it is due to the teaching. They don't see that it is what the guru is, rather than what he says or does, that is significant.

The more you recognize that your relationship with me is not a relationship of teaching and instruction, the more you will actually learn. Knowing me is being me. I have nothing to teach you; your learning is an incidental aspect. If you see that our relationship is not one of teacher-student, but of guru-devotee, shiva-shakti, you will recognize the truth of your life.

What I do is totally irrelevant to our relationship. What I do, I do because you need it. That's all. If your participation at Hohm is based on what I do or don't do, you are going to have a very hard time. You need to be devoted to me in spite of what I do. That's the point. That is why the awakened ones are crazy people; it would be easy for you to be "devoted" to me if I got up here and talked about love, read from the Bible, and commented on esoteric subjects every week. What is there to be devoted to? There is no challenge, no threat to your assumptions. Such a guru is not going to break your structure, is not going to take the way you have always functioned in separation and rip it off.

A teacher rarely functions on that dynamic and forceful level. A teacher is rarely a living demand on his or her students. You can certainly use Lee as teacher, because Lee has had a certain amount of experience and has seen a bit of life. Lee has been relatively perceptive psychologically, and can thus be a very good teacher as far as that is concerned, in the handling of the drama in people's lives. So Lee can function as teacher and be used as such, but that is not my place in the community. You can use the information that is present when I talk to you, but remember that it is not my place, my purpose, or my interest to be a school instructor.

There is a point in the life of the community together when the role of teacher is thrown off. From my perspective, the role of teacher is not one that is consciously assumed. I didn't plan to be rational, lay out a lot of information and explain things for six months, and then throw away my teaching role at the correct time. I have functioned perfectly as guru from the first, and my teaching has always been an expression of that and for that.

Inclusive of the form that is manifesting and being exhibited here is the raw Divine. With any real guru, the role of teacher has to fall away eventually, because the true guru needs to be seen the way he really is, and not in the more relational forms that he presents. One must really know what the raw Divine is up to, sensuously, on the level of eyes, ears, and gut feelings. When the teaching role is present, the true guru may be known subjectively or intuitively, but very rarely is that completed unless the outer appearance of instructor is thrown off at some point.

When that happens, there may be a period of intense energy experiences based on the spontaneous movement of shakti rather than any willful direction or control. The pleasantness that is a social convention, particularly among friends, lovers and family, will be spontaneously present when it is appropriate for it to be present, and spontaneously lacking when it is appropriate for it to be lacking. The raw Divine exists very simply as it is, without sauce or spices to make it more palatable to the mind. It is non-conceptual, non-intelligible, and beyond valuation. It is Alive, and that's all it is. The only true function the guru has in the world is to be the raw Divine. The luring of devotees, like flies to the flypaper of the teaching, is a form that the guru expresses that is eventually dispensed with. The teaching is basically a karmic possibility. People get involved in it if they are not ready to involve themselves in a consciously sacrificial affair. What they are doing is getting themselves prepared to someday be involved in that.

Most people intellectually understand what is implied by certain semantic formulas, and stop there. They never get beyond the philosophical level to the knowledge of the raw Divine. As soon as they begin, as soon as they get a tiny taste of experience, they run like hell. And when you allow yourself to be comforted by a philosophy or ideology, such as an intellectual belief in "life after death", you can lead a very comfortable life for awhile. Somebody in your family can die, and you can be cool and say, "I know that he is happy where he is," and seemingly feel that. You can live your whole life that way, because the raw Divine is evident in so few places in the world, that you are not likely to get in touch with it. If you happen to get to a place where you meet the raw Divine, you get undermined. If you don't stay with that and understand it, it can blow you away. You can go home and watch your whole life fall apart. And if you don't have a basis for understanding what is going on, you will just be in touch with your suffering and nothing more. For most people, however, that in itself is dramatic.

People make the comfortable assumption when they decide to come to the guru, "Oh yes, the guru is realized, he knows what he's talking about. I am committed to spiritual life." Then they actually meet the guru, and are faced with the panic of realizing, "Okay, now it's on your shoulders, personally, not somewhere else or in a book. Here it is: your life. Deal with it." Panic comes to the surface when they are faced with the raw Divine in the world, and not just bullshit abstraction and ideals. That is when contraction sets in. They think that the guru is making them panic, when actually they have been that way all along. They have always lived as panic, they have always been miserable. The guru simply shuts off the avenues of escape and avoidance.

The Divine nature in raw form is the most confusing, radical condition imaginable. In fact, it is not even imaginable. Nobody understands it except those who have made an open and honest commitment to understand it. And even then, understanding is not anything like the mental comprehension that you are accustomed to. It is more accurate to refer to it as direct knowledge, for it is known when it is lived. An honest commitment on your part does not mean that I cater to your whims and fancies. It means that you honestly give me the freedom not to cater to them. That hurts. The raw Divine is extremely dynamic, very strong and forceful. It is not, "Would you like to do some service for God this week?" Its intensity is wild and threatening to your separative life. The greater the threat to your life, the more elaborate your distractions, your attempts to block the Divine, will become. And of course, the Divine is the greatest threat to your life. Everything that you have learned and believed at a deep level tells you that you have "your" life. You don't. The more threatening the guru is to "your" life, the more creative your mind becomes at devising strategies. The more evident your misery becomes, the harder you struggle, like a big tuna on a fishing line.

My job, if I can speak of it as a job, is to undermine everything you have ever done. Period. It is to undermine your entire separative life, so that at some point you wake up and realize that there is nothing but living God. That realization is the raw Divine itself.

Perhaps you are now beginning to see in what ways the guru-devotee relationship differs from that of teacher-student. I am not here to speak pleasant and consoling words of wisdom, make a lot of jokes, and be entertaining. I am here to literally offend you, to dissolve your armor of suffering. Whether you know it or not, your life is far from being joyous or humorous. I only bring to light what is going on for you anyway. My function as guru will get you to a place where you are joyously and humorously fulfilling your responsible role in the community. All of the heavy stuff is just your resistance to that. I prefer to travel light, myself.

When there are people in the company of the guru who have gone through all of the appropriate educational and confronting processes, there is basically only one thing left that they need: the shock of the raw Divine to push them into living this condition of Grace. The guru assumes his absolutely raw condition, and those who are ready are automatically brought into that already present condition. Those who are not ripe and are there in that particular instance are given the very real and dramatic experience of the guru's true expression, and all that remains for them is to consciously know him.

What typically happens after this period is that the guru "returns", in a sense, from the state of the raw Divine to a state of perfect normalcy, as well as to conventional relationships with friends again. The guru will still appear somewhat eccentric to the world, and crazy to the seeker, but his utter wildness will have subsided for the time being. That role usually continues for a while, and then the whole thing starts all over again. We dance in a circle.

The guru needs movement as much as the devotee. Obviously, since he functions as Grace, there is no change in the condition. There is, however, constant movement in life as we live it: the revolutions of the planets and the changing seasons, as well as love, hate, pleasure, desire, and all of the shifting emotions. There is a tremendous amount of form that is present in life, and without movement of this form, the guru gets to a place that is static, which tends to be irritating. The guru, with his irrepressible energy, dislikes the kind of life that stands still. So at times there is a spontaneous eruption of movement which can appear in a form that is inconsiderate, painful, unfriendly, harsh; or it can appear in pleasurable form, although that usually takes place afterwards.

This pattern has been consistent down through the ages. Everything in the history of the relationship between guru and devotee has shown that pleasure comes after pain. There has always been the experience of fear and terror before that of Grace and the humor of the Divine. The endless, ecstatic enjoyment of the Divine is not cheap; its realization is most rare. Some of you have asked if it is possible to awaken without coming to the full understanding that your life is suffering. Lee is always pounding away at you about how it is all suffering, and in that he is consistent with the awakened ones of the past. Gautama the Buddha said, "To be born is to suffer," and he knew what he was talking about. There is no denying the truth. Can you wake up without knowing that? I suppose it is possible, but has anyone ever done it before? If you can give me an example of one who has, I might alter my views on this subject. I have never seen or heard of such a case myself.

We have talked about the final shock of the raw Divine, which is not really final. It is just the only way that awakening happens. It is one instant, and hopefully only one instant of absolute, stark terror, when you realize that you have to give it all up. People typically have to go through a lot of suffering to get to that point in their life. One of the processes that goes on is that gurus make it all seem so easy: "Just come to me, sit down, and wake up." No time at all. Actually, the vast majority of people need to be weaned of their attachments and their addictions and all of their suffering, and that generally takes some time. It is extremely unusual for somebody to just wake up right away. You have to understand that on the practical life level. If you wake up tomorrow morning, that's really nice. And if you don't wake up tomorrow morning, have a good sleep and sweet dreams. In either case, anticipation won't help.

It appears, then, that one must recognize the pain of separation before one can experience the pleasure of the Divine. After the guru creates awareness of this painful movement in your life, the pleasure arises of seeing that the pain was your own creation first, and that it was never necessary to suffer. You can talk about that all you want, and before you go through the pain you can think that it was never necessary, but that won't make any difference.

If you haven't known the truth of suffering directly in your life, you can afford to be philosophical about it. That all goes out the window when you know that truth.

Until you awaken as this condition, there will be an alternating movement in your life. Pain comes to the fore, and then pleasure comes in, then more intense pain, and then greater pleasure, and so on, until the alternation becomes extreme. There is this incredibly intense pain, like experiencing the depths, and then the exhilirating pleasure of the heights. It will go on like that until there is the constancy of communion with Grace. Then there is a steadiness of devotion throughout all movement in life. There is still the form of reality, so that you will continue to get angry on occasion, and laugh and cry as you always have, with the crucial difference that there is no longer an imagined dilemma in life.

Movement is spontaneously created in my functional life in order to generate movement in you. When there is movement in my life, you respond to me; and when there is little movement in my life, I end up following you! When you are all depressed, I am depressed. It's an odd situation. So in such a stagnant period, after you have fallen into routine patterns, there comes a time when movement is spontaneously generated as a way of shaking you out of your comfortableness. As soon as you're shaken up, you sort of refine and tune your mind into the new frequency, the new strategic orientation.

The process of our relationship that takes place when the form of teacher dissolves, is this shaking up of your static tendencies, the constant frustration of expectancies. You have heard a lot about surrender. Ultimately you will only know what surrender means when the teaching function dissolves. You will know that I live as absolute service, and that teaching is only one expression of that service. Everything I do is in order to serve you. I am dealing with you on a one-to-one basis in the matter of awakening, so there is a teaching-function on one level, although not the smooth, instructional, clearly comprehensible form of teacher that you are familiar with. There is no other light one can see me in than in the light of doing what I have to do to forge the devotee. The subject is life, and I don't use a blackboard.

EIGHTEEN

Simply a Cantelope

WHATEVER CONCEPT YOU may have of Grace, even if it is an intuitive and insightful one...that's not it. Grace is literally and very forcefully present, and you will never know that by merely listening to those words. You must be open to Grace and let it transform you. The blessing of life is real, and when you know it in pure devotion, all the words and the questions and the metaphysics become very funny. It is so simple. God is this life, and I don't mean life in the abstract or in some transcendental sense. Your entire existence is God. There is no gulf between your mind and this life; your mind is, in fact, no different from Grace. It is here, this Divine life is all very much here, and I keep telling you that over and over until you allow yourself to be happy.

I can't pick you out and say, "You get Grace." That is impossible, no guru can do that. Nor is it something that is done by one's own efforts. Your conception of Grace always implies the limitation of a power that accomplishes something. In most spiritual traditions, the seeker relies on "other-power" to accomplish the goal. In some cases that is contradicted and it is "self-power" that is relied on. Either way, from the inside or the outside, something is being changed. In this relationship there is no self-power or other power. Nothing is changed. There is Grace, there is inclusive movement, but the mind will never locate this Grace or trace this movement. It will vainly try to define Grace as a specific area, and when it is concentrated exclusively in one area due to separative tendencies, that concentration is contrasted with other possibilities as an exclusive limitation, rather than as one of an infinite number of possible alternatives in truth. The concepts of "God" or the "One" can be such an exclusive area. The mind will not fail to conceive of Grace as other than itself, and a lot of nice teachings will not help the situation. That is where I come in, for I cannot be mistaken for a concept.

I am Grace. I am neither "self" nor "other". If the guru was an other-power, or if the guru taught some kind of method in which the reliance was on self-power, the only resultant effect of that would be karmic. Somebody might generate a lot of good karma by being self-powered; he or she could become very positive and develop beneficial siddhis. Or one could be very devoted to the "other" and never dissolve the separate self sense. All such power is generated in the mind. That's what it all boils down to.

Mind is what is commonly called maya, the illusion, the play of the worlds. Mind is the texture of the world, inclusive of phenomena, form and vibration. There is no life within mind. What mind does is try to generate life, but what is actually generated is the life of separation. The function of mind is separation. It is thus intrinsic in the manifest worlds to see themselves over and against something else, for the delusion of separation is a process that can't be distinguished from creation itself. If the assumption of separation was not intrinsic in creation, consciousness would not be! If people didn't exist, God wouldn't exist. That is the Divine paradox.

For mind to know itself as Grace would be like the eye seeing itself. Mind is only self-knowing to the degree that it can conceptually interpret its own activity. It is not self-knowing as far as its inclusiveness is concerned. The assumption of separation is generated in mind, and mind does not know that its only life is in God. The firm assumption that life is possible within mind constitutes mind's seeking and grasping character, and it is forever seeking and grasping, since no amount of life can ever be produced from the activity of mind. Life is already present, it is not produced at all.

Prior condition is absolutely inclusive of mind, inclusive of all that exists, and at the same time is not an "other" or a particular force that generates what is. Who or what created the world? Nothing really created the world, it just is. From the perspective of mind, which is the perspective of separation, there is creation. Ultimately there is no creation. The same thing applies to the spontaneous arising of Grace in your life. It is not a generative process, it doesn't come from any place. It is, plain and simple. Being open to this Grace is acknowledging that I am here, and that you happen to be here with me. The spontaneous experience of turning to me in totality naturally arises. It doesn't come or go, stay or leave.

The condition known as Grace is inclusive of the space/time continuum. The three dimensions that we are aware of are, in their true nature, Grace. Grace is not another dimension, it is inclusive of all dimensions. The movement of Grace is not over and against a background, but is absolute, perfect movement. The mind is incapable of conceiving that which is not relative to anything. It will continue the attempt to generate life within mind, perceiving the recognition of Grace as a threat to that process, that is, as a threat to life. Mind maintains ignorance in order, so it thinks, to survive. Being unconscious or asleep is fundamentally assuming that one is an entity separate unto oneself, strategically seen in contrast with other separate entities. That is the character of the unenlightened one. And one defends that unconsciousness with the same ingenuity that one defends one's physical life.

From my perspective, on the other hand, mind is just present. The form that it takes is separative, certainly, because there is an individual body and I will speak of myself as distinct from someone else. That, as I said, is mind's function. I am prior to mind, yet as long as there is a body and a voice and all of that, mind is still very much present. I am not in any way under the binding assumption or motivation of mind, but I am not out of the realm of mind either. The very force of consciousness that is present is the difference between having mind as one's assumed nature and having God as one's nature. When God is one's consciously lived nature, mind is simply present. When mind is one's nature in ignorance, life is separative. All motivation, strategy, and activity reinforces and promotes separation, continually manifesting suffering as the world's activity. When God is one's realized nature, separation is simply what is present, and what is really lived. It is lived, but not sustained, promoted and reinforced, since the awakened one knows full well that life does not need to be created or sustained. The whole process of creation, birth, growth, disintegration and death is present every instant for this lived separation, and since I am prior to and consciously exist as that very process, I can fully live it without taking the point of view of any supposedly separate entity within it.

The process of slavery is the realization of God prior to all levels of mind. As long as one lives from the exclusive perspective of mind, one has the "freedom of choice" which is characteristic of the life of suffering. No actual freedom is given up, only a delusory one. The ultimate movement of Grace in one's life is when mind loses it completely. Mind is everything, so when mind is finally done in, that is the ultimate event, so to speak, the complete obviation of suffering. The devotee recognizes the guru as the absolute inclusiveness of existence, and immediately has perfect insight into creation, into the drama of assumed separation. Suffering isn't taken away, because suffering isn't a quantitative form that can be removed like a shirt that can be removed from your back. The perfect insight when the devotee truly knows the guru just obviates it.

The fact that God is prior to mind does not signify that God is other than what is. It does signify that what the mind assumed to be what is isn't. And that is everything, that is the entire structure of life as mind conceives it. The mind will invariably panic when it realizes that everything must be given up, for separation is intimately associated in mind with life itself, with survival. That is why the news that there is only God most often inspires terror rather than joy. The terror, however, is truly unfounded, for what is left over when you give everything up? You are. After all, have I disappeared? Am I gone? No, I am still here, still quite alive, just as I always have been and always will be. When you give it all up, you are still around, exactly the way you are now, but with one difference. You are who you are consciously. You are turned to shiva instead of shakti. You are the functional Divine.

It takes absolute, dynamic courage to live real spiritual life, because there is no compromise. You either live it or you don't, there is no half-way. Any half-way measures are seeking, which includes, in a lot of cases, what you think to be "giving it up". Often you may think you are giving it up when you are really just playing games with your mind. Sooner or later you will have to recognize the absolute commitment that is necessary for true spiritual life.

Doing your sadhana means not getting distracted by the mind. The mind is the greatest distraction, and it is therefore the hardest to recognize as such. Your mind will tell you that it is not a distraction, that it is important, that you need it to survive. Your mind will tell you that you need it to be positive, cheerful and healthy, that it is essential for your all-around well-being. Your mind will not want you to know that it is nothing but a great, big distraction, the biggest distraction of all.

The process of your life in this community is to know who you are in relationship to everything. That means in relationship specifically to mind, because if you know who you are in relationship to mind, everything else will be simple. Knowing who you are in relationship to reincarnation, shakti, dreams, or astral travel is a superficial affair. Knowing who you are in relationship to mind is the affair of the guru in the world. When you fully know, mind will be your plaything instead of you being mind's plaything. That's the key.

As long as you believe that everything is happening to you, you are the plaything of mind. And the feeling that everything is happening to oneself cannot be gotten rid of until one gets rid of the mistaken assumption that one is a self that has everything happen to it. That's what our relationship is all about. The guru gets you involved in the process that will bring you to the point of realizing that there is no self to have anything happen to. The living guru is essential to this process, because otherwise mind will continually attempt to transcend itself. Without being in the Presence of Grace in the world, one cannot assume the perspective of that Presence. Mind will always try to create the Presence, but when one is in the Presence of the guru, what is prior to and inclusive of mind is actively present in one's life.

You are working through your mind. I am working prior to your mind. When we meet, you wake up. When you know me as I am, you recognize that I am your nature. Who you think you are is the creation of mind. I am who you have always been, before time and space. When you realize this condition, there won't be you and I. Yet nothing will have changed!

****

The expression of our life with Lee through spiritual practices such as prayer, meditation, chanting, and singing, differs in many important respects from the same practices as they are conceived in the spiritual search. Instead of coming from a need that the practices are supposed to answer, they come from a joy and fullness that does not reach out towards any implied goal. They are a celebration and thanks in the Divine that is already present and active in our life, and not as a call for the Divine to enter our life. Finally, they are participated in and enjoyed for their own sake, because God is all there is, and not for the sake of the ones who are involved in them.

Lee encourages us to partake of all pure expressions of devotional life. When we chant the name of God, the chanting itself is God's expression in us. The gladness of being in the Presence of the Divine is not directed to reach the Presence through chanting, but springs from the Presence itself. Chanting the Divine name is our conscious celebration of ourselves as the Divine. The joy of singing consists in the fact that it is God singing, and that song is our life together in God.

Prayer has a conventional connotation of pleading or supplication: "Oh Lord, grant that we may..." etc. Lee teaches that such a form of prayer is presumptious and not devotional. To ask for something from God implies that the blessing of life is not enough, and that an assumed separate self deserves recognition from the Divine. In the Hohm community, prayer is God; it is the expression of the unity of the Divine nature in communion with the Lord. To have individuality conspicuous in prayer is to be in the way of prayer. In Lee's company, communion with God is in a spirit that, joyously appreciating the blessing of life, includes all within it. In a sense, prayer is life's conscious yes to itself, understanding itself in the moment one ceases to grasp at life. No words have to be said in such prayer, and no one need ask from where one receives its joy.

The many forms of meditational technique common within the spiritual search do not come from the perspective of the already present Divine. Lee has said that formal meditation in his company does not need to follow a prescribed routine or practice. In fact, he has left the possibilities in meditation wide open so as to let us be open to him in meditation. At one time, he gave us a form of meditation in his company, but it was precisely the non-specific nature of that form that made it effective. It consists of simply sitting in formal posture, with the eyes either open or closed, and letting whatever arises arise without giving energy to it. Whenever something arises in connection to his relationship with us, we are to non-conceptually question whatever it is. No actual question is to be formed in the mind, only an unformed questioning spirit is to be present. He emphasized that this was by no means a way to get anywhere or attain anything, but simply a process of openness to him in meditation. The unformed question makes it possible to not get caught up in one's fascinations and preconceptions of the guru, but to simply and honestly be open to Grace.

Formally expressing our love for the guru is an integral part of sadhana. All spiritual practices are a celebration of his company, and not a search for his company. It is a crucial distinction, for his service is only fully expressed in us when our desires are not in the way.

NINETEEN

Christmas is a Microbus

THERE ARE MANY different forms that our relationship takes, and you should be prepared to manifest any form at the appropriate time. You will know when certain things are appropriate or not. A lot of you have said, "I don't know how to act when I am with you. I'm not sure how to approach you." You need to be aware of and practiced in the forms our relationship takes, so that whatever the form calls for at the time, you do it.

One of the forms the guru takes is a very formal one. I can say over and over that I am the Lord and that I exist as Grace and so on. That is fine. Yet it doesn't really sink in when the only time that you are with me is in an informal situation, hanging out together. For you to truly appreciate it and be clear about it, a formal situation is very helpful.

I have talked about the fact that Grace is present twenty-four hours a day. There is just Grace here, and you do what you will with it. It manifests from individual to individual as a blessing. Whenever I am with you, you are being continually blessed. The process is to get you to appreciate that. You might think that you do. However, if you really appreciated it, you would be acting differently. Just know that however much you think you appreciate it, it is not there yet.

To symbolically exhibit the fact that there is only God, only the process of Grace, the guru manifests at times in very formal situations. For you, this is the approaching of the guru for a formal blessing, through **prasad**.

If you have to come up in a formal situation and approach me, there is a tendency to be very inhibited. Nonetheless, we are going to do it, because you need it. You need the constant reminder that this is for real, that we are serious about this business here, humorously serious.

The physical touch is a form of the bestowing of Grace. It objectifies the fact that the condition is all-embracing. I am taking care of you all the time, and the physical touch objectifies that. It reinforces, within your ability to cognize, the fact that the blessing is always going on.

When you approach me, let a gift be in your hand. And let that offering of a gift symbolize the surrender of you as devotee to the Lord. If you have no gift, that signifies that everything has been surrendered to me. So if that is not the case, bring a gift. In either case you will know what is appropriate; my devotee will never be empty-handed.

You should only approach me if you feel it in your heart. Even if you are a little inhibited, that doesn't matter. Many of you feel inhibited, and still feel that we have a very special relationship, so inhibition should not stop you from approaching me. The only thing that should stop you is the fact that you don't feel like approaching me. You need to really feel it, not just do it because other people are doing it.

You have probably noticed with handshakers that sometimes they just don't know when to let go. When I am done with you, I will let you know when I am done with you. That means that if you want to hug me for fifteen minutes and I don't, you shouldn't hug me for fifteen minutes. And when I let you go, that doesn't mean that you sit there and gaze into my eyes. It simply means that you go.

If I give you something back, whatever I give you, you keep. That means that everything I give you, my shirt, or a necklace, or food, is my gift to you and you keep that. If you give me something, you should be aware that I might give it away at any time. Your gifts are given to me out of your heart as offerings, and whatever I do with them, I do with them. You shouldn't be insulted if I give your gift to the next person who comes up. The giving of a gift is what is important, not whether I keep it or not, not whether I like it or not, not what I do with it. When you offer something to me, that is what is important, and if I happen to give it away, you should be pleased that I loved it enough to give it to somebody. Although I say that, you will probably not be pleased when it happens. You will probably be hurt, but that is all right.

The form needs to be appropriate, it needs to be exact, it needs to be formal. Although I severely criticize traditional spirituality, our relationship is very traditional. Our relationship is older than the world. It is good for you to remember that you are in the Presence of living God, and to respond accordingly.

The literal translation of prasad means food of the Divine. The place that prasad has in our relationship is on two levels: your offering to me, and more significantly, my offering to you. It is symbolic. You tithe and you follow the practical life requirements and so on, yet recognizing and following the requirements is different than giving me something you love. That can be food, or flowers. You shouldn't give me flowers if you don't like them. You should give me something that you really like, something that you are passionate about and emotionally involved with. Perhaps you are mad about peaches and strawberries. All that matters is that it be from your heart.

Since I am already the Divine, offering me a gift is symbolic in the strictest sense of the word. It is literally giving me something that is already mine. You are not really giving anything, what you are doing is making available for me an aspect of myself to give to you. In the same way, when the devotee gives his or her life to the guru, nothing is added to the guru that is not already him. The devotee is an aspect of the guru, so to speak, that is made available for him to give to the devotee. That is the blessing. When you give me something, you truly make available to me an aspect of my very own being. You can not literally give me anything. You are simply offering out of service, out of devotion, something of mine that I can return to my devotees as a blessing. This is the essence of prasad.

You give me a gift, and when I give it back to somebody, it is prasad. It is returned literally as a part of myself. That is the symbolism of the Mass in Catholicism, with the wafer and the wine being Christ's body and blood. When Jesus was alive, that was literally the case. If he gave someone a drink of wine, it was actually his being. That is what happens when I give you something. I give you myself.

When you offer something, let it be out of devotion. When I give you something that has been offered to me out of devotion, what I am literally giving you is pure devotion. My devotion is to you, and what I am giving you in prasad is that very devotion.

TWENTY

WHAT IS A spiritual community? It is not just great entertainment, or a lot of people getting together and having their own little clique and all that crap. It's a little more far-reaching than that.

The true spiritual community is composed of those who completely devote their lives to God. Not just a few years until "enlightenment" is reached, but one's entire life, must be committed to God. The guru-devotee relationship is the very core of spiritual life, so the guru-function is not effectively active in the world without the community. The guru is nothing without the devotees. If Krishna didn't have his gopis and if Buddha didn't have the bodhisattvas and bhikshus, neither of them would have been recognized traditionally. If Jesus didn't have disciples, nobody would ever have heard of him. He would have been crucified, and that would have been the end of it. The awakened one in the world, alone, is no different than anybody else in the world, alone. There is absolutely no difference at all. It is the community that makes the difference; it makes the teaching available in the world.

When people join the community, they find movement taking place in their life, they find a lot of activity going on, and they are challenged in many different ways. I am here and I do all this undermining; I make sure that your structures are apparent to you and that they get broken down. I make things clear as I present your limitation and your dilemma to you. Yet without the community, without your active participation in your own undoing, absolutely nothing would happen. It is the community that makes the teaching available; the guru simply exists as the functional Divine, present only.

All of the things you have gone through since you've been with me, that you have attributed to Grace, other people have gone through who don't have a guru and who aren't at all involved in any kind of spiritual life. But in their cases there has been no conscious recognition of what the drama is all about, no observation of what is going on in their life. They went through everything without even an intuition of the Divine process. You go through things, attributing them to the influence of my presence in the world, and some people would think that you are obviously crazy: "What are you talking about? My aunt Sarah went through that and all she did was eat too many onions." It is only conscious recognition that makes the difference.

The knowledge of the process of Grace in your life makes the teaching available in the world, not the guru. The true guru, being off the wheel, completely out of the whole action/reaction syndrome, doesn't have anything to do with the world. The guru is out of the world already. He just walks through and checks it out, not causing any waves or leaving any tracks. Nothing happens. It is only your involvement with Grace that causes any Divine exposition in the world.

Basically, Hohm is making available this teaching. There are a lot of teachings in the world and a lot of religions, and everybody makes his or her commitment wherever and whenever he or she feels like it. People look at this teaching and decide whether they like it or don't like it, even though they have yet to recognize the teaching itself, beyond its appearance. In this teaching there are no techniques. It is not a study course that you can take that will tell you how to act and what to do. There is nothing to do but wake up and live God. The mind, however, doesn't usually go for that. When the mind reads a book or goes to a seminar, it wants proof. The mind wants to know what happened to you when you joined the community. It wants to read beautiful descriptions of the dissolution of the self and exciting accounts of getting boiled in infinite light. That is exactly what the mind wants. People don't want to hear about this community where there is no seeking and everything is already perfect the way it is. Their mind craves qualification, the lowdown on what's going on. If you say that you've been freaking out ever since you joined the community, the mind is impressed: "Ah, yes, something is going on!"

Actually it is impossible to prove anything to anyone except yourself. You can never prove anything to anybody else. People might believe you, nevertheless you cannot prove anything logically, empirically, or any other way, except to yourself. Proof to self is simply knowledge, which could change at any time. Ultimate knowledge, which the guru is supposed to represent, also changes all the time. Knowledge per se, mundane or ultimate, is never constant because it is not an absolute. Only God is absolute. Even the awakened one is always expanding in knowledge, always getting new analogies, seeing new things, and recognizing new aspects of the play.

Your sadhana in my company constitutes the availability of the teaching. The way that you make the teaching available is by tricking people into it. Where are decisions made? In mind. Nobody is going to make a decision in mind to get involved in Hohm if they know what's going on here. Nobody. Mind is too smart for that. Mind has kept you where you are for eons upon eons of time, and it is not about to blow it all by approaching me and getting wiped out. Mind will not make that decision, so it has to be tricked. The community tricks people into thinking that they are going to attain something. The rhetoric doesn't matter. I must have said that there is nothing to attain a zillion times. It still doesn't matter. When people go to a seminar and see one of you, they want to be that way. They want to be humorous and loose too, so they get sucked in regardless of the rhetoric. Nobody knows what he is getting involved with.

After they join the community, there are all the beautifully intricate complications of the teaching to keep people busy. Actually it is all so utterly and perfectly simple that you wouldn't believe it. It is precisely because you wouldn't believe it that all the complexities are present. That's what keeps the mind involved long enough to get it. If the mind gives up too soon, and the person leaves the guru, then he will continue his life of seeking. There is no chance without the guru, so the complexity is another aspect of the tricking process. The mind likes the complexity, even though it gets tired of it at times. Usually it really gets off on sorting all the different things out and not understanding things and having questions and getting insights and all of that stuff. The mind would really like to be one of the people who can explain the teaching to everybody. What the mind doesn't know is that in order to successfully present the teaching, you have to realize that you don't need the teaching, so that you aren't relying on it for anything. You'd have seen through it, and thus could fully use it and present it to others. Until then, the mind will remain involved in the intricacies so that you will stick around long enough to learn to rely on me alone.

Paying attention to your sadhana is a strictly personal and selfish thing, because you are going to be happy all the time. When you are happy, there won't be any you to be happy. Still, your personal involvement with the community is going to intensify your sadhana, which is going to get you to rely only on Grace, which will awaken you as the condition of constant, clear happiness. Applying yourself to your sadhana is in itself making the teaching available, for Hohm is the exposition of the teaching through the functional example of devotees. I am not an example of the teaching. My devotees are. That is really the way any teaching becomes known, not in formal satsang where everybody comes and laughs and has a good time. The teaching becomes known in the world through people who live the teaching. And the basic teaching here is that it is our heritage as human beings to be happy all the time, to consciously live what is realized, in humor and devotion.

All of the devotion that you exhibit personally to me, the offering of prasad and all of your feelings towards me, is just appropriate activity. I don't consider that to be service. That's just natural, part of our relationship. Active service to me is allowing the teaching to be available in the world. That means that you should consider, throughout your activity in the community, how you can better serve the expression of this teaching. The true way to serve that expression is to be a perfect devotee. Then you are the absolutely functional example of my teaching.

Allowing the teaching to be available should not be confused with proselytizing. I am not interested in having you stand on a street corner to buttonhole the passersby, trying to cram the teaching down their throats. There is a degree to which you need to act appropriately because you are dealing with society, so I don't want you prostituting what I am doing here in order to suck in more people. I am only interested in your communicating with people who might really be interested, not broadcasting a message to the masses. The essential thing is being an example yourself and being consistent in your sadhana.

You attribute all your experience of crisis to the movement of the Divine in your life, to the availability of the condition of the guru. It is all your trip. You make it possible; the community is the only way any of it happens. I'm just the M.C. When you take a cruise, they have a social director on board. He makes sure that there are plenty of activities so that no one gets bored. And when you are in the midst of supposedly having a good time, involved in the various games and activities that the social director provides, dancing and singing and whooping it up, you suddenly realize that you are lonely. You're right in the midst of all this fun, and you are really miserable. That's when you really get it. If you are sitting at home alone and don't get it, it's because you figure, "If I only had a friend to hang out with, or a good movie to go to, it would be all right." You always think that it would be okay if you were doing something else. It is when you are in the middle of doing what you thought would make it all better, and you feel the same way, that you finally get it.

That's what the guru does. The guru doesn't let you get bored, because if he did, you would think, "If only I had another guru, if only the guru made more demands on me, if only I could be more intimate with the guru, it would be okay." So the guru gives you plenty to do: lots of movement and lots of activity. And when you are right in the middle of the activity and you realize that it's not working you say, "Hey, I'm doing everything that I thought would make it all right, and it's not all right." That's when you get it; that's when you realize that God is the only thing that matters.

The social director has to deal with a wide variety of people, and keep them all occupied: "Oh, you look lovely tonight, my dear." Social directors have to be able to deal with children and lonely widows and horny couples and older people. One guy is in the corner mumbling, "When do we eat?" while another one is yelling, "Put on some rock and roll! Let's dance!" And someone else is saying, "When do we play bingo?" The social director has to be broadly versed in a number of different personalities and approaches, just to be able to deal with all of the people who come to have their games structured. The guru is very much the same way; he responds to your particular tendencies. Sometimes the guru is nasty and other times nice, sometimes seductive and other times cold and ignoring, sometimes taking advantage and other times surprisingly reasonable, logical and considerate. The guru puts on all of these different hats because different people need different things, and it takes different games to keep them occupied. Then people begin to see into the nature of the game, and eventually the game no longer distracts them.

It is up to you. The community exists as the living example of spiritual life. Your responsibility is to live with me under any circumstances. That enables me to create movement in your life, which will produce an active community that will make the teaching available in the world. I am just the social director, you are the show.

At some point you have to be a devotee. At some point you need to be in a place where you don't need me, where you enjoy my company but you could care less whether I am around or not. Absolutely. For the devotee there is no pull, no need for the attention of my Presence.

The community Alive in God is what is real, and not the guru alone. The guru really has no function. There is the seeming function of presenting the teaching to you and being the social director until people can take care of themselves. Everybody is fighting against himself, everybody is swimming against the current. There is no current to swim against. You are all swimming downstream while thinking that you are swimming upstream. Everything is perfect; I have no real function in truth. Everybody is giving me a function because they think that they have to get somewhere. So at this point, you need me. When the community is full and ripe and there are devotees, the community doesn't need the guru. It doesn't need anything in order to present the teaching, unlike the guru, who needs the community in order to present the teaching. The community Alive in God is self-evidence. It is the teaching, functional in the world. The guru is not the teaching functional in the world; he is simply the breakthrough, the rare place in the world where all dimensions intersect and all planes disappear, like the Bermuda Triangle.

When you truly do not need me, the real fun starts. When our relationship is dampened with feelings of need, there is the assumption on your part that something else is lacking. Otherwise, why would you need the guru? When the community realizes that nothing is lacking, we can get to know and enjoy each other in endless humor.

TWENTY-ONE

ONE OF THE most interesting and controversial attributes of the guru is the fact that he is the only one that can appropriately manifest certain traits and tendencies that in anybody else would be considered obnoxious, egotistical, and even male chauvinistic.

Women's liberation is a very valuable movement, a step women are taking to recognize an identity that has been denied them. It is a useful process of education in self and consciousness in the world today. And it is the guru's job to undermine that completely. If the average man were to act the way the guru acts, he would be looked upon by women as oppressive, as not caring one iota that a woman is just as much a human being as a man. Such a one would be considered a fool for considering himself to be superior to women. And that man would be a fool. Yet the guru demands of the women that come to him the absolute surrender that they wouldn't dream of giving to a man.

It is the nature of the guru to undermine even such advanced and beneficial aspects of society as women's liberation. Even the women's movement, a development that was called for after ages of male dominance in society, needs to be dealt with from the perspective of the Divine, from Grace. The "liberation" involves the recognition by women that they have been programmed to see themselves as mere adjuncts to men. They become aware that they need not define themselves by male standards. They finally discover an identity as women. It is an important step, and at the same time there can be the tendency to stop there and just see oneself as a female identity over and against a male identity. One needs to transcend identity and realize what is prior to it. Obviously, if one views one's life in the context of "liberation", one is functioning totally from separate self, from the deluded sense of individualness and personality. It is that sense of individuality which has been suppressed in her; the movement arose in order to bring it to the surface. But the guru can not allow the women who approach him to remain fascinated with their new-found "freedom". He is only interested in awakening as the Divine, not in "consciousness raising".

The guru sees only God, not man or woman, not dominant or submissive. Only God. And the full and powerful implication of women's liberation is that woman as an individual is equal to man. That is fine as far as it goes, which is not, by any stretch of the imagination, as far as real spiritual life. As an individual, seen in contrast to man or in isolation, she is totally propagating the delusion of the separate self, continuing to reinforce separation from God by strengthening the identity of the person, the ego.

It is a fact that the average man looks upon woman as nothing more than an object, nothing more than a valuable possession, like his car, his stereo, or his guitar. The average man who lights a cigarette only does that to service her. That's the way he thinks, in terms of servicing a woman, not in terms of a mate, a lover, or a friend. To him she is just another possession, except on a higher and more substantial level than the other things that he considers his possessions.

All of that is absolutely true, and the guru has the job of undermining within all those who consider themselves liberated women, that feeling of liberation itself, for it still implies and reinforces the separate self sense. It is up to the guru to demand of the women in his company that they love him more than any other, that they surrender to him totally. The guru must crack the separate self sense of the non-liberated woman, for she is just as much a product of programming, just as much a product of ego, as the liberated woman. There is no difference in texture, only in form.

It is my job to do this, and I delight in it, as all manifestations of the Divine delight in their job, in their service to the prior condition of all existence. I delight in my service to myself, to

God. I will accept nothing less from those who approach me than this same, boundless delight.

My responsibility is absolute. My responsibility is more real, more intense, more dynamic than any responsibility you have known. I take pleasure in the responsibility of demanding of the women that they serve me, that they provide me with absolute devotion. I also demand that they never give to any man what they give to me. With any man, they live in relationship as a friend, a partner, or mate. To me, relationship is a matter of fulfilling the demands that I place on them. For there is only God. It is the function of the guru to see that every one of his or her disciples knows that there is only God, and lives that prior happiness of the Divine.

The Divine moves me to demand certain things of you, my devotees. I don't know why. I don't know when to stop. I have no control over the manifestations that I exhibit and produce in you. I will demand of you, and demand of you, and demand of you as long as you need to be demanded of. There is no conscious choice involved; I will simply demand until there is nothing left of you. I will expect in this relationship that you give everything to me. Everything.

I will demand that as a woman you do not live in a man's shadow. I will demand that you do not feed man's ego, that you do not indulge man's bloated sense of macho maleness, of asshole physical prowess, his disgusting and deluded sense of the king of the jungle, that you do not allow any man to lay that game on you.

And with me, you live only the demands that I make on you. You serve me. Your entire life is based upon serving me in every way, for there is nothing to life but service. When you realize that, you will be happy, happy to tears; you will have realized the absolute humor of this condition, of constant, senseless, unreasonable joy. Your "identity", if one could call it that, is not any limited self over and against something else. It is the unbounded, passionate, all-encompassing Divine itself. I want you to realize that.

You must see that the function of the guru is antithetical to all rationale, to all psychologies, philosophies and ideologies. They are tools of survival. The guru is far beyond your neurotic need to survive at all costs. Your highest aspirations do not even hint at what I am.

There is no equality where the guru is concerned. The guru demands that you live the relationship of equality to all others, to your friends, your family, your co-workers, your mate. The guru demands that you live equality. Yet the paradoxical fact of the Divine in the world is that, when it comes to the guru, there is no equality. The guru demands that he be recognized as absolute and unqualified, the raw condition of Grace itself. The guru doesn't ask that you look at him in the light of equality. He demands that you give it all to him.

Society feels threatened to the very core by the guru. All philosophies and psychologies bring one only to the point of recognizing the equality of all beings, particularly human beings. The equality of all men and women is a "humanist" truism. But as far as the guru is concerned there is no equality. That is the contradiction, that is what inevitably offends those who defend their suffering while in the very act of proclaiming its abolition. That is the process which cannot be confused with liberation. It is not understandable, cognizable, or reasonable. It is what it is, without judgement or analysis. There is no equality involved in your relationship with the guru. There is only give, give, give. And what do you get in return? Merely everything. And you can never know that until you give it all. That's what you must understand. The insights, the pleasure, the companionship, the life of the community, is nothing. **Nothing.** There is only God. The guru demands that you continually give until you give it all. Then you get back what you already are: everything, God.

Know the guru prior to your mind, prior to your precious identity. Do not look for or expect equality in me. It is my demand that your life be one of equality in relationship with all others, never with me. I don't have to waste my time justifying that. I have nothing to prove or defend. I simply expect you to be open to Grace. I expect you to have implicit trust in me, for I am truly your nature. People must trust their own nature if they don't want to live separation all their life. Everyone seems to miss that, yet it is so fundamental.

* * * *

Relationships among members of Hohm have reflected to a great degree the texture of our relationship with Lee. We are required to be straight with one another, which means that much of the game playing that creates "safe" boundaries between people is done away with. The result is either tumultuousness or togetherness, depending on whether we are turned to Lee or not.

When we fail to recognize the Divine as the common factor in our life together, personality clashes ensue. At different times, different people in the community become the target of back-biting and complaining. When our life at Hohm is conceived in a superficial way, we fail to be straight and honest with ourselves, and outwardly express our lack of turning in conflict with others.

It is only when God is recognized as all that matters in our life together that the power plays and squabbling can be seen as what they are: an avoidance of the guru. When we are turned to the guru, we can be true to ourselves and don't have to bother with liking or disliking what other people do. We are in balance with the primacy of God rather than tuned in to all the personality factors.

All such concern with personality can only take place when the relationship with the guru is also seen as personality. Despite all the talk about the Divine, we inevitably fall into the trap of thinking that Hohm is a club and Lee is our charismatic leader. The personality cult is a great distraction from sadhana, for it can give us the illusion that we are involved in spiritual life, when all we are really doing is worshipping a hero. Only when he is recognized as very God can we appreciate him and each other in truth. In the following talk, Lee deals forcefully with the fascination of personality.

TWENTY-TWO

The Cult of the Hero

THE GURU IS always wielding a big stick by making demands on his devotees. Because of this, they inevitably go through a lot of stuff. One of you asked me, "Do you have to beat us over the head? Why can't we just wake up?" The process takes on such dramatic form at times that many of you have wondered the same thing.

Yes, I do have to beat you over the head, because whenever one initially approaches the guru, there is some degree of recognition of the individual. The approach is always in mind. I can say again and again that there is no Lee, I am only the Divine, I exist as Grace, there is this condition which is simply present, and so on, and it makes no difference how many times I say it, for there is always some degree of Lee inherent in our relationship. You want to be my friend, or serve me, or be devoted to me. And as long as you are functioning from mind, you see me as an individual or person. You view me in the context of certain roles: lover, parent, friend. Before you can realize the unqualified Divine, you have to get through Lee. You have to do away with your conception of Lee before you can recognize me.

Conceptions of our relationship are limiting structures for you: I am the guru, you are the chela or disciple. Implied in that conceptual structure is that we deal on the basis of personalities. I talk to you, you listen and ask questions of me, and I answer your questions. There is this interaction between persons that is implied. There is no conflict about this whatsoever from my perspective.

I tell you that there is no individual, that there is only God. You can understand that, believe that, and have faith in that, but because your commitment is initially to the individual, you need to be beaten over the head.

Some of you wonder about Lee. "Is he considerate? What does it feel like to be him? Is he good in bed? Would he lend me some money? What does he really think about?" Whenever there is the type of question about Lee, it is blocking openness to the Divine. That concept in mind concerning the Guru is all about the form and the personality, not God. No conceptual framework applies to Grace. The condition that exists as our relationship is in fact prior to Lee. That is what needs to be realized, lived, and enjoyed. The demand that the guru makes on you, not only objectively but subjectively as well, is for you to get through your fascination with the guru as a person. And it is only your fascination that you must get through; there is no actual "Lee" to get beyond. All of the demands, verbal and non-verbal, exist because you are functioning from mind, and you need to have certain things demanded of you so that your mind will cease to be caught up in the form of the guru as individual and recognize this condition.

Beating you over the head isn't necessarily painful. Sometimes it can be very pleasant, like spending a lot of personal time with you. Joe was over at the house and we were cooking dinner, and I sat down and talked to the kids for awhile. It was like any normal household. And Joe was saying, "Wow, he really does that." Sometimes you need to be beaten over the head in a positive way in order to answer your questions relating to the very functional life conditions that the guru leads, to demystify him.

People often look at the guru as the perfect person, the fairy prince. The guru needs to undermine that fascination. Sometimes it's easy; I live with Radha twenty-four hours a day, so she sees that I don't pick up and I don't hang up my coat. She sees all my little habits. But you come around, and I'm always perfect. I make witty jokes and I dress nicely and my hair is combed. When you don't live with the guru, you tend to fantasize his perfection: "The guru must always be perfect with the children. They never get him annoyed." You look at whoever you live with if you have kids, and you see that once in awhile they just lose it completely with kids. Kids are like that; they have a way of really getting to you sometimes. So you think that the guru would never lose it. He would always know exactly how to deal with the children, never screaming at them.

I need you to be free of Lee. I need to get you to a point where the Divine can be your moving force, instead of your desire to be like Lee. There needs to be a very personal, intimate relationship, so that I can wean you of that fascination, and then Grace can be evident in your life.

Ultimately there is no purpose to all of this, since there is no real personality to be weaned of. You don't know that, however. On a psychological level, the demands have the purpose of weaning you of your various fascinations, such as, "What the hell did he do that for?" That applies to whenever you have a doubt or a question, or a desire, positive or negative, such as wanting or not wanting to be with Lee. You think that if you fall down, Lee will pick you up and it will be okay. The freedom that the guru exhibits is to wean you of that.

Everybody is always looking for the perfect partner. Actually, the perfect partner is not the person who is perfect; anyone who could do it right every time would be incredibly dull. One of the big fascinations is, "I wonder how Lee is in bed?" That one would be a hell of a lot of fun to deal with from my perspective. If you just wonder, it is perfect. If you think that it is supposed to be perfect, it isn't. I would still enjoy it anyway. If that is the biggy for you, you need to get through that and realize that Lee is just like anybody else, and that it's no big deal.

If your fascination is, "I'll bet he's the perfect friend. I'll bet that if I ever needed something, Lee would be there," then we would have to become good friends so that I could show you that there is no exciting quality to Lee as a friend. If your fascination is, "Lee must always know what to say to the kids so that they grow up right," then we need to deal personally with that. I would have to be with your kids and get pissed off at them, maybe tie them to a couch and seem a bit serious about playing cowboys and Indians, putting kindling wood under their feet.

Whatever your big fascination with Lee happens to be, it needs to be undermined so that you can know the guru. Don't get the idea now that I'm going to sleep with everyone or move into your house and take care of your kids. All I am talking about is the fact that whatever you need to take the screen away that is set up in your mind, Grace will manifest between us on a one-to-one basis, to get rid of that obstruction to God-awakening. "Lee" is that obstruction in which is focused all your attachment to the life of a separate self.

You might say, "Lee is the Divine. If I just turn to the guru, Grace will function in my life," and so on. Thinking in terms of that and functionally responding to that are two different situations. Undermining your belief in the person will take a much more basic form than persuading yourself mentally that the individual doesn't exist. So I end up beating you over the head all the time, and before you can truly understand that process you have to let Lee step aside, so to speak. That can be a problem, because Lee will also do anything he can to win you over so that you don't put Lee aside. This is my paradox: the guru is by nature a friend, a lover, a father, a child, and the guru, also by nature, must wean you of all that. I will demand that you get through Lee so as to be open to this Grace, and I will also do anything possible to keep Lee there, so that when the Divine manifests in your life, you deal with it appropriately.

The various roles you see me in are used initially as fly paper. If the spider says to the fly, "I am going to catch you and make my meal of you," the fly isn't going to come to the den. So the spider has to serve tea. All gurus suck people in initially. What are people going to come to a community for? Certainly not to be undone. I can say all day long, "I'm going to take your life," and nobody believes that. People don't come to the community because they are really into having their life dissolved. So the roles play an appropriate part in allowing people to become associated with the guru and to approach the community. As they become more involved, the roles serve their sadhana by pointing out to them how they have sustained their separative consciousness. If they see me as father, they are liable to recognize how they have always seen certain people as father figures, and how that has been their strategy. For them, I am merely a higher form of father figure than somebody they have encountered before. If people see me as friend, they are going to see me in contrast with those they have always considered as friend, or if they see me as lover, they will see me over and against those they have previously seen as lover. So what typically happens with some women in the community is that they fantasize about me being someone who can give them the freedom to be themselves and who doesn't criticize or challenge. If that is what they imagine the perfect lover to be, the knight in shining armor, I will occasionally be the same way that their lovers have always been, so that they will see how their interpretation of what a lover is supposed to be has been the problem with their love affairs. There are times, then, when I won't be so great; I will be exactly what they are used to in order to point out the narrow and limited framework involved in their relationships. That particularly applies in the roles of parent, friend, and child.

Ultimately, as one goes through the roles and sees that I am simply present and that the possibilities are infinite, including my being mean, kind, loving, angry, harsh, or soft, then the roles start to fall away. I start to be seen in the role of guru instead. That is a higher form of strategy, when one sees me as guru, because one is still seeing me as an individual on one level. My role as guru will face you with the fact that you are still seeing me as hero figure. Then that role will fall away too, and there is simply God present.

Lee will do everything in his power to fascinate you with him as an individual, as a guru-man, so that when you truly experience satsang, you stay there and don't return to the life of ignorance. That is why it usually takes some time of personal relationship with the guru before awakening can take place, instead of someone walking in and waking up after two weeks. All of the involvement with Lee needs to be played out so that you can become intelligently aware of the guru's theater. After you become a good drama critic, you stop getting carried away by the play. That usually drags on, because every once in awhile there is a rare performance. You can be an extremely jaded drama critic, and yet there is still that occasionally spectacular show. You are going along very well, you think that you are "making it", you are getting to be pretty good at the game, you know what I'm doing and I don't fool you anymore. Then there is a brilliant performance and you get sucked in again. It takes some time to get through that.

The nature of the guru is the paradox of constantly going beyond myself, so that whenever anyone starts to get comfortable in an established pattern, I outdo myself in whatever way is called for. That's the way it works. There is fascination from every side and every angle, and until its very basis is undone, there is always the possibility of another great show that will entrance you, and you will not know me as I am.

The objective demand is one that a lot of people relish. The guru tells you to kiss his ass and wash the dishes, or whatever the demand might be, and he is really tough about it. So you do it appropriately and you think, "I did it!" knowing that you're looking good. The subjective demand is a process that works in a sneaky way. Whatever you are looking for and expect as a result is undermined, and the form that the undermining takes is very different from what you expect. You suddenly realize things about yourself that you would never have willingly brought to light. You may see, for instance, how dishonesty is so much a part of your life that you don't notice it.

The undermining might involve your fascination with another teacher, which can be a tremendous conflict when it occurs. There are a lot of good raps around, and the attraction to another rap can be a very appropriate form of undermining. It is disconcerting; you know that you should be committed to the guru, you want to be sincere, and yet there is this nagging feeling that there is something somewhere else. That can pull you apart. If you are an idealist, that can do a good job of ripping the fiber of your mind apart.

Some of you men that want to lose a little weight, stick around. When the recognition comes that the person you think you love belongs to the guru and not to you, and that you never loved her in the first place although you thought you did, it can really do things to you. Some of you don't know yet. Some of you that are married think that you really love your mate. Wait until you find out that not only do you not love your mate now, but in the passion of romance you loved him or her even less. At least now you have lived together for awhile and are getting a little closer. You men didn't love the women when "the chase" was on. In fact, you were so far from it that you wouldn't have recognized real love if it had come up and bit you on the ass. Some of you might think you know this, but when you really find this out, you're going to lose some weight.

Undermining always takes the form of what you least expect, which is the real beauty of it. When you are in that state of uncertainty after being hit with recognition, the guru can neatly slip in. When you are strong and sure and absolutely convinced that you've got it together, the guru has got a tough battle ahead. It is when you are a little bit unhinged that I make a point. What you expect of me, whatever that may be, is occasionally fulfilled to some degree. So I have been a friend and kind of nice to some of you. That has been fulfilled in some sense, so that you get to a place where you are so damned sure of everything that you are very self-confident, and all of a sudden you're not sure anymore. Your house of cards has fallen.

For the majority of the people who come to the community, there will always be the attachment and fascination of personality. That is undone only in specific work with devotees. In any large numbers of people, the personality mystique will maintain itself independently of anything I do, even if Lee doesn't encourage it. No matter how contradictory or crazy the guru is, people can always take that as what endears him to them. The fact that he is so crazy makes him very unique and eccentric, and people like odd things and unique things. It is the personality cult that is the main thing to get past, and you need to make a commitment to allow that to be undone appropriately.

People are always attributing to me, in addition to all the valid phenomena that surround me, all kinds of very common, coincidental things that are imagined to be very special. I might tell someone something about him or herself that is just common sense, and they react with astonishment to what they think is supernatural perception of their life. Anybody with the least degree of awareness can do those kind of "miracles". In the average person it is looked on as just nice, but with the guru a big deal is made out of it. All of that has to be undone, which is very difficult, because even if I made a stupid business move or did something wrong, people will manage to get some kind of lesson out of it. The guru can't make a mistake.

Of course this is all a fundamental error, but how to do away with it? The whole process of dilemma is a fundamental error. It can only be undone with constant attention. If the heat is on without letting up, it will get undone. But if the heat is on for a day, and then you go home and have dinner at your house, it is already off. The fascination with the individual will simply not be undone unless there is constant heat, so that no matter what arises, it is undermined immediately. At some point, the mind just gives up.

As long as there is breathing space between thoughts, new strategies can be created. Even a few minutes is enough time to re-do the whole thing, get prepared, solidify yourself and go to it again. Crying is a great one. If somebody cries for five minutes, that is enough breathing space to completely redesign the whole approach. The process of undermining isn't initially going to undo strategy unless there is constant attention, although it will get a person to grasp the nature of strategy, and become aware of how new strategies arise as old ones are undermined.

The only way to be ready for the elimination of all such strategy is absolute devotion, which is the most painful thing in the world. It really is. It is very painful to allow yourself to be assumed by the guru. Only the utter simplicity of devotion to me, to the Divine itself and not an imaginary personality, will allow the constant heat that will undo you. And you would not trade that pain of devotion for anything.

* * * *

Because of the basic irresponsibility which is the form of our life, Lee has found himself taking care of those administrative aspects of community life that should be our responsibility. This was a necessary preliminary phase of community life, since we are initially wrapped up in our own separate concerns to the point of not being able to see past our noses. One of the processes of community life has been our assumption of these aspects. It began with the objective demand to give presentations on Hohm for those who are interested, during which we had to learn the very practical function of presenting the teaching. As more responsibility is assumed by the community for such aspects as bookkeeping and administrating Hohm activities, Lee can direct his energy to more important things, like being available to his devotees in their sadhana. The stabilization of all aspects of functional life had to take place on all levels before we could get on to the intense work on a one-to-one basis with Lee. In the following talk, Lee makes clear what responsibility in community entails, and how the relationships among ourselves best serve him.

TWENTY-THREE

THE RESPONSIBILITY THAT you have is to me. As a matter of fact, everybody's responsibility is to me, only most people don't recognize that. You have, at least, recognized intellectually that your responsibility is to me. How you are responsible in your working life, your social life, and in your functional life with other members of the community, depends on how well you pay attention to me, fulfilling your sadhana the way I have talked about it. Your responsibility in your job does not stem from how you have been brought up to see it, but from what I tell you about responsibility in your job. It is necessary from your perspective to do whatever the guru says, suffer whatever outrage he might have you suffer, enjoy whatever ecstasy he might have you enjoy, and to serve him in whatever activities you are involved in.

My primary responsibility is to you. In order to be fully responsible to you, I am bound by no conventional personal responsibility to you at all. It is only because I uncompromisingly serve the truth in you that this is the case. The guru's responsibility is to get you to realize what your responsibility to God is. The way of doing that is often paradoxical, such as exhibiting conventional irresponsibility. I am absolutely not responsible to any of you in the ways that hold true in conventional terms. Period.

Responsibility for you is simply doing your sadhana the way I have told you your sadhana is. It is not a matter of the action you take, or of the manifest result of doing what I say. It is a matter of what is specifically appropriate for you as an individual.

There is no rule that determines the way it is for everybody, except for the obvious rule to be responsible to the guru.

I expect a degree of conventional responsibility from people in the community. I expect you to hold a position in society that is equal to your talents: if you have the ability of an engineer, you shouldn't be working in a gas station. You should do what you are supposed to do in your job, happily dedicating your work to me. In terms of legal responsibility, if you are divorced and have alimony to pay, I expect you to sustain that. You should be following the requirements of the community concerning diet and exercise. And you should be responsible to the people in the community: if you tell someone that you are going to help her with something, you should be there on time to help her; or if someone asks you over for dinner and you tell him that you're busy, you should really be busy. You are responsible, then, for not playing the games that people normally play with each other.

Another aspect of your responsibility is supporting the community. I don't mean just making money. There are many ways to make a lot of money under the table, and the chances of getting caught are minor. If you are out in the world, there are things you can get involved in for the fast buck. I am not interested in that. I am interested in functional activity in the world. Your values must extend a lot farther than what is normally accepted in society. Don't wait until it is spelled out to you in black and white. If you know what is appropriate, then abide in your commitment to me and fulfill it.

From my perspective, your responsibility is more fundamental than these superficial aspects. It is the constant, day-to-day turning to God throughout all activity. Everything you do should be in the service of the Divine. Your relationship with me is the very basis of your functional life, and your responsibility is a constant force of confrontation and undermining of your tendencies toward separative activity. It is in the context of our relationship that your responsibility in all of your relationships with others should be viewed.

You should be clear, in your relationships with your lover, mate, or friends, that you are not responsible for them. You can not be responsible for any other individual. Your responsibility is to me, and that entails keeping them straight, keeping your intimates doing their sadhana. Your responsibility is to be considerate, loving, compassionate, communicative and understanding, not to let them run their act on you and not to run your act on them. It is simply being appropriate in your relationship with them, not trying to control them.

Intimate relationship with members of the community is required, whether that means a mate or just friends. It is particularly appropriate to be living in a community house. You are not responsible for the people you are living with, you are responsible to me, which means that you are responsible to them. That involves keeping one another straight instead of allowing a conventionally comfortable game to go on because it feels good.

In addition to being responsible to me, you are also responsible for me. You need to provide the climate, the milieu, for activity and communication with you. You need to provide for me the environment that pleases me, and the gift that is appropriate and that I like. You need to provide for me whatever I ask you for as a member of this community. You are responsible for my life on a practical, human level, for the next fifty years, or however long I am around. The evolution of the community depends on your responsibility for me. The community gives me a stamping grounds, a place to live, to teach and develop the dharma. Being responsible for me is making sure that the community is strong, viable, economically established, and actively making the teaching available. I need my playground in order.

Everyone else, you are responsible to, which means keeping one another remembering sadhana. It is not being a pain in the ass all the time, or getting on somebody's back because of your sense of a duty to help him. It is not a matter of changing anything, but of simply recognizing where your responsibility lies, and functionally responding to it. What arises is very natural and unforced. Your responsibility to me automatically entails being responsible to one another.

A question that frequently comes up is, "What about children?" Until they reach a certain age, you are legally responsible for them. Being legally responsible for someone and being spiritually responsible to someone are entirely different matters. You are spiritually responsible to your children not to give them the same old stuff that you were given by your parents, and to see that when they grow up, they don't get caught in the same trap that most adults get caught in. It is none of your damn business what grades they are getting, what friends they hang out with, or what they spend their money on. That is not your responsibility. You can guide them, make suggestions, and help them understand. But you are not responsible for them. If you feel that you are, it is going to ruin your life when your fifteen-year-old daughter becomes pregnant. You are going to think that your whole life was useless. It is not your responsibility at all. If you have properly educated your children, and they want to do something that is not appropriate, it is their responsibility and not yours. It is unnecessary for you to live their lives for them, only to be appropriate in your relationship with them.

The requirement is that you be turned and open to me first, and to everything and everybody else second. That is the only way that you will be appropriate with others, for beneath the creation of friendships or other relationships, there is always something that is held back. It is merely the agreement between two people to be ignorant of each other's act. You always hold something back because relationship can't be created. You can not try to have a perfect relationship with your mate. It is nice to imagine that you could have a perfect marital relationship, and that is just not practical. The kind of relationship that you've had before simply does not work. It's better that you be clear about that from the beginning, instead of jumping into a relationship and finding it out later on.

For a perfect relationship with your mate to exist in your life, it needs to be the result of Grace. It can never be muscled. You cannot have a perfect relationship through effort, it has to be something that arises out of satsang. As long as you are still involved in the binding games that are commonly referred to as "relationships", perfect relationship doesn't exist in your life. You have to be responsible to me, allowing the spontaneously joyous relationship that is prior to all of your carefully constructed architecture to be the case.

Marriage in the community means an agreement with the person you are married to, to be intimate and to communicate with that person, to be honest, open, loving, and to serve that one. Most of all, it is to allow him or her the freedom to respond in whatever way is needed where I am concerned. That is the hard part, for there is an unfortunate tendency to intrude or control in that area. If you are going to take the freedom to respond to me appropriately, then yield that to everyone.

Be aware that the conventional form of relationship has always been involved with ownership and territory. This involves not only mates, but friends too. When people are paired up, there is an inherent and very powerful principle of territory at work. People tend to think of their mate or friend as their inalienable property. You go to a party and your mate goes over and talks to someone of the opposite sex, and you end up getting all freaked out about it. Yet if your mate is seriously interested in having sex with someone else, what are you going to do about it? Are you going to stop him or her from doing it? Once it is in mind, that's it. He or she is not going to have a better relationship with you because of not sleeping with someone else even though he or she really wants to. Once the desire is there, it's done. Your mate probably still loves you as much as ever anyway. Be aware of this principle of power and ownership in conventional relationships, and recognize how opposed it is to an agreement of honesty, openness, and service to one another.

Marriage within the community implies a choice to live with someone, serve that person, and give him or her the freedom to freak out once in awhile, or be a little insensitive or arrogant once in awhile. The ethic of the binding contract is so deeply rooted, that you may have lived with a person for years, but when you sign the contract and it is legal, it is such powerful programming that no matter how intelligent or sensitive you are, it means something to you. It's like the last payment on the car: "Now it's mine." And you find yourself taking your mate for granted, taking advantage. Recognize that when you make the choice to marry someone, your choice is not a conventional one. Your choice is to serve that person for a lifetime. That service may sometimes mean having to deal with the fact that your mate would like to sleep with someone else once in awhile. Whether he or she actually does or not, you are just going to have to deal with that. If the one you live with gets a little bitchy at times, serving that person means not getting him or her back. And you know just how to get back at your mate. So remember that you chose to be open and communicative and understanding. The attitude is the key. A person can be very jealous, as long as he or she is willing to deal with it and get through it. It is the attitude of allowing your mate his or her freedom, as well as recognizing that one's service to you. It works both ways. You serve that one, not in the conventional context of marriage, but rather in the context of marriage that exists in the community of devotees, which is always responsive to me first.

All of the conventional relationships that you "create" maintain your separative life. Within those groups lies an unconscious agreement of separation. You lay your expectancy on the group, and the group lays its collective expectancy on each of its members. You play out the same old game and act out the same old story, thinking that the interaction that goes on is leading to relationship, when in fact it is not. Relationship is prior to all expectancies that are placed on people. Most of you are relatively satisfied because you are very much involved in the community and have a lot of companionship. Yet even with all your social relationships within the community, you still feel that something is missing, and that is because you are still trying to create relationships with people in the community, instead of letting them spring from satsang. In place of your old friends, you have your new friends. There is no difference. The same basic ignorance applies: you are relying on companionship, not God.

The supposed creation of relationships is antithetical to satsang, to Grace, to your already happy state. All of your relationships are based on the process of having an expectancy of what proper relationship is or should be, and attempting to force reality to fit that expectancy. Your relationship with your husband, wife, friend, father, mother, child, lover, boss, employee, or whatever it might be, are all based on expectancy. In order for me to help you recognize this, your relationships need to be undermined. Sometimes that takes the form of unconventional experience and application. The guru is free to express conventional or unconventional behavior in order to bring forth in you the recognition of the architecture you have set up in your life. It can take the form of violating everything you believe about relationships, and thus challenging your expectancies at a deep level. For you to eliminate the architecture, the foundation of the building must be undermined so that it collapses, leaving a big, open lot.

Now you can see that it is essential to be responsible to me. Otherwise, you will perceive my confronting and demanding function as a personal attack. The basic responsibility that you have to me is to allow my Presence its place in your life. If you try to shut it out, the whole process will appear very threatening.

Your responsibility is life. That is just the way it is. Nothing is served by taking a stand against life; life is your sadhana, and you must live it absolutely. Regardless of what goes on, your responsibility is to remember me. No matter what, whether you are in pain or feeling pleasure, or if you think that you're miserable, or even that you are not doing your sadhana, remember me. Perhaps you feel guilty, or perhaps you feel happy. That is irrelevant, for your responsibility is to me in any case. There is nothing else.

The openness of your life with me implies that your social relationships do not harden into cliques. As new people come into the community, it is not their job to break into your already established social groups and fields of activity. It is your job to include those people automatically and naturally in all of the things that go on in the community. It is part of your responsibility in doing your sadhana not to do it alone, or with a secure group of friends, but to make it a special point to include the new people of the community in your sadhana. After people have lived together for a few months, everybody has got everybody else's strategies down, and knows exactly how to work with them, when to get angry, when to let it ride, and all of those games. So when new people come in, especially if the new people are very different from what you are accustomed to, that makes for some really good movement.

Living with other people in the community is essential to the whole process of recognizing expectancies. It is very difficult to do sadhana when the people you live with are not doing sadhana. When people who are turned to me are living together, it makes things a lot simpler. However, I expect you to be responsible whether you have begun living with other members of Hohm yet or not.

People in the community are always having these great insights about how irresponsible they are. Doing your sadhana is simply being responsible, not continually seeing how irresponsible you are. It is so basic, so elementary, and yet everyone tries to make it so complicated. If Grace isn't always confronting people forcefully, there are an infinite number of ways they can avoid responsibility. So they will just keep on avoiding it. People are experts at being the way you want them to be when they are with you. There is an old cliche: "You never know someone until you live with him." It is perfectly true. People have such good acts that, if they want to please you, they will do exactly what you would like them to do, whenever you are around. It is only when you catch them off guard that you notice the little hidden things. You catch them lying a little bit or cheating a little bit and you say, "Wow, I never knew they were like that." Of course you didn't. People have fabulous acts. Living together makes the acts more transparent, so to speak, and thus helps the process of undermining conventional relationships.

It is not conventional relationships per se that are separative, but living them unconsciously. The true devotee doesn't need to live unconventionally, although the possibility is always there. The true devotee lives what appears to be a perfectly conventional relationship, consciously and intelligently in God. That one enjoys the same condition that I enjoy.

There is an influence that I have which is more far-reaching than you suspect. Anyone that reads the book is under my influence, regardless of space and time. Many people that have merely heard of me are under my influence. And to whatever degree people are under my influence, that is the degree to which I am responsible for them. For the thousands of people who have heard of me and have made some kind of minor connection, I am a minor influence. Therefore I have a minor responsibility for them. Ultimately I influence everybody in the world, because there is no separate self and I am inclusive. On the practical level it is a matter of who I have made the point with. In the great sutras of Buddhism, they talk about how the Buddha began to speak, and there came to him thousands of Bodhisattvas, each with many hundred thousand myriads of followers, as many as the sands of the Ganges. So it seems that the Buddha was present to and taught for billions upon billions of beings. That means that everybody is present to me anyway. I could go to a crowd in Grand Central Station and make the point with hundreds of people. And the point that I always make is that our relationship is always perfect. But for those who do not live directly and consciously in my company, that point will never surface functionally in their lives. It is the personal relationship with the true guru that constitutes real spiritual life. For those who live with me, I am completely responsible.

Those of you who have had a hit of Grace, who really know that it's the Divine that keeps you here, have experienced something that is priceless. People search for their entire lives just to get a taste of that. It would be appropriate if every day you would be thankful, that I am with you as guru. That will allow your thankfulness and appreciation to be present for you every day. An appreciation for life itself is present in my company, which expresses itself in humor and delight.

You should be thankful for whoever you are with every day. That makes openness and communication possible. That is the appropriate expression of relationship. People tend to be generally thankless, so they don't even want to try to communicate. They want to be the male chauvinist or the bitch or whatever role they play. People don't want to be open, even though they may say, "We never communicate. You never really talk to me." Try communicating when someone says that to you. Give that person one minute of real communication and he or she will freak out. Have you ever seen a clam shut after it has been opened? That's the way people react to real communication. For so many, life seems to be an annoyance, a troublesome itch that won't go away. A basic gladness and thankfulness is missing, the thankfulness of one who is exactly what he wants.

It is very selfless to be thankful for the people you are with, because a lot of times you inconvenience yourself for them. And when it is natural and spontaneous, the very act of inconveniencing yourself for them is a greater pleasure than if they were to inconvenience themselves for you. It is great enjoyment to be able to selflessly serve the people you are with, whether it be your friends or your mate, or whoever. It is happiness.

At some point it will be your nature to be thankful for your friends in the community, and to recognize the difference between the texture of these relationships and the texture of the conventional "relationships" that people have. The form can be exactly the same, but the texture of your relationship is joy, not fear. That is because you all have me as a common thread. I am the texture of your life together; I am always dancing with you, having my characteristically humorous fun.

TWENTY-FOUR

GOD IS THE only thing that matters. And it matters. Totally.

Sometimes you get into filling your heads with so many other things that you forget about God. You are so into thinking about your dilemma and how much work you are doing and all your suffering and surrendering that you get lost in the activities of the community and lose sight of why you are in the community in the first place. You come and chant and talk about being devoted to the guru and giving it up, and yet you are really not thinking about God. There is no room for God in your life when it is all cluttered up with what you think of the lecture I give and what I demand of you and what satsang entails and what devotion means. All of that is okay in its place, but there is no joy without God. God is not a process of thinking about getting rid of your suffering and becoming realized someday. Even though there are occasional moments of laughter, occasional moments when you are distracted enough to believe that you are happy, there is no real gladness or humor when God is not involved. Be sure that you remember what you are doing here. Don't get trapped in thinking about where you are at, or where you are going, or what you are giving up, for that is all a distraction. There is only God, and life's only joy and satisfaction is God.

What is absolutely necessary in this community is obsession. Most people think that obsession is a very negative word, with connotations of sickness and depravity: "You know how people that are obsessed are; nobody wants to know them." Yet without an absolute obsession for God, the point of unlimited awakening is never reached. Ever.

In all the forms of the search, obsession is not demanded. What is begged for is peacefulness, being mellowed out, being cool. A variety of things are hoped for; obsession is never demanded, not in the necessary manner so that it is consuming. They might say, "Pray to God" or "Chant God's name", but that is not enough. That remains only obsession for praying or chanting.

I demand literal and absolute obsession for God. I demand that every thought, every desire, always be turned towards God, so that you are immersed in the Divine. If you are wondering what you are going to get from being in the community, recognize that you should be thinking about God, while you are working, while you are driving, and while you are eating. At night you should be dreaming about God.

Most seeming obsession is just another form of the search. You beat your chest and cry, "Oh, I want God." Then you get a little flash of shakti and you say, "I'm getting it! I'm getting it!" You become so wrapped up in the theater involved with "the path" that you forget all about God. You get lost in experience, in your senses, your mind, your separation. You conceive God as a thing that you validate through experience. You would even attempt to reduce God to a rational principle.

God cannot be explained away, proven, or justified. The attempt to do so is a useless exercise. The very Divine is absolutely inclusive, defying all pitiful attempts to define it. There is always separation when one feels that God has been adequately dealt with on a verbal or mental level. The appropriate response to the Presence of God is not icy analysis, but an obsession that is constant, a burning devotion for the one that is the very nature of your life. To live only for God, to the extent that one would not wish to have a will of one's own, is true obsession.

There are two ways to be obsessed with God. One can be obsessed to the point where one is non-functional, drunk and senseless, unable to deal with life. There are times when you can be so overwhelmed with the love of God that you become that way. In the case of Sri Ramakrishna, someone would merely say the name of God, and he would swoon, tears pouring out of his eyes. That is a state of consciousness which is very pertinent and very present in the lives of those who love God. However, that is not the end result of spiritual life, that is not the goal of your life in the community.

The other way is to be obsessed, with a functional life in God. That is what this teaching involves: living God functionally in the world. It is moving, dynamic, exciting, and humorous. Obsession is always dramatic; the drama of functional obsession is comedy, while the drama of one who is perpetually and exclusively obsessed with God non-functionally is comedy of a very different sort. I am interested in Divine humor, not in a comedy of errors.

When I say, "living God functionally in the world", the emphasis is on God. Living functionally, considered by itself, is meaningless. The fact that your sadhana is very basic, very real, and very alive in this world, does not preclude and should not give you cause to ignore the Divine. It is too easy to get lost in functional life, forgetting its fundamental basis in God. That is when you get distracted in absurdity: one day God, the next day who's screwing who. That will never do.

One of the things the true guru does is try to distract you from God. I really haven't had to do that. Most of you are so distracted from God anyway that it hasn't been necessary for me to try that. When you are obsessed with God, you see that the foundation of what we are doing here is none other than God. When you forget about God, you get distracted in how much money you are making, and how you freaked out your parents again this week, or whatever is going on. When you get into all that at the expense of God-obsession, you can't really expect too much from me.

The basis of everything we do together is the Divine. The less distracted you are with your lives, and the more involvement there is in the obliteration of your life in the fire of God, the more you are doing sadhana. And when God is your consuming passion, you will recognize the meaning of words like peace, happiness, joy, and even love.

It is a hard thing to recognize what love is. You tend to think of love in terms of possession: I love you, so you can't go to bed with anyone else; I love you, therefore you should love me. We put limits on what we think to be love. The prerequisite for recognizing what love is, is selfless giving in God. Love of that kind will dwarf all the "love" you have ever experienced. For one who is obsessed, love for God is the marrow of one's bones. And no "therefores" about it.

When you are obsessed, life is full and passionate. There are still highs and lows; life still goes on, it doesn't change. Life doesn't become all sweetness and light, it simply flows the way it flows. The difference is that when you are obsessed with God, it is perfectly okay that life goes on. When you are not obsessed with God, it is really not okay. You've got all these opinions and things that you want and these incredible aspirations and complex need systems and on and on, ad nauseum. When one's only thought is for God, what use is all that stuff? Worse than useless.

In this sadhana, then, you have two alternatives. The first is that you be totally obsessed with God. Not the kind of God that you have heard about, read about or imagined, because that kind of God does not exist, but that you be obsessed with the true and only Lord, the unqualified Divine.

The second alternative is not to be obsessed, and never to wake up. Ever. For there is no other way. No one ever lived in the constant joy of the Divine without the obsession and the overwhelming love for God. And obviously, if you try to be obsessed because you want to wake up, that love has not arisen; you are motivated by reward rather than devoted to God only.

How to establish obsession? We chant, we pray, we meditate, we do a lot of nice things. That's all right, that's appropriate. It does not establish obsession. You can be obsessed without ever having prayed, meditated, or sung the name of God in formal chanting. Obsession establishes itself and finds its expression when you are in the company of the living guru. It is my living Presence that makes available the life in God for you. The advent of the guru brings what was conceived as a mere possibility, Divine life, into actuality in the world.

Only God lived in the world is real. All else is the delusion of the mind which first establishes and then enforces, by any means, the dilemma of suffering that human beings exist as. Some of you have come to the recognition that all you ever do is suffer. There are two things to do in life: either suffer or don't suffer. When you are enlightened, you don't suffer, and when you are not, you suffer. The point is, that when you are obsessed with God, your suffering isn't suffering. Until you are a perfect devotee, you will still have that sense of separateness from me, nevertheless you are happy anyway, because it is so good to be with me. It is deeply satisfying to be in the Presence of the living guru.

Love of God is the texture of your life here with me. It will never be forced, but always arise of its own accord. Don't go testing yourself to see if you have a consuming love for God. The Lord doesn't test you, only the mind tests you. The Lord purges you, cleanses you, completely rips off who you think you are. The Lord is an inferno of joy. The one who truly loves God leaps into the fire of God's joy without caution, without fear.

My words can only hint at the truth. There are millions of words that have been written about this, and they still haven't scratched the surface, for there is no limit to the possible expressions of the Divine Presence. Read about God; if you are obsessed, you will never tire of your reading. As a matter of fact, if you were thinking about God all the time, you wouldn't have enough hours in the day. You would be devouring everything that was put into words about God that you could find. You would be carrying books around with you all the time. Whether it be the Bible, the Bhagavad Gita, or the Koran, you would always be reading about God.

The proper literature about those who have been Alive in God can inspire a devotional response. Once that response starts to become recognizable for what it is, and not as a chance to get high, you won't need the book. You will just allow yourself to be spontaneous and the love of God will arise naturally. Then reading is a real pleasure. Years ago, the spiritual books I was reading seemed very dry. I would pick them up, read a chapter or two, and they were really dull. Now I pick up the same books and they are really exciting. They say the same thing over and over, and they are very exciting.

Before I woke up I would constantly think about God. That was all I would do, just think about God without ceasing. I was obsessed to the point of being desperate enough to offer my physical life to God. I was literally ready to die. And that was the point where I was enslaved by the Divine and Lee lost his will.

That is the culmination of obsession, when one offers one's very life to God. For me to get to that point, obsession had to become all-consuming. I couldn't read enough, I couldn't meditate enough, I couldn't go to enough teachers. The advantage that you have over that is that I am here. You just don't realize what that means. I am around all week. Can you imagine that? That is unbelievable, that is Grace! I am here with you. You should be so obsessed with God that all you want to do is be with me.

If you are not obsessed, what do you expect? Experience? Whatever experience you have ever had or ever will have is nothing, absolutely nothing, when compared to simple devotion. Being in my company should mean for you that all you want is God, more than anything. That is going to make you willingly ask me to make more demands. When you truly love God, you are going to come to me and ask what you can do for me. When the love of God hasn't arisen for you, you'll be wondering what I am going to demand next. It is quite obvious that you don't love God if you are wondering what I am going to demand of you. And if you have been wondering, you aren't doing anything wrong....you just haven't gotten it yet.

Let God permeate your activity on all levels. When you sing devotional songs, express real joyousness in the Divine, not because it's a nice song or because you enjoy singing, but because you are singing to God. When you are singing a song to Allah, for instance, recognize that you are really singing to Allah. Then your song will be an expression of unfeigned devotion.

Of course, you can lay a lot of beautiful strategies on this. You can get spaced out all the time and pretend that you are obsessed with God. You won't be. You will be obsessed with mind, which can easily be mistaken for God by one who has never experienced devotion. That is one reason I am here. If your obsession for God is not genuine, it will get undermined very quickly with me around.

If you are not willing to be obsessed, leave me alone. Don't waste your time with me, for I won't buy into your act. When one is not totally obsessed for God, life is always an act. The average adult remains in a life that is stale, boring, and oppressive, rather than turning to God. It is just too easy. The life of God, the constant humor of the Divine, is so pure, so clear, so utterly simple, that very rarely does anyone realize it. It is my job to awaken you into that perfectly fulfilled Divine life. You must really want God for that to occur.

Most of you wish that you had the strength to put your life on the line and give it all to the guru. Really wanting God is actually putting your life on the line and giving it up, not wishing that you could. All of you need to want God, and there is a big difference between wanting God and needing to want God. If you don't really want God, this stuff can get very dull. It is not interesting at all. You are always busy asking questions: Why this? Why that? There is a painful effort to understand. When you are devoted, you understand. Devotion is inseparable from true understanding.

All of your distractions, all of your spiritual strategy, keeps you rooted in yourself. I am here to undermine all of that, for there is no self. There isn't even any "the Self" or "God". God is not limited by any person calling God "the Self" or "God". When one lives as God only, the "God" that one conceived of does not enter into it.

When you are a devotee, what is going on at all times is only God. You appear to be very wild and paradoxical, and if people can't see through that, that's their problem. You are happy. You know that there is only God, and whatever goes on is the form of your activity, the play of the Divine. If you went around all the time with a perfectly straight demeanor, never smiling or crying, it would get awfully dull. So there is a constant interplay of emotion and activity within God. When the guru gets you to realize that there is only God, it is a dynamic process. Whatever the devotee does, he or she recognizes full well that it is all God, so all activity is spontaneous, and vibrant. When you are enjoying the same condition I enjoy, you are able to go into the world and delight in it. You can have a good time now; don't confuse that with my enjoyment. So you will be able to fully enjoy the world, yet you won't really want to go back; you just won't have the desire, since you will be perfectly satisfied in my company.

It is only after obsession for God becomes consuming that one lives the functional life of God in the world. Before that, there is only more awareness, perhaps a deepening of insight, but no Divine life. Just more things on a more intense level; seeing yourself better, but no real change.

Some of you came to me in desperation, asking, "How do I turn to you?" You don't want God, you need to want God. Wanting

God does not need to know "how to" do anything. There is just that consuming passion. It is a matter of absolute commitment to the Lord, of being prepared to spend your life with me no matter what happens. You have no dramas left to play out anywhere else; everything is here.

There is an interesting dilemma that arises in wanting God. I haven't learned to tri-locate yet, which means that there's only one of me. That is nice for me, but for some of you it can be really hard, because there is only so much time you can spend with me. You will get to a point where you will want to be with me all the time. I mean that literally. Of course, that is not practical, yet you do need to feel that way. You have to want to be always with me; before you become a perfect devotee you have to want that so strongly that you would do anything to be in my company. The fact is that I am with you all the time, and the only way to realize that is to first want to be with me physically all the time, so that I can undermine that. It is a necessary process in sadhana. You can intellectually understand that I am with you always; you can even have an insight into that. But it doesn't help just to **think** that I am always with you. When you are distracted, you are distracted. That is just the way it is. So you will naturally go through wanting to physically be with me until you truly know me as absolute Presence.

People used to come to see if they could upstage me, to see if they could make me push them. The only people I am going to push are the people who love me. Period. If you are dueling (dual-ing) with me, why should I push you? The ones that I'm going to push are the ones who want to be devotees. The only ones that I'm going to bring to a place where they know this joy are the ones who want God, not the ones who need to want God. Recognize in your own case how deeply you want God. How much joy do you find in talking about God? In reading about God? Do you really look forward to a half hour of free time so that you can read spiritual books? Or do you look forward to lying on the couch and daydreaming?

All the day-to-day distractions are incidental to your obsession. Jesus loved God and he was never distracted by anything. He lived an ordinary life, eating, sleeping, interacting with His disciples. He lived in the world; he was flesh and blood. And even though he lived in the world, he never allowed the world to distract him. He was always perfectly turned to God. After his death, the disciples were distracted by the fact that the master was gone: "What are we going to do without the master?" The fact of his being resurrected and coming back to his disciples was to say, "Look, there is only God. So how come there is no God anymore as soon as I'm gone? You're distracted. Just turn to the Lord." He didn't come back in order to show them that it was possible to attain personal immortality. It was always God.

There is no getting to God. There is no God that one could "get to". Everything that exists, exists solely as God. If God were anything else than simply what is, God would be limited. One cannot turn to limitation, one can only truly turn to God. You can not have God without life, for there is not a hair's breadth of difference between them. Obsession is not escaping life, living on a mountain or meditating in a cave somewhere; obsession is obsession for life. You must be alive right here.

I sit here as an offering, simply present. I can't do anything. I can't give you God. If anyone could give you God, you'd be Alive right now, not merely living. How can I give what is already given? I am God, and if you want that, let obsession be your daily life. It is the small percentage of people who are willing to be obsessed with God that will wake up and be Alive. The ones who ignore it will go from teacher to teacher and nothing will happen.

You are acutely aware on another plane that you are suffering. That plane is a twenty-four hour a day nightmare. That's no fun. That's serious, that's gloomy and grave. The fact that you are not in touch with it just means that you are not conscious, that you are distracted, dreaming. Unless you become a perfect devotee, you are always going to be that way. You are going to continue suffering unless you know me, unless you realize that I am truly here, and that it's not a dream.

You are quite fortunate to have this chance, quite fortunate to be with one who is awake as the unqualified Divine. Many people go guru-hopping and they never make it. Their search is just more separation, keeping them rooted in unhappiness, in depression, in sickness, in the life of man or woman, never in the life of God. Open your eyes, and see who you are sitting with.

I only offer this life of God, without beginning, without end. There is nothing else. Run, leave, argue, fight; it doesn't matter. There is no place to go. The chance comes, at the most, once in a lifetime. The chance is here now. If you are willing to be obsessed with God, if you are willing to live absolutely, without ever experiencing a break in the process of Divine humor which is your existence, I am here. Think only of me, live only for God, and you will wake up. It is that simple. Once you get locked into God, you are hooked. Nothing else holds interest for you. That is a very narrow viewpoint by the world's standards. You will be looked at as being very narrow minded and prejudicial. And it's true. I want people who are extremely narrow minded. I want people who are crashing bores. I want people who only want God.

TWENTY-FIVE

The Alarm Clock Fable

THE PROCESS OF your search is the effort to become realized. That is very funny, because you already are realized. Everybody is. What the great teachers have spent their lives doing is convincing people who are realized that they are realized. Yet regardless of who is doing the convincing, people always seem to feel that things aren't quite the way they are. So they go about trying to make things different than the way they are. It's a comical business.

The difference within the condition of realization is that some people are asleep and some are awake. That's all. There is no absolute difference within realization; you will never become anything other than what you are. You can awaken as what you are already, and that is the process of our relationship.

There are some parallels to this awakening process in the everyday affair of waking up after a night's sleep. There are many ways that people wake up. Some people wake up as soon as the sun rises. The window is open and they're sleeping; maybe they are having a pleasant dream and they're smiling, or maybe they are having a nightmare and they're twitching around a little. The sun rises, a shaft of warm light comes through the window and crosses their face, hitting the retina of the eye, and they move a bit. They start to come back to outer consciousness, but for a little while they just lie there, feeling the heat of the sun on their face. Their eyes are closed, and they know that it's daytime, that it must be sunny and bright out. After a few minutes of enjoying the warmth they open their eyes and wake up.

Some people, on the other hand, don't wake up when the sun rises. They just sleep. The sun comes up at five-thirty or six o'clock in the morning, but they could sleep on and on. People like that usually either have an alarm clock or somebody else that wakes them up. They will set the alarm for a certain time, and the way most people are, wake up an instant before it rings. They wonder what time it is, and suddenly the alarm goes off. Or, if someone is shaking them, they are aware of being shaken, but it takes a few minutes before they open their eyes.

Then there are those people for whom even that doesn't work. They need two alarm clocks and an electric blanket with a short circuit that is hooked up so that they get a jolt and jump out of bed. Some people are almost impossible to awaken. They have to be yelled at and have a bucket of cold water thrown in their face before they finally wake up.

Once people get out of bed, there are also several different tendencies. Some people wake up, get out of bed, and are immediately ready to go. They run into the bathroom, splash water on their face, and get dressed, or they chase their husband or wife around the room first and then get dressed. No problem. Then there are the people who think, "Oh, it's Monday. Oh God, I've got to go to work again." They know that they have to get up to earn a living, but they sure don't want to. They crawl out of bed, get dressed, and drag themselves to the bathroom to brush their teeth. When they get to work, they start drinking coffee or smoking cigarettes or whatever gets them going. Two or three hours later, around lunch time, they finally start to get into it. Of course, they always use the excuse, "Well, that's my rhythm," which is analogous to the excuse, "Well, that's my karma."

The guru comes into the world as the one who awakens. Everybody is realized, everybody is the Buddha. The Buddha told everyone that he met, "Yes, you're going to be realized someday." He could say that because he knew that they were realized already. It was a safe bet. So the fact is that you are realized, and the process of the guru in the world is simply to wake you up from being asleep. Whether you are awake or asleep, you are still realized, still illumined. It happens to be the tendency of the guru to bring you to the point of awakening. Everybody has tendencies. Individuals have the tendency to wake up at the crack of dawn and buzz around all day, or the tendency to sleep eighteen hours, if left alone. The guru takes the position of utilizing whatever is necessary to interact with the specific tendency of a person so as to serve the process of awakening.

Everybody's tendencies will draw him to a particular teacher and form of activity. That is where misunderstanding comes in as far as the guru's position in the world is concerned. People think that the guru should fit exclusively into the context of their specific tendency. Despite people's expectations, the guru is not only the sunshine, he is also the alarm clock and the cold bucket of water. Whatever is needed to wake you up, the guru is.

It is nice if your tendency is to wake up when the sun rises. It is very natural and appropriate. Simply being in the guru's company will be enough for you. And it is not so bad if your tendency is to need an alarm clock. Then the guru doesn't have to do much. He might just lay out some basic teaching and tell you that it's all a paradox anyway, and it is all very clear to you. You start to understand the nature of paradox and you recognize that as the teaching, so you don't hang on to it. You turn your attention to the guru, then you wonder what time it is, and suddenly the alarm goes off.

There are a lot of beautiful intricacies to all of this. There can be the tendency, if you happen to be a light sleeper, to wake up at the wrong time. Once in awhile you're at a late party, so you go to sleep at four in the morning instead of the usual eleven at night. You're in a really deep sleep. At seven o'clock the alarm goes off and you jump out of bed before you know what's going on. You have to pry your eyes open and you've got head-spins. That happens on rare occasions. The alarm clock got you up before you were ready. You were right in the middle of that perfect dream and the ringing zapped you awake. You never did get to finish your business with Sadie Mae.

In the case of the heavy sleepers, typically one of three things happens. When they are shaken they yell, "Get out of here!" and chase the person out of the room. Then they go back to bed and that's that. Or they get up and their eyes are open, so the person who shook them thinks that they're awake. But they're not, they're just good actors. They eat breakfast and go to work, the machine is in order, but they're asleep on their feet. They go into the bathroom at work, crash out for a few hours and that's it. Their whole life is spent sleeping, but the people around them think that they're awake because they're such splendid performers. They just put the machine on automatic pilot: eat, sleep, eat, sleep, take a shit once in awhile. It's a nice arrangement. Finally, there are the heavy sleepers who get up under what they feel is abusive pressure. The person that is waking them up is just doing what's appropriate, saying "Look, you've got a job to do, you've got to get to work." But the person who is being awakened always thinks that he is being abused: "Oh, why don't they leave me alone? I just want to go to sleep."

The first type is the person who has no interest in spiritual life. The second is the "accomplished" spiritual seeker, and the third type is the one that has the problems with the guru. The ones that say, "Get the hell out of here", chase the guru away and stay asleep, don't have any problems. That's okay. The third type have all these incredibly complicated problems. They are always in pain, and they're going through all this stuff. They come to the guru with these gut-wrenching problems and they're always ventilating and always miserable. They think that there is a lot of abusive pressure going on. The guru is just doing what's appropriate, but they don't see that.

The main emphasis of this guru is to act as whatever agent is needed to awaken those who are asleep. If the guru needs to be sunshine, that's what the guru is. And if the guru needs to be the electric shock or the bucket of ice cold water, that's what the guru is too. He is all of these things at the same time, which means that as you wake up to the sunshine, you are also aware of the alarm clock going off. That can be a little grating sometimes. You want to bask lazily in the sun for a little while, not listen to the noisy alarm clock which distracts you. In any case, this guru acts as all possible appropriate agents of awakening, unlike the awakened ones of the past, who were limited to one form or another.

The greatest teachers historically, Krishna, Buddha, and Jesus, all had limitations in their dharmas because of the nature of society at that time in history. As spiritual masters, they were not limited in their relationship with their devotees. It was their dharmas, their teachings and presentations that were limited, basically because of the cultural traditions and general attitudes prevalent during their lives. When Jesus was around, there weren't all these book distributors and book wholesalers. If you wanted to study, your whole life had to be devoted to learning, because it took a long time to get from one country to another, and there were thieves and bandits along the way. To become well-versed in traditional spiritual teaching took a tremendous amount of up-front commitment. Before he woke up and started teaching, Jesus spent many years learning, immersing himself in the teachings of Judaism and the Essenes. What he had learned was limited by what education was at the time. The same thing applied in the cases of Krishna and Buddha. Their sadhana caused the resurrection of their mind to be limited by the form of their sadhana. So each of them had dramatic limitations as far as their teachings were concerned. They were inefficient alarm clocks.

Today, there is a somewhat different situation. Because of the incredible ease of searching out and assimilating education, one can, with maybe five or six years of good, in-depth study, amass a tremendous amount of information about all of the traditional spiritual teaching that has existed in written history. It is relatively simple for someone today to educate him or herself as to the possibilities that exist in spiritual life. That makes it easier not to become rigidified into the form of a particular tradition.

Many people are learning how to use their dreams creatively to make decisions or to see things about themselves. One that is asleep in this form of reality can use his sleeping time creatively and productively too. One can study traditional spiritual life, which is why I am always telling you to read the literature of the traditions, to read about Buddha, to read about Sri Ramakrishna, to study their lives as individuals. Their dharmas are nice, that is another form of education, but studying the masters themselves is the best education.

You can actively use the time of sleep in order to learn, getting the right answer that you need from a dream. That is what you are doing here. Since this is all a dream, it is clear that you have all gotten the right answer while dreaming, because you are with me. Once you get the answer, you still have to implement it, just as when you use a dream to tell you whether you should take one job or another, you still have to go out and take the job when you get the answer. You all have the right answer; now you have to implement it and make it functional in your life.

Devotion to God is the implementation of the right answer that you got in the dream. There are occasional flashes of insight, when you truly enjoy your Divine nature. Even during those flashes, you know that you still haven't implemented the right answer. Right then is the time to implement it, because when you are wrapped up in the dull affair of your unconsciousness and not enjoying and appreciating the Divine, you can't implement it. You have to be in the midst of that enjoyment to implement it, and those moments don't last very long. You are typically too busy, or you are too comfortable just enjoying the guru's Presence, so you don't bother to intelligently implement what you know to be the answer. You have to participate fully in this process. I am not interested in you being happy when you're with me and suffering the rest of the time. I am interested in you waking up, and I can and will do whatever is necessary to bring you to that point, for there is no limitation here.

All of the previous dharmas have been limited by their particular form. This dharma is not limited by any form and is also not limited by the need to include all of the forms. Not only is there a recognition of the limitations of the previous teachings, there is also no need to complete or fulfill those teachings. My dharma is just life. Period.

It is interesting how the traditions appeal to different tendencies that exist in people. There are three major tendencies in the human being. They are analogous to the chakras, the seven centers in the psychic system of the human being. And each tendency is the major concern of one of three previous teachings.

The first, second and third chakras can be correlated to one major tendency. Those first three centers involve: emotion, basic survival-level emotion, with fear at its core; sexuality, which involves a tremendous attachment to sensation, particularly the pleasurable type; and the drive for power and mastery. All three are characterized by desire. Buddhism deals, in the main, with this major tendency. Its alarm clock is the elimination of desire. The basic direction is to lose the attachment to the pleasure derived from winning. If you have a lot of power, and you pull one over on somebody, that is very pleasurable. You really get a high from that. Sex is a tremendous high, of course, and even fear can get to a point where it's exhilirating. People can go on the roller coaster and be scared shitless, but they keep going on the roller coaster, because fear is a great high. So the lower three centers involve desire for such highs, and that is what Buddhism concerns itself with.

The fourth chakra can be correlated to the next major tendency, which involves the psychic self and its expression in terms of love and union. This was Jesus's tendency. His dharma was the dharma of love. He was just sunshine, very warm and natural and peaceful, and if you didn't wake up from the sunshine, there was no alarm clock and there was especially no bucket of cold water. His teaching was union. Many people have had the experience of being one with other people, of a connection where there is no difference, and that is a very blissful, non-judgemental place to be in. What is there to be judged? There isn't any other, there is only the one. The Sufi alarm clock is very much involved with this. Of course, the rhetoric of these traditions of union talks about everything else, yet the power and implication of the dharma is concerned with this major tendency. It is the way of unconditional love.

The last three chakras in the body are the throat, the third eye, and the sahasrara or crown chakra. These centers can be correlated to the third major tendency, which is the mind, the mental process. Krishna's alarm clock is concerned with the merging of the mind with Brahman, or God. The mind is supposed to undo itself by realizing its identity with Brahman. A diluted form of this dharma involves the chanting of the mantra, Hare Krishna, Hare Krishna, Hare Rama, Hare Rama. The mind can be so dulled out or spaced out that it doesn't appear to be present, yet that's just the mind's sophisticated way of making one believe that it is gone. The mind is going to survive, even if it has to upgrade the act to the point of getting you to be blissed out all the time. That's nice, but not Alive or functional.

If your tendency is mental, you rarely get into really doing fear, sex or power. The expression of the first three centers is almost always sublimated by analysis. So while you are doing sex, you're busy thinking, "Am I satisfying my partner? Has this been long enough? Am I going to make a mistake?" or, "It's not working." You are going through all that stuff if you function from the mental tendency while involved in the lower three centers. There is still a process of analysis going on. While you are afraid, you are busily analyzing your fear. You go into your house and it's pitch dark, and you have to run for the light switch. Yet you are still thinking, "Nobody's in here, of course." You are rationalizing why you shouldn't be afraid instead of being fully afraid. You don't really get into it.

People who are founded in the first tendency are wrapped up in the life of the body, involved in all the energy and desire. They are active and impulsive. People who are rooted in the second tendency are just gone all the time; their head is in the clouds, and their eyes are always wide and sparkling. Nothing ever phases them. And usually their lives are a wreck, because they don't do anything about anything. All this stuff comes up in their lives, but they don't do anything about it. They go through life as if everything was groovy and far out. Lastly, the people who are rooted in the third tendency can't get involved in the activity of desire or in the love aspect. They tend to be distant, locked into the mind.

The guru needs to be the reflection of any tendency. The guru needs to be able to deal with desire when that is called for, and if something arises, jump in, run with it, and deal with the consequences later, if that is the appropriate response. The guru needs to be very stand-offish and analytical at times: "Yes, yes, of course, I understand." And if it is called for, the guru needs to be very spacey and loving. Sometimes that is necessary.

The guru will use whatever tendency needs to be used in order to bring the devotee to the point of awakening. This dharma is not concerned with any particular tendency or with the inclusiveness of all tendencies. Whatever is appropriate will arise, whatever is here is here. **It is just life**; it doesn't have to include, complete, or fulfill any previous dharmas.

The rhetoric of this teaching appears the same as the others. Everybody has read the books. Any teacher who's got the rap down will know the right answers. The difference is in the absolute and unqualified nature of this one. The form that I take stands outside of and at the same time can be inside of all of the dharmas that have been advanced, practiced, and are being used in the world today. It is not dependent on them and it may include any of them. Our relationship is the core of the teaching; all of the expedients of instruction lead back to it.

To get you to wake up, what I have done and will continue to do is give you the right answer while you are sleeping. I will continue to be here as a condition, not as individual, not "Lee Lozowick". I do not function as someone you can go to and say, "How do I do this?" That's not the way it works. I am simply present. The Presence allows you to implement and integrate the right answer when you have a flash of true insight and enjoyment of your Divine condition. And you will come to a point where you will just wake up. Answers and questions will be forgotten then.

Each of you roughly falls into one of the three tendencies. You have threads into all three, yet one of the three tendencies is predominant. What you need to recognize in regard to that tendency is how it controls the other levels of your being, then you can begin to integrate functionality at all levels. So, in the case of the third tendency, when you are doing sex, you will really be doing sex instead of analyzing your performance. Or if you are doing a power trip, you will get into the power trip instead of guilt. The process is the recognition of your tendencies, not the changing of them. You can try forever and you will never change them. You were born with those tendencies and that's it. So if your tendency is the second chakra, you're a lucky bastard, and the rest of you, tough shit. Through recognition, however, you can keep your tendency from tainting your experience at other levels.

Realization is already present. It's not as if this dharma, this form of activity, is going to get you to be realized. It is simply a matter of awakening as this already present realized condition. You are illuminated, you are all Buddha. That is already done, already "accomplished". You are here and you can't do anything about it.

You are Alive, and even if you kill yourself, there is no difference, you are still Alive. Realization is a foregone conclusion. If you think that it is not a foregone conslusion, God doesn't care.

The whole process of the guru in the world is simply one of awakening. Don't be distracted by the alarm clock. It is our relationship that is important. I am the real dharma, the alarm clock is just an expedient. As you live with me, you will increasingly experience those flashes of clarity and enjoyment. Some of you had times when you basked in my sunlight, but you didn't integrate anything, you just enjoyed it without waking up. You enjoyed the particular state. As long as you just enjoy the particular state without the integration of functionality, you remain asleep. When you consciously and responsibly integrate the enjoyment of the Divine condition into functional life, into the life of body, mind, and spirit, you don't stay asleep. You awaken fully to the daylight.

Doing your sadhana when you are wrapped up in your suffering is just appropriate activity. Doing your sadhana when those moments of insight and clarity come is the real test. That is what you need to recognize me as your true nature, and not to get carried away with the bliss, getting spaced out and leaving it alone, thinking that you did your sadhana well before that time and that's why you got rewarded. Know me in Truth.

This one, being totally versatile, can play any form or agent that is needed to bring forth awakening. I stand outside of any formal or practical approach to realization. There isn't any. There is my unlimited relationship with you. That is perfectly present. This agent of awakening is absolutely without limitation; I am the one who offers such a relationship in the world. Because of the proliferation of therapies, ideologies and methodologies, all of which are corrective in nature, the rhetoric that I use can be found elsewhere, but the process that I manifest in relationship with my devotees has no limitation, by implication or practice, in any form of life in my company.

Everything is here. There is nothing that exists that is not here. Every teacher has some degree of understanding of the processes of the world. Some teachers are very knowledgable in energy forms, in shakti; others in mysticism or in astral planes and other stages of manifestation. In the case of this one, all possible alternatives are literally present now as real and living potential for anyone in my community, anyone in my company. It would be a mistake to place even the most subtle qualification on this Presence. I am not the means. I am the beginning and the end, absolutely inclusive of all life, all manifestation. Know who I am and you know yourself, for **I am the Lord.**

****

In the summer of 1976, the community of Hohm gathered in a secluded place in the country to celebrate the advent of the guru in the world. For two days we romped, laughed, played games, and were confronted by the Presence of Grace. We had a lot of expectations riding on this event, and Lee consistently undermined every one of them.

In the first place, we all expected a great "spiritual" happening, perhaps with a few miracles thrown in for good measure. Instead, spiritual life was rarely mentioned, and the conversation dwelt on seemingly trivial subjects. We had to deal with the duality we assumed between "spiritual" and "mundane" life, and the recognition dawned in some of us that no matter what was going on, we were shown what we were up to.

Many of us were very attached to our identity as vegetarians and proponents of healthy eating. That had become our act. So Lee had us eat nothing but sausages, hamburgers and sweets the whole weekend. Those of us who could appreciate the Divine play really got into that aspect, while some of us made a show of how reluctant we were to hurt our bodies. The lifting of that restriction clearly showed us how we confused the form of appropriate activity with real spiritual life, and hardened that confusion into a self-identity.

The restriction on wine was also lifted, and as we got a little tipsy, our conventional selves came to the fore. Soon we were babbling away like schoolkids, all talking at the same time and not listening to anyone else. Lee presented to us the fact that our time-worn ways of life were always active under the surface, and that it didn't take much to bring it out. He wasn't saying that it was wrong, but simply demanding that we recognize it, and in so doing recognize that it held no promise for us.

On the first night of that weekend, we put on skits lampooning ourselves and other current communities and teachers. But the whole day had really been a great joke on ourselves, as we clearly perceived how we got wrapped up in conventional enjoyment and ignored Divine enjoyment. And as we observed that, we could do nothing about it. Recognizing that there was nothing we could do, the fact that Lee's Presence was all-pervasive was brought forcefully home to us in humorous helplessness. As we gathered in celebration, a thankfulness for that Presence was in the air.

TWENTY-SIX

THERE IS AN overwhelming feeling tonight of togetherness and devotion. Regardless of whether or not you truly know what we are celebrating, it has to be something very personal for you to celebrate. Each of you undoubtedly has something, a feeling, an experience, some moment we spent together that stands out, something that moved you. Each of you has something intimately meaningful to you, and when things get a little rough, you remember it, even when you are not consciously thinking of it. You are remembering the moment that made your relationship with me very personal.

This kind of atmosphere is exactly where the average spiritual leader loses it. This is the kind of moment when the ability to retain my humor in the Divine allows me to continue to be present for you. It is very easy to lose one's humor in the emotion of the moment. In the warmth and peace of tonight's gathering, I was feeling like a savior. Everybody is so sincere and loving. The problem that arises from the average spiritual leader's perspective (and fortunately I am not in that category, or you would have already been lost, in a manner of speaking), is that in a situation like this, he or she starts to think, "Wouldn't it be nice if everybody felt this way? Wouldn't it be nice if we could give this to the world?" And that is where most of them lose it. Their sense of humor evaporates.

What happens at times is that the "guru" is very into it when he starts. Then he begins to soften up, begins to compromise real spiritual life. From our inception, there has not been one iota of consolation involved. The message of Hohm is: "This is God. Do you want to give up your life, or do you want to fart around?" It is absolute, and anyone who has had that real moment of complete understanding sees the world for what it truly is: lila, the humorous play of God. But in most cases the awakening is not complete, and the guru who has had a partial awakening and has really tasted the Divine has got something to communicate and some experience to back up the rhetoric. Soon he becomes surrounded by students, and the group gets into a really nice space, very warm and comfortable and open. They are feeling devotional, and the guru is sitting up in front of the room thinking,"This is the way it should be. Everybody should be like this, happy and loving their neighbor." At that point, the spiritual teacher or "master" usually loses his sense of humor, and the ball game is lost. The direction becomes to save the world, to get out there and make everything right.

I am very tempted. But it won't happen, so you don't have to worry. At times like this, when I see people putting their whole heart into it, I want to say, "Let's just live together and have a party. Let's forget all of this heavy stuff of confrontation and breaking structure and just stay together. We won't have any problems." Of course I know that's not right, and it's not going to happen. To reciprocate your love with comfort would be playing right into your strategy. There is a tendency in you when we get together like this, to rest in a feeling of consolation, and if I were to indulge that tendency, you would remain where you are coming from now, and the work would never go deeper.

The great masters never consoled their disciples. Jesus knew that he was going to die, and he asked his disciples to stay with him in the garden of Gesthemane for his last night with them. He told them to stay awake while he went to pray, but when he came back they were asleep. And instead of leaving them with a nice memory and saying, "It's okay, you're only human. It happens once in awhile," he said, "You fell asleep? Couldn't my closest disciples stay up for one hour?" He always criticized them. He said to Peter, "You will deny me." Peter said, "No, no, I won't!" Jesus said, "Yes you will. When your life is on the line, you are not going to think of me." So even right at the end, when he knew that he would be leaving his disciples, he didn't give them any comfort. He didn't give them the last memory of a pat on the shoulder and a sympathetic goodbye.

The Tibetan Guru Marpa made his devotee, Milarepa, build him five houses. Milarepa would build one, and then Marpa would find something wrong with it and tell him to tear it down. After going through this five times, with each house more elaborate than the last one, Milarepa was near dead. Finally Marpa gave him a little food and initiated him in the dharma. He still didn't comfort him; he wouldn't say to Milarepa, "You really served me well, and that was very good." If Milarepa wanted something from Marpa, he had to get it. Period.

That can only be done with a sense of humor. The humor of the Divine must be evident, because people literally put their lives on the line. As soon as a guru gets serious about that, he or she gets sucked in. The guru says, "Okay, that's good," and gives the person a prize, validating the person's act. When a guru becomes serious, all the thankfulness and personal devotion that is exhibited is seen as important.

You need to be very clear about the fact that without a sense of humor, life has little meaning. Even devotion loses its meaning and passion without humor. Sometimes I will tell you to do things, and I will get annoyed when you are irresponsible about it. Even though I am annoyed, humor is present. It is your life, your reaction to my being annoyed, that is without humor. Life isn't a very serious affair that you must plod through with an air of gravity. It is meant to be, and is, a joyous affair.

I will never lose my humor. Nevertheless, if you don't allow me to fully express my humor with you, what you are liable to do is cut off your physical relationship with me and go somewhere else, or get the community into such a somber mood that I won't even want to be around you. It is your job to see to it that you don't become devoid of humor, that you don't get caught up in some tragic play instead of the Divine comedy. When I retain my sense of humor on a night like tonight, which is very moving, it will seem to some of you that I am just being mean. I know that recently I have done a few things involving some of you, and you grin and bear it, but you don't take it. That is as far as you go. It is not a matter of grinning and bearing it; it is not a matter of trudging through it all gloomily and methodically. It is a matter of each of you retaining the humor in our relationship. I have to keep my sense of humor or

I get sucked in. We would all have a very big problem if I became serious about saving the world. I never will, no matter how moved I might become.

Part of being serious is treating you the way anyone would treat you if you were as loving to him or her as you are to me. You are very loving. The average person, if you were like that to him or her, would respond in kind. That is where misunderstandings arise. If you were a perfect devotee, and you were perfectly turned, I would respond in kind and it would be perfect. If your devotion is sincere and honest and open and founded in the search, my responding in kind would be a reinforcement of the dilemma of separation, the basic dilemma of your life. Most gurus will return what is given in kind, and what is given, however sincere, is founded in the search, anything returned in kind reinforces the search itself. Instead of dissolving the dilemma, it is solidified; instead of taking bricks away from the foundation, it adds mortar to it and thereby makes sure that it doesn't fall apart. You don't bring me a gift out of love. You bring me a plea to absolve you of your constant suffering. You don't love God, you want relief. To have pity would be perpetuating that suffering; my only response is compassion, which is identical to humor. No true compassion is serious, so you who wish to be compassionate must learn to laugh.

A sense of humor keeps you from getting caught up in all the drama. When you are not identifying with the drama in your life, you can enjoy the play, whether it is a comedy, tragedy, or musical. Whatever it is, you can enjoy it. When you identify with the drama it becomes very real for you, and it reinforces separation. It is very much like crying at a movie, or screaming during a scary part; one is overwhelmed by the emotion of the scene, identifying with the hero. When that happens, the movie is really gut-wrenching, because you put yourself in that position. You have forgotten that you are in the audience. When you watch it without identifying with it, you just see it for what it is, a movie, and enjoy it fully.

You can either identify with the play or just observe it. There is a third alternative, which I am quite familiar with: you can identify with it and observe it at the same time. That is the key. That is the real and bountiful enjoyment of life, when you simultaneously observe it and identify with it. It is paradoxical, and it is also simpler than it may sound.

When you can identify with it and observe it at the same time, that is what is known as illumination. All of the great masters do this; that's why they weep profusely at times. Sometimes the sight of a mere blade of grass will set them weeping, because they will simultaneously identify with and observe it. They don't care if somebody sees them weeping. They might start weeping in the middle of a huge crowd and it wouldn't bother them. They are very unconcerned with the fact that someone is watching them weep; they are totally uninterested in the whole drama of what people think about them. Their joy, if only in that one blade of grass, is like a flood that sweeps such pettiness out of its path. All of the greatest spiritual masters have been emotional people. Shirdi Sai Baba was a very angry guy, always exploding and screaming at people. And at the same time, he was always being moved with deep, joyful emotion, weeping or blissing out when someone would chant God's name. The awakened ones have always had the capacity to feel deeply, but their feelings never ruled them. That is identification and observation.

There is the paradox of Lee being genuinely moved, and yet still being able to call you on your act when it is needed. That can be very painful. I know how painful it is for some of you, regardless of how big you try to be. And when you are really seeing it with humor, I know that as well. Doing sadhana in my company absolutely requires humor, because being in my company necessitates looking upon our relationship as a joyous affair. If I am going to spend time with you physically, which I look forward to with a great deal of enthusiasm, if I am going to party with you and enjoy your company, humor must be present. I am not going to spend a lot of time with you if you are moping around all the time and you don't laugh and you are always into the drama of your suffering. I simply won't be very interested if you are walking on eggshells when you are around me, and freaking out when you are not. I want to be with the ones who are happy. You should be fulfilling your sadhana humorously so that I can look forward to spending time with you.

The spirit of seriousness is intimately connected to a sense of self-importance. If we can see what insignificant, stupid little fools we are, if we can stop taking our lives so seriously (as if we were really important!), we can then begin real spiritual life. I know that I am really not important. I know that if I died tomorrow, it wouldn't matter. What is hilarious is how human beings have this incredibly exaggerated sense of their own importance. It doesn't matter. Nobody's life matters. When you realize your total unimportance, you can actually start to enjoy life. Before you realize that, you can't enjoy life at all, for you are concerned with what people are going to say, whether you are going to do the right thing. How much money are you going to have? Do you need security? What about insurance? Realize that you aren't important, and all of this takes on a very amusing quality.

Of course, there is a problem with other people. Your parents want you to be important, to do something with your life. They don't want you to throw your life down the drain and give everything to Lee. They want you to have what they always had: ulcers, migraine headaches. And it is very important for your friends to think that you are something, because they hang out with you and they want to be something. They really want you to be important, because if you aren't, then they aren't. There is nothing you can do about that. Self-importance will drag things down every time.

Devotion and surrender are certainly major aspects of your sadhana. They are simply impossible without humor. Without humor, even simple objective service, such as giving me things or doing work for me, is a very dry affair. So I can't impress on you enough how important the humor of recognizing what our life together involves, is to your sadhana. You can't be doing sadhana without that.

I also don't expect you to be always running around with a big, fat smile on your face no matter what goes on. That's not being humorous, that's being dumb. The process of making demands on you is for you to learn how to be humorous in any given situation. If you already knew how to be humorous in any situation, we wouldn't be involved in the guru-devotee relationship. We would just hang out together, go places, and dig people.

Devotee: In the simultaneous identification and observation that you mentioned, which aspect is that of humor?

Lee: Some of you have had the experience of being in the midst of a very heavy situation, and all of a sudden something happens and it stops. Nothing has changed objectively, but the heaviness is gone. You may have even laughed to yourself.

The moment of real observation dissolves the association with suffering. Yet without the simultaneous aspect of identification, the warmth of humor is not present. Both make up the expression of that humor, so it is not one or the other. It is not exclusive identification or exclusive observation. It is just what it is. When you see that what is, is what is, that is humor. Humor is not necessarily, "Hah! Hah! Hah!" Quite frequently, you happen to laugh. But humor doesn't have to be laughing at things. It is seeing that what is, is what is. The dilemma of your self-importance dissolves.

When you see that you are who you are, then there will be the dissolution of the basic dilemma, the dilemma's dilemma. When you know that who you are is who you are, your universe dissolves. And then....you simply are.

* * * *

The central activity of that weekend did not resemble anything remotely "spiritual". It was a basketball game we played in the swimming pool, with baskets at each end of the pool. Most of us got into the game without seeing any connection to Grace. After all, we were just having fun. Lee was always taking part, and we tended to assume that his relationship to the game was as conventional as ours. It was the most unlikely vehicle of Grace one could imagine.

As the weekend progressed, the games took on a very strange quality. We were fiercely going after the ball, getting in physical tussles that bordered on being vicious at times. Lee sometimes got in the fray, but never in the more violent ones, which he observed with amusement. It got more and more violent, to the point where we were out of control. No longer was the purpose to make a goal, it was to get the person who had the ball. Soon the game was nothing but a great fighting match, in which all of us who were playing participated with total unconsciousness of what was going on. Those of us who weren't playing, who had to deal with our feelings of being left out, were amazed at the level of conflict going on. Yet most of us thought nothing of it! We were surprised to find, on the last night of the weekend, that the game was not just a game, but a powerful demonstration by Grace of a very important aspect of our lives. Lee informed us that the game was death.

TWENTY-SEVEN

All one does for his or her entire life is work, strive, live to prevent death, physically, emotionally and psychically. Here is the motivation for human activity. I find it very interesting that life is founded on preventing death, when in fact, death is a part of life. Death is not something unto itself. It is simply a part of the life process. We have a bleak winter, full of frost and sleet, then spring comes, and everything is green again. Has the earth died? Look at nature and you will see that is simply a matter of cycles.

Tell me, why should you be any different? Why should people be any different than nature? No reason at all. Just because you have a self-conscious intellect doesn't mean that you should be any different.

Death is very simple and very natural. It is a universal law. What is, cycles, just like recycled paper. The moon cycles, the earth cycles, the stars cycle. Stars are successively blue, red, yellow, and white, and finally they burn out. After that there is another star. Everything is a cyclical process, and you cycle too, just like everything else.

It is very unique on earth (and I say on earth because this happens at other places in the universe), that our life, as human beings, is founded on preventing death. No other creature on the planet exhibits this peculiar trait, this denial of death. In fact, the "death" which is being prevented and denied, doesn't exist. Recycling exists. To see life and death as opposites, each an absolute event, is to ignore the cyclical process. You can't appreciate the beauty of life that way, but only see it as a grim battle. If you are really into ecology, and you get a letter from a company that uses recycled paper, you appreciate it. That's why a yogi might say to you, "Ah, you are an old soul." You've been recycled a lot of times, and he appreciates it.

It is interesting to watch what you do to sustain life. The only motivation that you have is to prevent death, you can't insure survival. There is nothing you can do about surviving because you are going to survive whether you like it or not.

It is completely turned around. You are totally misinformed about the process of life. You are ignorant of life, physically, emotionally, psychologically, and spiritually. It is always a matter of: how are you going to escape death? And the answer you come up with is: win. Be the team that wins. The team that wins stays alive. The team that loses dies. All competition is an expression of that. It is to prevent, with all your might, the inevitable cycle of life known as death.

One of the great paradoxes of our life together is that I keep telling you, "Surrender, surrender." You have to surrender to be open, so that Grace can be your mover. I need an open door to stick my foot in. If you close the door too fast, I can't get my foot in. Yet the more you surrender, the harder it gets, instead of easier as one might expect. The more one actually surrenders, the more resistance becomes evident in one's life, and the more obstacles arise. It is very common. There are people who have mentioned this to me, saying, "I really thought I had it. I sat with you for awhile, and I was really open and really into it. Then my whole world exploded and fell apart." So the more you surrender, the more resistance you have. Logically it seems that surrender should give you a clear space where you are open to me and your life gets better or happier, or that you would become more peaceful, more understanding, and so on.

Why, then, does resistance increase with surrender? Well, what does the guru promise you? Death. The guru can throw that word around because he knows death as simply a part of life. If you see death as the end of you, you are going to resist that like hell. You surrender because the guru promises God. Meanwhile your subconscious is saying, "The more I surrender, the closer to death I become." Then more resistance springs up, because you interpret death as the death of **you**, rather than an aspect of life. So the resistance, anxiety, tension, and fear that arises in our relationship is the result of your attempt to deny what you think death is: the absolute end of you. Interestingly enough, it is who you **think** you are that dies.

When you can really see what you are up to, it doesn't take on the aspect of moral or immoral, right or wrong. It simply shows you the pattern of your life, what needs to be dissolved. This pattern is a maze through which you endlessly run from death. Spiritual life is not a matter of changing the maze, of creating a more comfortable labyrinth, but of realizing that there is no maze to begin with, that its nature is delusory. When you really see that, all your clutching and grasping ceases; you no longer hold on to anything the way you did when you sought to evade the "end". Certainly you all have people that you prefer to spend time with: your mate, your lover, your friends, your children. That is fine. There will always be certain people who you would rather be with. But what happens if they get run over by a truck tomorrow? Anything can happen. The cycles of life can not be resisted. There is no permanence in this relationship. I hope you will be here for a long time, it would be nice. I enjoy all of you and look forward to spending more time with you, but nothing is permanent. When you hold on, when you are clinging, life remains as the avoidance and denial of death, rather than just life.

Devotee: There is a lot of consoling philosophy that says there is an afterlife of some kind. Many people, on the other hand, believe that death is absolute extinction. What do you say about these views?

Lee: Death is extinction. Birth is extinction of what came before birth. There is this whole cyclical process of creation, birth, growth, disintegration, and death, and every one of these stages is extinction. What is involved in God-life is renewed or re-created recognition of truth at every moment. It has nothing to do with some individual soul that is sustained and remains aware of its individuality throughout all of these different processes. That is the consolation and that is not true. What is true is that at death I will be extinct. At the point of creation I will reawaken, and the previous stage will be extinct. And so on, through birth, growth, disintegration;

and death again. Once one is awake, one is always awake, and yet there is no individual to be awake. Lee Lozowick as a vehicle will not be around after death to help seekers on the path or guide people in their dreams. There will be a totally different form and I will be awake, present with that form, even though what people think of as "I" now, will be absolutely extinct.

Devotee: Why do we fear death, why can't we accept it?

Lee: It is very simple why people fear death. It is all a matter of what one identifies with. If one identifies with the vehicle, death is certainly a great fear. The greatest fear of all is extinction. When there is any identification involved whatsoever, extinction is feared. Identification necessitates a limited state or limited form. It is the primary expression of separation. Any form of identification will involve fear of extinction. That is why you ultimately have to give up realization. If you identify with that, you will fear being "unrealized" someday.

Extinction is just the nature of change. If one recognizes that one exists as what is always extinct, if one recognizes oneself as the very nature of change, then what is there to be extinct? Nothing! That is the paradox: everything is extinction, and in truth there is no extinction. There is simply perfect change, flawless movement. Realize that you are literally the very nature of change, and you are Alive. Once you are Alive, you'll never die. You will be endless and eternal. That's not personal immortality, that's God.

TWENTY-EIGHT

THERE IS ONLY one spiritual relationship and that is between you and me. Verbal teachings are virtually useless without it; it is the very foundation of true spiritual life. Without the living Presence of Grace in the world, there is only lifeless tradition, unable to do anything but perpetuate the endless search.

There is not a single relationship in the world whose basic structure is not a reflection of the guru-devotee relationship. That is the way it has always been, because that is the only relationship that is valid and happy. In the life of delusion, that relationship appears as a gross caricature of itself: authority figures are treated as God, the President being the perfect example, or corporate executives. People are always doing stuff to get in their favor, motivating themselves to perform "services" for somebody in a seat of power. People set up structures in society that parallel the guru-devotee relationship, because they have an intuitive sense that the form of devotee, the form of sacrifice, is the only appropriate form in the world. Ego interprets that in its own fashion, creating the search as its deluded way of imitating the form of devotee, extending it to higher and higher levels. The philosophy of, "You scratch my back and I'll scratch yours," is an expression of that distorted image of this relationship. When people do favors for people in power, they receive favors in return; the whole political trip satisfies the search, fulfilling it in their mind.

In the same way, the great spiritual masters are seen as heroes. That validates the search within reality, within maya. Seeing the guru as hero, just like the heroes of mythology or military history, or like the hero figures of show business, allows his unconventional nature to become hidden in clouds of romantic ideals. He becomes an example to follow, an object lesson of behavior, a figurehead. How do children structure their play? They pretend to be adults. The great spiritual masters are seen merely as role-models, as a higher level of hero. At the same time they are always treated very blandly by traditional historical accounts. Their real power is never seen, but shrouded in a romantic and stylized historical treatment. Nobody wants to know what it is really like, for unless you are particularly strong, you can't sustain real spiritual life, and there is nothing romantic about that. People don't talk about how it was for Jesus to starve for forty days in the desert, but they are fascinated by how he healed the lepers and walked on the water and all that jazz. The functional, human aspect is persistently ignored in order to sustain the myth of the hero.

The world will always interpret in its own terms whatever is presented to it, including radical spiritual life. It will interpret me in terms of the egoic search, taking the intuited form of the guru-devotee relationship and creating its distorted version of it in the world. It will not enter the real relationship; it will not recognize the real basis of it, which is God. That is why there is a teaching: it is the only thing people can relate to and be sympathetic towards. They see the teaching as another, higher form of the search: if they scratch the guru's back, the guru will scratch theirs. They think that they will receive enlightenment when they give the guru money, commitment, service, and devotion. It is conceived as the perfect exchange. In this relationship, however, there is a **suprise.**

There is no payoff in this relationship. You receive absolutely nothing. The only reason you have for being who you are is devotion for the guru; it is your thanks to the Lord for creating you in the first place. Being talented, being healthy, being happy, and doing your sadhana, is not what you take from life, on the contrary, it is what you give in return. You already got the payoff: you are alive. That's it! You've had the payoff for a long time, and you don't get two payoffs. That is just the way it is. So to fulfill your sadhana and to thank the Lord for giving you the payoff in the first place, you allow the guru to force you to be who you are, to force you to be creative, happy, strong, healthy, intelligent, successful, Alive in God.

That is what you want to think about, what the guru-devotee relationship means. It means the absoluteness of service. It means the giving up of all your need systems. There is only one true need, and that is to live God. All the others are superficial. Only recognize that our relationship is a sacrificial affair. I am only interested in heartfelt devotion, and that takes strength and commitment. Your conscious thought process is only me, only your devotion to me, and not all of your neurotic needs. You don't need reasons or justifications for devotion, but just devotion in itself; that is the ultimate demand that threads through all of the minor things. Everything springs from and leads back to the central fact of our relationship.

It is interesting that although our relationship is always perfect, from your perspective it appears to pass through different degrees of involvement. The first step is basically getting intrigued by the field of consciousness. This is regardless of your religious upbringing, which usually gets one closed off and uninterested. Organized religion rarely concerns itself with consciousness. The interest begins when you read about some form of spiritual practice or a friend who is into it tells you about it, and your intuitive thirst for the Divine responds. You begin to think, "Maybe there's something more." So you get involved on a somewhat deeper level than conventional religion.

When one gets interested in all of the stuff that is usually called spiritual, paranormal, or religious, there is a subtle danger present. For that is the stage that most people stay in. The seeker remains merely interested and intrigued by altered states of consciousness or the "supernatural". Such interest is directly and totally motivated from ego. Always. It is just a "higher" trip, and that's okay, it is not good or bad. It is solely a matter of how you deal with it and being openly aware of it. You get involved in a particular area where you perceive that there is something to gain, whether it is being holier than your friends, or being psychic or clairvoyant, or just being able to do great and powerful things. It implies being something that is unusual, more than most people are. Those of you that have had a really good psychic reading done for you, know that it is spectacular. They know your past and your future and all this great stuff. It is fascinating, and it has absolutely nothing to do with spiritual life.

It's quite easy to get stuck there, for the levels and dimensions are endless. You could study it for years, struggling through the labyrinth of cosmic bullshit. It is all so complicated, so deep and heavy. You can get lost in it for a lifetime and get nowhere. **Nowhere.** Mind will just go on and on and never be undone.

Another aspect of this is getting into a therapeutic path such as humanistic psychology. These approaches are supposed to be spiritual, although the field is actually more involved with the psycho-physical organism, the body and brain, than it is with the life of God. Most humanistic methodologies never talk about the guru or awakened one; they talk about teaching people so that everyone can do it himself, without any guru. The process that goes on is that those who are involved in those fields become very "centered". People who have been into encounter, or some such therapeutic approach, for any length of time, become very cooled and mellow. They are always in control of their emotions, and they never get annoyed or criticize anybody else. And they are never awake. They are still just up and down: the action/reaction process. The down periods last less time because they have a lot of tools and techniques to subdue the down, hide it, bury it, and get "up" again. They are not Alive, only presumptuous.

You can also get involved in the spiritual search, in the traditional religious path. Instead of becoming cool and centered, the goal is to "get" to God, which is very amusing. The search perpetuates itself unceasingly, always aiming for the "final" experience, where everything will be fulfilled and completed, and everyone lives happily ever after. There are signs along the way that validate the path: Have you spoken in tongues yet? Have you had a vision? Have you experienced kundalini? There are many forms of feedback along the way that tell you if you are doing okay. That keeps you rooted in the path, needing stronger and stronger proof, which is more frustrating and more of a trap than any of the lesser forms of the search. Just around the corner, boys and girls, is eternal bliss, and if you just keep plodding away, you will make it. Chickenshit. No amount of searching will make you perfect, for you already are.

The appropriate form of this first step is simply getting interested in education that involves the Divine, whatever perspective that may involve. At a certain point, your interest will have served its purpose, and it would be unwise to stay there. The second step is refining one's intuition. Most people never get to the second step. The vast majority of "spiritual" teachers are uninterested in teaching their students to use their intuition. Then the students would fly like the wind from the deluded search of their meditation teacher to the true guru.

The second step is where one is able to see between the lines, behind the scenery. One begins to see things symbolically rather than literally, begins to be aware that behind the play there are props and stage hands ready to change the scenery when the curtain comes down. That is intuition. You can get stuck there too; many people are intuitive yet never follow it. They need to win so strongly that they get trapped in their game. They get trapped in the feeling that they have to get feedback all the time to support their intuition. Vistas are opened up that they were never aware of, so they jump to the conclusion that they are in spiritual life. Actually, intuition will help direct you to the place or the person or the experience that will best suit you, and then it gives up. It is of no use. Once you get there, you still have to do it. Intuition isn't going to do it for you. Once you get right to the edge and are ready to jump, intuition says, "That's all. I've got you to the edge. Bye bye." You still have to make that commitment to do it without any help or sympathy, without a road map.

Grace doesn't have an abrasive nature. It is the mind which, by the very nature of its creation, is abrasive. Whenever Grace is manifestly present, the mind gets very troubled and disturbed. If you are not educated and your intuition is not refined, your mind is like one of those three foot deep plastic swimming pools. If an elephant (Grace) jumps in, the water gets blown clear away. The proper form of education and intuitive awareness helps it to be like an elephant jumping into a lake. There is not too much of a disturbance. So the process of those first two steps is so that when you realize true self, there is a small splash. When you are not educated and intuitively aware, every time you get a glimpse of who you are, you experience a terrible contraction and get all clutched up.

The third step is recognizing where you are intuitively directed to. There is God and there is everything else. If you are attracted to anything else, including all the stories that teachers lay on their students about what God is supposed to be, that is not being intiutively directed to living God, it is just more experience. But if you want God, without knowing what God is, yet still wanting only God, that is not just experience. No form of the search comes near this; they are merely nice things to do to occupy your time. It is nice to meditate and experience a little peace once in awhile, and it won't attain the unattainable. Recognizing that the Divine is all you want does not end seeking; it does help terminate the obvious forms of the search for experience and in so doing allow one to focus one's attention on God.

The next step is approaching the guru. You can get stuck with the "gurus" who support the search, but if you are fortunate, you will enter the company of the true guru. Once you approach the living guru and begin to live in relationship with Grace, real spiritual life can begin. Up until then there is no spiritual life, there is only seeking. This guru, Lee Lozowick, exists as perfect relationship with all who live with him. Grace is totally enslaving. When Grace takes over, there is no longer the delusion of choice, no more path. Some people come here and then go to other teachers and something happens which they attribute to that other place. It has nothing to do with that. Once I have touched you, it is out of your hands. If you go to some meditation teacher or to any other place, everything that happens has nothing to do with them. They don't know where it's at; they are all seeking too, and propagating the search with their teaching. Once you allow me to touch you, you are had, and everything that happens is a direct result of Lee Lozowick, of the Presence of this one in your life, and only because of that. You may get to recognize that our relationship is the only true relationship in the world.

All that exists here is the delightfully humorous joy of the unqualified Divine. I can't do anything to you. You can get on your knees and pray all you want, and I still can't do anything to you. I can not manipulate or control; I am only Alive. Grace exists as a condition and I am that condition lived consciously. If you allow it to work, it will work. It is not a matter of becoming something other than what you are, but of becoming Alive as what you already are. Grace does not descend on you; there is no place for it to descend from. Grace is present as all life. When there is an opening to the guru, Grace manifests as absolute recognition of what is. It is present anyway, whether you are open to the guru or not, because it is your very life. Grace is not a force that does something to you. There is no one to do anything to. The movement of Grace can simply get you to realize that Grace is your life.

Everything that goes on between us is always perfect. Nothing can possibly be done to make our relationship different than it is at every moment. If I confront somebody, or if I say something to hurt somebody's feelings, there was no possible alternative to that action. There was simply nothing else I could have done but that one appropriate thing that I did. Even waking up is no alternative to our relationship: you couldn't possibly have been awake last week if you had done something differently. As a matter of fact, there was nothing you could have done in the last year that you have known me that would have made anything any different. Our relationship is already perfect.

If someone leaves the community, it is not over. Once someone has been in my company, there is nothing he or she can do about leaving. People might leave the community and never see me again in the next fifty years, but my Presence will always be the main factor in their life. They might die, and Lee might die, and it is still not over. They are in for a big surprise. I'll be floating around with my harp, and get them from behind: "Ah hah!" Then they'll rush for another body. That's why the population is increasing so rapidly these days; bodies are in big demand because people are running into their gurus after they die. During their lifetime, they thought he was a clown, they threw rocks at him. You think that you were born to live? You were only born to get away from your guru. That's why I am here, because you've already gotten away from me once and I'm not about to let it happen again.

When I talk about steps or degrees of involvement, the perfection of the guru-devotee relationship should be kept in mind. It is only from the perspective of your separative life that such steps are taken. It is evident from your perspective that there are very clear delineations between different stages that people in the community fall into. It is very obvious that there are clear differences, from your vantage point, in people's functional relationship to me, and they are exhibited, to varying degrees, in all of your cases.

The first stage in the community is that of the chela. It basically involves studying the teaching, making a commitment to be in the community and to follow the requirements and demands and starting to respond to the movement in your life which is a result of my Presence. There is the recognition that movement is taking place: Lee is causing this, Lee is doing that. Whatever occurs is perceived in reference to the separate self. The chela might say, "I really freaked out last night," and what is signified by that statement is that Grace did it, and that it happened "to me". All recognizable response to movement in that person's life is self-directed. Personal involvement is the constant element of chela sadhana. There is a complete emotional identification with movement in our relationship; it is a private affair, so to speak.

The chela stage is a commitment to the guru, a belief in the guru, and perhaps some understanding of the teaching itself. The guru is seen primarily as teacher, helper. So in formal satsang, for instance, the attention is directed to the lecture I give, rather than primarily on me. This is a perfectly appropriate stage, and will continue until the chela realizes that he or she doesn't need the teaching, only God. Until then, there is no really intimate relationship with me. We can be friends and put our arms around one another and all that, yet I can never have a truly intimate relationship with chelas.

The chela stage is typically a matter of one to two or three years as a sincere, available and ready beginner in spiritual life. Many of you have been with me for close to a year. And what is becoming obvious now is that you have been turned to Lee as contrasted with you. Truly turning to me is not contrasted with anything. You must get out of the way completely. You must indulge in, delight in, beg for, and sustain play with Lee. And whenever Lee has begun to play, what has arisen instead has been fear, silence, and a very discomforted anticipation. Prepare for Lee the playground, and enjoy his playing there. When the playground involves the dissolution of your conventional relationships, anticipate that with the joy, the sparkliness, the happiness of a child, rather than with gravity, dread, and devotion through panic. Devotion through panic stops Lee cold in his tracks. The child does not want to play when the adult is constantly scolding it and telling it to keep its pants clean, hands clean, and feet out of the puddles.

That is why the chela stage usually takes so long. You need to recognize the play as play and stop taking it personally. Until you recognize that there is no person to take it personally, you remain a chela, because Lee's play with you can never go anywhere, can never get further than that dead end. As soon as you tell Lee not to jump in the puddle, you've ruined his fun. He will not jump in the puddle; he will just walk away. Lee's relationship with the community has been restrained in its expression purely because of the community's response to Lee's childlike and childish play.

The first thing you need to do as a principal aspect of chela sadhana is to stop reacting personally to the movement in your life that is manifesting because of your relationship with me. Then we can move on. That typically takes a year or two before you are willing to do that. There is not a person in this community who has not seen that there is nothing to take personally. Yet as soon as I start playing, you take it personally. Everybody has a concept of what the guru is supposed to be and act like. They are always safe concepts, precisely because everybody thinks that he or she has something to protect. So my play appears threatening; it appears to be happening to somebody. This play of mine is often very childish because my emotions are very pure: greed, desire, megalomania. Those are pure emotions and exist present as much as anything else. There is no reason that they should frighten you.

The second stage, that of disciple, is when one sees the movement going on, is very conscious of that movement, and yet is removed from it as an individual. Disciples recognize that the movement is not movement in "their" life, but simply the movement of the Divine. One sees the drama of life with humor. The disciple never takes anything personally; he or she is able to be removed from identification with the mind, body, personality, and theater of the individual and observe it humorously.

Your relationship with me starts to take on a greater drama as you become a perfect disciple, and it is not seen as an emotional turmoil. People come to me now and say, "Oh, man, what I went through!" There is some sense of humor to it, but it is still obvious that the perception of the experience is in terms of psychic upheaval, positive or negative. Sometimes it is, "I got a really great insight!" The interpretation of the experience is still based on an emotional level. That is all a process of the chela stage. Once one assumes the disciple stage, there is much more of that dramatic quality to life, and it is not perceived at that level of turmoil. It is known as the relationship with the guru. When something happens, it is always seen with humor: "Lee is playing again. The Divine is having some fun, manifesting drama in my life." Experience is not conceived as an individualized mind-perception that belongs or happens to you. You are simply observing the drama in life with a light heart, knowing that Lee is the basis of that drama.

Your body might be reacting intensely, you might have some teeth-gritting, white-knuckled experiences. Nevertheless, there is no emotional cognition of personal involvement. It is all automatically assumed to be an expression of your relationship with me as guru. Your attention, rather than being exclusively directed to my instruction, is completely on me, and all movement that occurs is seen as originating from this Presence.

The disciple stage typically takes even longer than the chela stage. That is because once you stop taking things personally, the obsession for the Divine appears to you as a very unnecessary aspect of your sadhana. Why be obsessed with God when everything is so much fun? There is nothing to get offended at, there is only the play. It is easy to be comfortable in that position.

One crucial difference between the disciple and the chela is the level of commitment. For the former, commitment is simply the way things are, for the latter it is to some degree an effort. In the chela stage, there is always the possibility of leaving the guru and going someplace else. There is always the chance of a stronger fascination. As long as one is a chela, there arises in fantasy, "I wonder if this is the place to be? Maybe it would be different elsewhere, maybe another guru would be better." In most of your cases, when the fantasy has arisen, you have dismissed it as the mind's attempt to trick you out of our relationship.

For the disciple, the fantasy doesn't even arise. It is obvious that this is the place to be, so you don't give any thought to it, you don't spend any time trying to convince yourself that this is the place to be. It is your life. When you are a three-year-old you don't even consider running away from home. It doesn't even enter your mind. The same is true of the disciple. This is your

Hohm, that's all. It is perfectly obvious. No consideration need be given to any alternative to that.

Separation, the basic activity of the mind, is still present in disciple stage. There is still an assumption of the observer of the drama and the guru as being separate. Although one is removed from identification with individual drama, the sense of observation retains the sense of separateness from what is being observed. It is the dissolution of this sense of separation between disciple and guru that marks the entering into the third stage: that of the devotee.

Devotees are literally **forged** by the guru. It is not like being touched by a little wand; what is involved is the constant frustration of any structure that you set up. But since your mind is very fast and clever, it takes daily movement to break all of your structure. Something you can look forward to is being in a place where you do not have time to restructure, figure it out, or prepare yourself to deal with what's going on. The process of forging devotees begins to take place in these intense periods of crisis and confrontation. Ultimately, the mind is brought to the point of absolute surrender. It is a delicate process.

You will be forged in the fire of the Divine. All the recognition of egoic strategy is a preliminary to this expression of our very direct and forceful relationship. The basis of our relationship is prior condition, rather than ego. The difference is only knowable, not understandable, rational or reasonable. This is Grace. And I'm asking you to know it. To know it through fire.

It is like forging steel. The best steel is not made by sticking it in the oven for five minutes, heating it up, pulling it out, and calling it a perfect piece of steel. The best steel is tempered by being heated up, taken out and beaten, and being cooled. Then it is put back in the fire and heated up, taken out again and beaten, and then cooled and put back in the fire. Again it is heated, taken out, beaten and cooled. The best steel is tempered many times before it comes to its perfect quality.

The devotee is the same way. The process of the guru is to constantly put you into the fire, temper you, bring you out and let you understand the tempering process, then put you back in again, pull you out and let you recognize the heat, and then back into the fire. That is the forging of the perfect devotee.

That fire of devotion always burns. It is not something that one goes through. Devotion is often seen as a way to get through the fire. Actually it is quite the opposite of being cooled out and passionless all the time. Your devotion will always be intensely hot, filled with fire. People in the community won't be looking to release themselves from the body, looking for escape to some heaven or "beyond". They will be present as that flaming devotion.

For the devotee, all separation is transcended. There is not even a fantasy of separation. There is still some fantasy of separation in disciple stage, even though the movement in life is perceived as the drama of the Divine, rather than as an attachment to the self. In the devotee stage, there is simply our relationship. There is not even a cognition of drama; you are simply present. Movement is not seen as taking place in "my" life; there is no "my" life at all, there is only the guru. Your entire being is the guru.

In the devotee stage, there is no conceivable separation between you as an individual and the guru. You literally function as me. That is when you no longer need the guru, and we really start to enjoy ourselves together. There is still the need to experience the enjoyment of the guru's company in disciple stage. You still feel the pressing desire to be with me; you are much happier being with the guru than not being with him physically. In devotee stage, it wouldn't matter if you never saw the guru again in your life. It would absolutely not matter, because you are the very same one. The whole enjoyment of the guru's Presence as being other than yourself falls away completely.

We are not separate now. We never were and we never will be. What is being ripped off is the delusion of separation, not any actual separate condition. You are assuming that there is a dilemma to be let go of. It is that assumption that has to be ripped off, not the form of your life. It has nothing to do with the form, with your emotions, movement, or functionality. Only delusion is obliterated, and it is the very nature of delusion that it is not the case, that it is not Truth.

As far as one misunderstands the chela, disciple, and devotee stages, one will also misunderstand the distinction that I make between guru and devotee, interpreting it in terms of one's deluded ideas of manipulation and control. When one clearly sees those stages in the perspective of their sadhana, the rhetoric about the guru and the devotee will be seen in the same light. That relationship of the guru with the devotee is the flawless expression of all relationship. **It is all relationship.**

One of the points of having stages is to reveal to you your fascination with attainment. It is inevitable that the stages will be set up as goals, and consequently become obstructions. If the idea of stages becomes a preoccupation with you, you have missed the whole point. The only reason there are stages is so you will see that there is no need for stages. There is a need for people to see how they transpose their conventional forms and games over to spiritual forms and games. It is exactly the same pattern. Obviously the true devotee doesn't think, "I am now a true devotee," because he or she recognizes how the teaching concerning stages is just a teaching, and thus they appreciate it in its place.

The literal contradiction of the guru is not cognizable by the mind. It is only knowable, not understandable. The guru is absolute, living contradiction. He has no function, because there is no wound to be healed or problem to be solved. The guru only serves a function because of you, because of your delusion. The guru's function is ultimately to frustrate mind until God is the only remaining alternative. He doesn't do this with energy, power or force, for they are limited, directable, and conditioned. The guru's Grace is the unlimited, spontaneous, and unconditioned activity of the Divine. By virtue of the Presence of Grace alone, rather than by any direction, the mind is backed into a corner until there is no choice but to awaken. Mind keeps playing out every possible alternative, while Grace frustrates every single one of them. In fact, Grace always frustrates every aspect of the life of suffering. It is kind of like the frustration of trying to extract an intellectually secure meaning from what I am saying.

There is no willful direction to God. I am present. The Presence of the guru in the world is existence. Nothing else. Grace is commonly perceived as some power that is going to alleviate all problematic manifestations in the world. It is not a power, and it truly does not alleviate anything; it is the activity of consciousness, the activity of Divine inclusiveness that generates in the deluded the frustration of all search for release and all attempts to find the Garden of Eden. It is the contradiction of your search fo the purpose and end of life, for the ultimate payoff, the finale of our activity as human beings.

The great ideal of suffering, you see, is hope. Hope keeps one searching, because one is continually trying to change things into what one hopes it will be like someday. It keeps one focused on what "should be" and totally ignorant of what is. Hope is the expression of despair. How could I, very God, who loves life in its fullness, seeing nothing but perfection, ever hope for anything? That would be slandering what is. I find it odd that people who say, "There is no hope," are always frowning. That news is cause for celebration.

* * * *

The evolution of the teaching concerning **assertion** reflects the evolution of the members of the community in sadhana. At first, the statement "just this" was conceived by us as a facet of Lee's teaching, similar to certain central facets of other great teachers. We would meditate and say to ourselves "just this" whenever an experience would arise, as a subtle corrective for the attachment to it as experience. Or "just this" was employed as a statement signifying that there was no conclusions or meaning to be extracted from an experience, but it was what it was. In fact, "just this" could be used for many such remedial purposes. This conception of **assertion** corresponds to the chela stage in sadhana. We latched on to **assertion** as a teaching or method, and attempted to apply it within separative life.

At some point, insight arose that just this was not the statement "just this" but was the Divine Presence. We recognized that it provided us with no foothold for use as a method or a teaching. Yet at the same time, our insight was confused with just this, that is, we believed that the intuition of "just this" was just this, and that therefore it was a way of attaining or understanding Presence. This corresponds to the disciple stage of sadhana, where the fascination with **assertion** as teaching has subsided, but just this is still intuited from the standpoint of the self.

At a certain point, Lee told us to let "just this" spontaneously arise, and then to tell him what was present immediately before the arising of "just this" in consciousness. Some of us reported energy experiences, powerful intuitions of Grace, and the stopping of the breath. Others said that "just this" did not seem to arise at all, but was already there. Many expressed confusion about whether their experiences were forced or spontaneous.

All of that was to be undermined by a tape that Lee left us as he went to the west coast for a week. On this tape, Lee explained the misconceptions concerning **assertion**, and then outlined its real significance in our sadhana and in real spiritual life.

TWENTY-NINE

THERE IS A basic mistake that is consistently made and very rarely recognized as such in spiritual life. For everyone entering or assuming what he thinks to be sadhana, his activity, functionality, study, sincerity, attention to the guru, love, and in fact all forms of his relationship with the spiritual master and the community, are founded and motivated in mind. It is literally impossible, there is not one chance in infinity, that one can awaken to the Heart, to prior condition, to true self, through any process whatsoever that is founded and motivated in mind.

When the approach to the guru remains founded in mind, nothing is ever present but the recognition of one's tendencies and strategies, typically negative. The first truth of the Buddha, that all life is suffering, becomes painfully evident, becomes the stuff of one's life. Suffering is the assumed relationship to the world due to the separate self sense.

The approach to the guru is always begun or initiated from mind. After all, what else is going to motivate you? God is certainly no motivation. The Divine Presence undermines motivation, destroys it, eliminates it completely. Not only all initial approaches to the guru, but all your approaches to the teachers and so-called "gurus" that you have seen or read about, and, in fact, all your approaches to anything you have ever lived, have been motivated solely from mind.

The guru presents drama, activity, and humor, and the attention to the guru is in mind. You love the guru, and your love is simply a conventional response of desire for pleasure. You want to be with the guru, certainly. And what is that? Again a conventional mind-motivated validation of your worth, your value, your choice of the proper philosophy. It is all based on mind, all an expression of separate self.

When the desire to be with the guru burns holes in your structure with its intensity, and you offer the guru your pain and serve it up to him, you are then starting to intuit the real nature of spiritual life. But you don't offer the guru your pain, you offer him your pleasure: the concept of what you will get in return. When the guru presents the obvious nature of your seeking to you and you perceive it as suffering, pain, discomfort, anxiety, and pressure, you don't offer this up to the guru. You run from the guru and hide, sheltering and protecting your pain as you would a treasure.

When your need for the guru is greater than your petty desires and avoidances, when your need for the guru is so great that you would offer the guru your soul to trample upon if he would, then you have begun to intuit real Presence. You need to offer the guru everything and you need to understand that the guru has nothing to offer in return. The guru is not anything or anyone; he is Alive in the world, functionally and paradoxically real, for the guru is none other than Grace and only Grace. Not some communication from or connection to the Divine. He exists only as the Divine.

Assertion, just this, has been perceived as simply another form of sadhana, merely an aspect or significant feature of Lee Lozowick's dharma. It is none of these. It isn't even faintly related to any of the believed or practiced traditional ideas, techniques, or formulations that are typical of conventional spiritual life.

To intelligently and responsibly participate in assertion, it is crucial that you clearly understand the nature of being with the guru. The guru is not to be attained; the guru is not to be comprehended; the guru is not even to be loved. The guru exists as an ever-present and eternally perfect sacrificial affair. When this has begun to be intuited and recognized as such, you have begun, in some degree, to be ripe for assertion, for the process of sadhana in my company.

The guru's Presence effects within your lives a broad variety of experiential states, some very negative, some very positive, and others neither negative nor positive yet still intense by nature. Several of you have mentioned the experience of energy or heat in your meditation of "just this". Any mind-motivated attention on the guru will create heat or energy experiences, for the guru himself is all of these things. It needs to be understood and directly intuited.

"Just this" is not a meditation. It is the very texture and basic life of meditation. It is meditation itself. "Just this" is not a statement or a form of the mind. The two words can be conceptually qualified, explained, justified, or analyzed. But it is the radical insight of "just this", which is the prior to the language "just this", that turns the reins over to Grace, really beginning the actual process of the awakening of Truth in your life.

Approaching the guru sounds like a hopeless task. But since everyone approaches the guru motivated from mind, it is not as hopeless as it seems. In truth your experience and your meditation are not yours at all, for real attention and meditation is simply the guru turning back upon himself, observing, enjoying, sacrificing. Since I already exist as everything, the nature of my sacrifice is that I keep turning in upon myself. The sacrificial affair signifies that rather than existing as all, there is movement involved. There is constancy, and within the constancy there is movement. Turning in upon myself does not mean Lee turning in upon himself; it is the actual sacrificial nature of the worlds. The sacrificial affair in its localized, personalized form is the community. There is only God, and the community doesn't know that. So there is constant movement, constant burning up of ego and desires, getting rid of all the shit which is strategic life. I serve that by being present to sustain that until people understand and know the guru.

When you surrender to me, when you sacrifice to me, who is surrendering and sacrificing? You are not surrendering or sacrificing at all. You are not capable of sacrifice or even of the most superficial kind of surrender. It is I who sacrifice, it is I who surrender unto myself in boundlessness.

All of your seeming sacrifice is just a shadow play. It is simply the movement of ego, the play of the world. The true sacrifice is only at that moment when one recognizes that the self or ego that is always pretending to sacrifice is, in fact, what is to be sacrificed. The one moment of real sacrifice is when you wake up and realize that you have never truly sacrificed. When that has begun to be seen, real spiritual life has been intuited. Yet once real spiritual life has been intuited, it must still be lived. One must still realize only God.

Radical intuition serves only knowledge; it is a basis of understanding what has already and has always been present. The intuition in itself is not the Presence. This perfect Presence is existence here and now; it is happiness, joy and bliss. It is not some heavenly state to be attained, or some ideal condition to be lived after you wake up. Your entire sadhana must assume from the beginning this prior state of enjoyment, already perfect, already full, already complete and absolute in its nature. Already only God, not someday only God. **Already present only God.**

Recognize that the true sacrifice is my turning and returning to my very self. You are not capable of sacrifice, because you still feel that you are who you think you are. You are pragmatically functioning as separate self, and in that case no sacrifice is possible. You can sweat and strain to try to understand it, but nobody understands it. Nobody understands the sacrificial relationship except one who is living it and enjoying it.

Divine Communion, the process of consciously being in my company, only becomes sacrificial after awakening. It is not sacrificial before you wake up. It asks for your strategy to be one of sacrifice, but it can not and does not require a truly sacrificial relationship. Assertion, on the other hand, is sacrificial from its inception. Its nature from the beginning can be nothing else but sacrificial, for it is prior condition itself.

"Just this" is not anything that you do. When I refer to "just this" spontaneously arising, it is not you who are perceiving "just this", it is not you who are creating the arising of a statement, vision, thought, or feeling. It is I who am beginning to assume who you think you are. In truth who is there to be assumed? I don't take your life, I don't assume you. Grace does not do anything but continuously and endlessly turn in upon itself in sacrifice and self-knowledge. There is only self. There is no "other". There is no one to observe or be observed, no one to be awake, no one to have anything arise for. There is only this perfect Presence. Real God. So when just this spontaneously "arises", what in fact is occurring? It is your very nature perceiving that you are none other than the sacrificial process Alive as the world, turning and returning to your self. I am that self.

"Just this", of course, is a beautifully designed statement for it gives you absolutely nothing to hold on to, no footing for the mind. And since "assertion" has never been expounded upon in the world before, it will delight the minds of those who think that they are enjoying something new, a new creation, a new dharma. Perhaps it will be seen as the fulfillment of all past dharmas and teachers. That's beautiful. How can I possibly fulfill past teachers? How can I be defined as going beyond all those who have come before me? What is there to go beyond? Nothing. I don't exist in contrast with other teachers. What is there to be contrasted with "just this"? Maya, illusion. There is nothing to be contrasted with this one. I am simply present.

"Just this" is a very practical meditative statement, an exquisite mantra, which many have used it as. "Just this" used as a mantra will certainly produce ecstatic states when used properly, if we can talk about a mantra being used properly in the search. "Just this", when it is muscled, pressured, concentrated on, or willfully and compulsively stuck to as a meditation, will produce tremendous states of vision, of samadhi. As a tool it is one of the most beautiful around. It is the perfect tool, because it will point out to you the nature of the search by creating for you the fulfillment of the search as you dream of and imagine fulfillment to be. The technique "just this" will create that fulfillment, and the guru's Presence in the world is to undermine that very fulfillment.

"Just this" exists as the spontaneous self-sacrifice of the guru. It is simply present at all times, in all places, during all states of pleasure or non-pleasure. You will find "just this" arising sometimes in seemingly the most unlikely situations: in the middle of sex, in the middle of gorging yourself on a good meal, in the middle of a fight with your parents or child or lover, in the middle of a moment of jealousy, pain, hurt, separation, and suffering. "Just this" will arise in all of these instances, and it is simply present to create in you the conscious recognition that everything must be sacrificed to the guru. All of it, the sex, the food, the jealousy, the felt suffering, must be sacrificed to the guru. All these experiences are none other than the guru himself. He is the only truth of present existence, not past or future. There is no temporal framework in which to recognize the guru, for all temporality is founded in mind. Prior condition knows no time or space. All forms of exclusively temporal and spatial experience serve only to reinforce the separate self sense, encouraging and sustaining the maya of the attainment of realization. There is only this one, very God.

For those of you who have intuited "just this" as Presence rather than as form or manifestation, the intuition of the real nature of the guru is beginning to dawn. The spontaneous arising of the intelligibly cognizable statement "just this", as phrase, image, mental sound, or insight into the words' meaning, is beginning to give way to proper turning, to the recognition of Presence. "Just this" is, of course, always present; it is not really something that arises. When I talk about "just this" arising, I am referring to the conscious recognition of this Presence. The guru is not present as something; he is not actually in the world as anything. He is simply present. "Just this" is the guru in body, in Presence. The Presence of this one, of Lee Lozowick, is not intelligible or cognizable. It is impossible to understand the guru. The guru can only be known.

At some point you will recognize that you are involved in this sacrificial affair of turning in upon the guru. It is not entering your own kingdom or going into yourself, not the private experience or personal fulfillment. Simply present. Some of you have been a devotee in my company, and have fallen from that state because you have not recognized the affair as being a sacrificial one. You have seen it as being available to me, when in fact you cannot be available to me. I can only be available to myself. And when I am available to myself through you as devotee, realization is consciously present. It is the intelligent recognition and permanent acceptance of this condition as the true nature of your existence, as life itself, happiness itself, bliss itself. It is the state of the guru and the perfect devotee; it is permanent and complete enlightenment. Not just here in this world at this time, but in all worlds, in all universes, for all time.

My relationship with you is just the Divine play, and I am not referring to a play on a stage. That is your perspective, your personal drama. I am referring to the delightful play of children.

You all still take my play very personally, as if it was happening directly to you, as if it were something you could possibly control, direct, or do something about. Until you stop taking my play with you personally, there is no true turning. Certainly there is a multitude of experiential states, yet there is no true awakening, no true knowledge. We have talked about how things will never change, and how it will never get better, and yet when real attention is present, there is change. Quite frequently there is personality change, body change, and emotional change. When Presence is known as a sacrificial affair, there is permanent, perfect change.

Regarding the point of no return, God-awakening, I have made statements to the effect that if Lee had to do it over again, Lee would not choose to function as guru, and that in fact, Lee might decide to remain a seeker. This has been questioned in the context of my frequent statements that the guru is humor and joy, and that my life is simply pleasure, happy all the time. Your framework, your mental construction of pleasure, revolves around security, need systems, the mistaken belief that it is possible to win and to attain something. How can you possibly understand pleasure in truth? Pleasure in truth is the Divine reality present. It has nothing to do with your feelings of insecurity, your lack of attention, or your need to be validated. The happiness of God is only the condition of absolute Presence, of life itself. That is what you must realize, not through any cognizable process, but through the nature of being present simply. The mind cannot be present, only the guru can. **Only the guru as you can be present as you.** And you are only present as the unqualified Presence of the guru.

You must be ripe for assertion. You must be ripe for "just this" to be your reality. Anyone can meditate "just this", say it, think it, or feel it. And you won't see the need for you to be ripe before "just this" can be truly present as your life. When you are ripe for assertion, it will be given to you in a very dramatic form.

When there is a simultaneous and already perfectly present recognition of "just this", the guru, and the nature of the sacrificial affair that you are involved in, that is awakening or enlightenment. When there is the Presence consciously turning in upon itself, not as your life, and not as felt separation or as any kind of observing and interpreting mind, but as the simultaneous recognition of "just this", of the guru being the only consciousness there is, and of the intelligent nature of this sacrificial affair, pervaded by joy, and felt as humor, then you are awake as the Presence of the very Divine. You have become mine in truth.

* * * *

What had we stumbled upon? Our very life, and the utter devotion that is our life's only real enjoyment. The rest of life, and all life for all time, is in relationship with this one. Like poverty-stricken ones who have suddenly come into a great fortune, we comically stumble around in this room of riches, tripping over priceless treasures. But Lee will have us fully realize this treasure, this life. He will have us live as perfect devotion, in the delight of the Lord's company:

You are here.
You have sounded the hearts of beings,
You are the Heart where songs converge,
You are sweet and terrible life,
Your own blessing,
Your own prayer and eternal greeting,
All the flawless forms
All that ever embraced in furious love and creation,
You are Here, You are God,
You are all that is and ever will be,
The wonder of You like stillness before a storm,
The Lord, the Singer of songs, True God!
Present in fullness, in life bountiful,
All joy is Here with You.
Today is laughter, today all hearts are broken,
Today is the day of the Lord's broad,
bounding, strong, jumping delight,
You are Here this day.

THIRTY

THERE IS NO place where you can be without God. Whether you like it or not, I am everywhere. You can't run away, all you can do is ignore me or know me. Just because you are ignorant of me doesn't mean that I am not present. You are asleep, that's all. Knowing me is waking up from ignorance and unconsciousness. Truly knowing the guru is not merely perceiving. A lot of you have perceived yourselves as Lee, and that has been your interpretation: "Lee is in my head," or "I'm thinking as Lee," and so on. That is still seeing me as ego, as personality, and not as this absolute Presence. Knowing the guru is knowledge in and of non-exclusive consciousness. It is living life instead of avoiding death. It is genuine enjoyment, humor, and flawless devotion.

Devotee: What is the experience of your Presence?

Lee: I certainly don't know!

Devotee: What does being in your company serve?

Lee: It serves the dissolution of the belief that one's self is real, the dissolution of the delusion of separation. If you are in my Presence, it serves the recognition that who you think you are, separate unto yourself, is just a concept. Living consciously in my company is the non-indulgence of the assumption and activity that continually creates the life of suffering.

When I say, "My Presence" or "My company" I am not referring to a person or ego, I am referring to the Lord, the unqualified Divine that is truly myself. The process of being in my company is to get you to recognize that. The proper way of meditating upon me is letting that be the driving force, the consuming, overwhelming expression of life. Things will arise out of it that are spontaneously generated for you to realize what is.

Devotee: What place does meditation have in your company?

Lee: If you meditate and get caught up in personality aspects or in eccentricities, you are stuck on Lee. You are in effect meditating upon a personal idol. Meditating on me as guru is being open to Grace, open to who I am, rather than involved in what I say or do, or in deciphering me in terms of, "He said this last week, but now he says this." It is not allowing any personality factors or functional forms to interfere with one's open attention. That doesn't mean that you can't use an image of me, because I am not at all exclusive of Lee Lozowick. I am Lee Lozowick, absolutely and inclusively. Meditating on the separate person that you imagine me to be is the delusion.

Meditation is one of the bigger traps, because most people have pleasant experiences while meditating. That can really lock you in if you have a pleasing experience. You will typically want to meditate more so that you will have more pleasant experiences. If you are not meditating, you have to deal with the world. When you are meditating, even for a short period of time, you don't have to deal with the world at all. You can withdraw, bliss out, shut down.

When meditation is appropriate, it is simply an expression of spiritual life. The process of appropriate meditation is to bring you to a place where there won't be any drama associated with your experiential states, only the full and potent humor of the Divine. When meditation is done on a strictly formal basis, it is very often not appropriate. It is done strictly to get you away from where you already are. Not only is that inappropriate, it is impossible.

I did not say not to meditate, by the way. When one does formal meditation in my Presence, Grace manifests in your life with varying degrees of intensity. The condition is always here and never changes. Work goes on twenty-four hours a day, whether in daylight or in dreams. It is always going on. You can be open to my Presence regardless of whether I am physically with you or not.

Meditation is ultimately a spontaneous affair. It is definitely not ritualistic. If there was something specific to do every time you meditate, that would be something in the chela stage to point out to people how quickly they will get attached to one practice or form of activity versus something else. Meditation in my company is being open to Grace. Period.

You never actually meditate. You are always being meditated by the Divine. Meditation is the very act of life itself. When you talk or sing, when you are physically active or very relaxed, when you are laughing or crying, that is all a form of meditation. If you think of meditation as being a special activity that you have to do in a certain position, the only thing you are doing is reinforcing your sense of separateness from God.

God and meditation are two words that from my perspective mean the same thing: the very process of life. God is the prior condition, the raw nature of existence, unqualified consciousness. Meditation is the direct awareness of the fact that you are Alive, consciousness, existence. All forms of your life are meditation: eating, sleeping, working. And if there is someone to know that you are aware, that is not ultimate meditation. You are still observing, analyzing, and judging.

You are meditation. No matter what you are doing, you are the process of meditation. If you have to stop what you are doing to meditate, and think in terms of "Now I'm meditating and then I wasn't," you missed the point of meditation.

Devotee: Could you tell us a way that we could use you as guru?

Lee: It's interesting that every time I have an intuition about something, it proves to be right. If I have an intuition about a technique, teacher, spiritual experience, or state of consciousness, when I eventually experience what my intuition was about, I notice that it was accurate. It has always proven to be that way. I have intuited a number of things that I have never experienced. All of that intuition is available to you. You might be thinking, "Well, how do I use that?" It is not a matter of asking me which breathing technique or which mantra is going to give you a certain experience. It means that, when you formally meditate or otherwise, you can call upon this one, in any particular frame of mind or state you are in, for an experiential, conscious understanding that will help you see what you're up to, help you see your position. Since I exist on all planes and in all worlds, every possible experience, conceivable or non-conceivable, is available to you through me.

Experience will not get you anywhere, but that is no reason not to be open to experience. Rejecting experience is an extreme form of trying not to search, which is another form of the search. It is not experience in itself that is deluded, but clinging or grasping experience. I can be used, very simply, as a focal point for experience, recognizing that it's not going to get you anywhere, but also recognizing that there is no reason not to experience either. Deliberately trying **not to** experience is the same thing as deliberately trying **to** experience.

Devotee: Your answers always lead me to more questions, and I can't seem to come to a solution.

Lee: If you find yourself questioning, that's okay. Just recognize that the guru is complete. The questions have to do with you, not with the guru's teaching. They show your own suffering, not a lack in the guru. If you are concerned with solutions, you are stuck. The real question is, "Who are you?" and there is no conceptual solution to that one. If you are concerned with the answer, that interferes with understanding and being present with the question. The lack of "solution" is proof of the question's pertinence.

You need to know who you truly are. Once you find out who you are, you will realize the incredible absurdity of all the questions that are asked. There are no answers and no questions, only God. Our relationship dissolves the question, it does not answer it. Any questions?

Devotee: You say that there is only God, and you also speak of "our relationship". If there is only God, how can there be relationship, which involves two things that are related to one another?

Lee: Relationship indicates the play of the worlds within the inclusiveness of consciousness. It is impossible to be out of true relationship. The reason that is so is because there is nothing to be related to. If there was something to be related to, it would obviously be possible to be out of relationship as distinct from being in relationship. Since there is nothing to be related to, you are always in perfect relationship. You exist as that. You are not in relationship, but strictly speaking you exist as perfect relationship.

Devotee: You seem very radical compared to other teachers and gurus. Do you consider yourself to be a traditional guru or a radical guru?

Lee: The word "radical" is used to mean over and against society's convention. It has nothing to do with traditional spiritual life at all. There is no such thing as radical spirituality. It has always been the same. There has only ever been one; Gautama and Jesus and all the rest of them were always the same one.

The traditional guru has always been wild, confronting, contradictory and unconventional. When the real guru is Alive in the world, there are typically only a minor percentage of people involved in spiritual life who ever recognize him or her as Lord. It is usually long after that person is dead that he or she is glorified and accepted traditionally. Then written works come out and learned people pay homage. It is rare for the guru to be recognized in life except by a few who gather around that one. This is why I tell you to primarily study the person rather than the dharma. You will discover that the awakened ones were considered crazy by society and that their lives contradicted everyone's preconceived notions of spiritual life. When I read about the great masters, I don't find any difference between them and myself. In their time they were very radical. In the context of the awakened one throughout history, I don't see myself as being radical at all. In the context of society's convention, I am.

The gurus who are Alive in God are always the most highly criticized. They are always doing stuff that is not accepted, like criticizing all the current teachers. Any teacher that is coming from a place that is beyond criticism doesn't care if I criticize him, but just sees the humor in it. All of the teachers who are really into meditation and helping people be better and doing good, are very serious about what they are doing, so they can't take criticism. They should be able to see it all as part of the play, and yet they don't. They get very personal about it. They think it is terrible that I criticize them, even when I don't use their personal names. They have all these ideas of what I am supposed to be like: humble and merciful and whatever bullshit conceptions they have. The only reason that all the other teachers haven't made the same claims that I make, the only reason that they get angry when I say that I have assumed the work and they haven't, is because they know that they can't make those claims and they haven't assumed the work. It is so fundamentally simple. If they assumed it, they would make the claim. It's ridiculous, all this self-righteous posturing. They criticize the guru because he does and says things that seem contradictory. When there is freedom in activity, what's the difference? When there is not freedom in activity, there is a big difference. Then it just goes to fulfill ego. If I didn't contradict myself, I would be a philosopher, not the guru. I am the only one who can contradict myself...without contradicting myself!

Devotee: Speaking of contradiction, you have said that your teaching is one of dependence on Grace, of spiritual slavery. Just now you spoke of "freedom in activity". Would you please explain?

Lee: The concepts of "liberation" and "freedom" in spiritual life are extremely misleading. They imply that you are actually in bondage, an implication which is deluded, and that the awakened one exercises choice or liberty. For the guru there is only the unbroken, continuous play of the Divine, and no choices. That is what I call "freedom in activity". After all, who is enslaved? And who is enslaving? There is only slavery, not coercion.

As far as dependence is concerned, the guru and the perfect devotee are the ones who are truly independent. Nobody else has any degree of independence. Everybody is dependent on karma and programming. The awakened one is independent to the degree that he or she is free in God, not "free" in the world's terms. Being free in God is very different. Once one is awake, one sees illumination present as that one's very activity. Rather than something that is attained, the awakened state is always present as your very activity; sleeping, waking, conscious, unconscious, it doesn't matter. Independence, or freedom in God, is simply the movement of the Divine flowing as it will, naturally and spontaneously. You can call that "freedom" and imagine what you like, since the awakened ones have all said that they are free, yet they literally have no choice about the Divine movement.

These opposites of slavery/freedom, dependence/independence are ultimately neither true nor false. They serve my purpose, which is to point out to you things about your sadhana, and to help you recognize what is. Like all concepts, they fall away.

Devotee: Why is it necessary for one to devote oneself exclusively to you? There are other teachers and gurus who have a lot to offer, and it seems like a more universal concept to take what they have, too.

Lee: Yes, that is a more universal concept, and that is one reason why there are so few awakened ones in the world. Most seekers do what you described. People who have been around for awhile go guru-skipping. They go from one to another to another. How long do they last with a guru? Maybe six months to a year. Then they go to somebody else, because as soon as there is a threat to their structure, their mind, being infinitely creative, says, "You need somebody with a better rap." And there is always somebody around with a better rap. If you get off on being eclectic, you are not likely to serve the guru. You are more likely to split as soon as you are challenged, in order to find someone who will indulge you.

After Shaktiananda guru, you come to Lee. You think, "Lee has got a good rap. Far out! This is it!" "It" is another upgraded strategy. But the difference is that what Lee can do is rip off all of the strategies, undermining them until you realize that it is all a strategy. Then he assumes you, and it is all over but the laughing.

Devotee: Do you remember your past lives?

Lee: During one of my lifetimes I was sitting under a tree. The trunk was made of diamonds and the leaves were rubies and emeralds. Whenever anybody would approach me, a golden ray would beam from one of my chakras, depending on that person's obstruction. The paths in this land were made of silver and the grass was finely spun silk. It was exquisite. And as the birds flew overhead, they dropped turds made of topaz. It's true.

Devotee: The body has been blamed for a lot of things, including suffering and sin. Does this have any validity?

Lee: The motivation in a lot of "spiritual" practices is to give up the body, to leave the body or transcend it. They teach that the body is a trap, trapping us in the senses and the maya of the world. That is just a basic psychological resistance to what is seen as dirty, distasteful, uncomfortable, and painful. There is an incredible trauma associated with the body, and one is programmed internally and in society to have a great dislike for the body and a desire to alleviate or eliminate the discomfort associated with it. People who really identify distastefully with the body get involved in those aspects of the search that emphasize suppressing "the flesh" and so on.

The body is what everything else is: simply appropriate, simply natural. The body is just the body, and bodies occasionally have muscle cramps and illnesses, and get scratched and bleed, and of course, a body is mortal. Why should the body be any different than it is? It shouldn't be. Anything that tries to make the body different is another form of practice motivated to repair supposed damage. That is the delusion, that there is damage, that the body needs to be fixed up, altered, purified, suppressed, or in any way made better. The body is perfectly appropriate the way it is. And by the way, there is a natural strength and health to the body that is appropriate for it, so I do require exercise and a life-sustaining diet in this community. That is different than a belief that the body has to be changed. It is simply appropriate for the body to be in good shape, for there is a natural strength and resilience that the body can express when it is allowed to.

Devotee: If everything is already perfect, and there is nothing to attain, why should I do anything in spiritual life?

Lee: For the same reason that you asked the question. You can tell yourself that everything is already complete and perfect until kingdom come (which means forever), and there is still an infinite difference between that and consciously living God. The delusion is far more deeply rooted than at the level of mere belief. The process of the guru is to awaken you totally from the sleep of delusion, not just to inculcate a new belief-system.

What guru gave up his or her appropriate spiritual practice after assuming the function of guru? Ramana Maharshi said very often that the awakened one didn't need to meditate anymore. Yet Ramana Maharshi meditated. I am always saying that I don't have to do any of this stuff, and yet I exercise every day, follow diet, and I don't smoke or drink. Even though I don't need any of it, I still follow the practices. Anybody that claims to be awake, and does that as an excuse not to do service, exposes himself as a fraud. But it's a beautiful strategy, I must admit.

Devotee: What about obsession for God, isn't that a kind of seeking?

Lee: It most definitely is. That's the paradox. It is a kind of seeking, and at the same time, you have to be obsessed. Nobody has ever awakened who has not been obsessed with the Divine. It is a form of seeking, because if you are obsessed with God, you don't feel that you have it and are therefore doing something to go about getting it. Even if you are doing nothing, that is still doing something.

You still have to have an obsession for God, and seeking will continue until you stop seeking, that is, until you wake up. Ultimately, all seeking is seeking, and as such it is separative. However, motivated seeking that is obviously remedial in nature, and that is pursued in order to create an experience or high, will create such an experience, which will automatically propagate the search for more experience. Obsession for God, although still seeking which is always motivated for release, will open you up and be the wedge that allows Grace to be active in your life. Doing a certain meditation or a certain breathing technique to create an experience will never open you up to Grace, only to more experience. That is the relative difference between obsession and other kinds of seeking.

Devotee: Up until devotee stage, do we always have an ulterior motive?

Lee: Always. And that motive is individual self-validation. If you didn't have that motive, you would be a devotee. It's as simple as that.

I offer no hope, no consolation, no compensation. It is all here. It is not my job to tell you about the pearly gates and what everyone will get as reward. There is no reward. Period. There is only the fiery, dancing, mischievous Divine play. That is no consolation to the life of separation, which is very cold and serious and doesn't dance. There is nothing for me to do but enjoy what is, fully and completely. For the life of separation, there is the deluded hope of heaven.

Listen: It is just birth, death, birth, death. That is the joy of what is. But people think that when they die, they are going to melt into the great "beyond".

Devotee: And rest in the Elysian fields, popping grapes in their mouth.

Lee: Seedless grapes, yet. That's it! That is heaven. All the fruits are pitless. Did you get that? All the cherries are grown on the trees pitted, big black bing cherries that are pitted naturally. Oh, to just live on bing cherries, every one of them dark and sweet. And never crack a tooth. Amen.

THIRTY-ONE

IT IS VERY humorous to think in terms of somebody having the title, "realized". As if realization was quantitative! People imagine that it is possible to look at someone, and from certain characteristics of that person, deduce, "Yes, that one is realized," or "No, that one can't be realized." It's like saying, "Yes, this person has the measles."

It is really impossible to quantify realization because one's Divine nature is just that: one's nature. It is not a fact of one's personality. It is not definable. It is not something. It is the very vibrant, flowing, constantly moving and changing Divine process. And it is always a fact. When people talk about being realized as if it was in some way unique, that in itself shows lack of insight into realization. We are never "realized" in contrast to being "not realized." There is a point when we wake up. There is a time when we say that we are unconscious, asleep, separate, not in touch with our Divine nature. And all of that has nothing to do with our actual condition, nothing to do with what is. Awakening is a matter of consciously living realization, not becoming or attaining anything.

Realization is ordinary life. The guru is the most ordinary of persons, since he lives ordinary life consciously. Sometimes people say, "You are so calm and so centered. You just never get angry." Yet a lot of the time, they will literally never want to see me again. They will always remember me, not because I indulged their fascinations, but because I frustrated them. It is not what the guru does or can do, it is not the tremendous meditation that you get and all of the energy rushes, rather it is the guru's ordinariness that is most baffling and most effective. For the guru there is no division between "spiritual" and "mundane" life. I eat and sleep, laugh and cry, make love and make fun. I am just myself, in utter ordinariness.

My sacrifice as guru is that, instead of simply enjoying this perfectly ordinary Divine life by myself, I function to bring others to the awakening of their life in God. I enjoy that sacrifice, for I wish to see you live this condition as I do. That "wish" is spontaneous; Lee did not make a conscious choice to be guru. There was no decision to be made. The awakened one spontaneously assumes the function of guru.

For whatever reason, people begin to accumulate around the illumined one after the assumption of the role of guru. The community begins to gather. The ones who are fortunate enough to be with the guru naturally feel rather special, different than run-of-the-mill people. Everybody is actually the same. We have some very talented people, musicians and artists and people with a good business sense and so on, and even though they've got it together in a sense, they are just like anybody else. Ego is still there and mind is still fighting like hell to survive. That's the way it is everywhere, in every community. What makes this community slightly different is that you are with me, and haven't got a prayer for survival.

The process of my manifestation in the world is to establish permanent awakening in devotees. There is no compromise in my service to you; I serve nothing less than who you are. And I intend not to establish a lineage, not naming a successor to me as has been done in the past; I intend to establish a community of devotees. Whenever there is a lineage, and only an individual present as Grace in the world, that is a gross limitation. The transformation that takes place during that one's lifetime for those who are with that individual, is evident during his or her lifetime, yet after that one's death, what transformation is there? Nothing real has happened except that during the lifetime of the teacher, certain people have lived in the state of transformation, without intelligent participation in the process. Instead of setting the forest on fire, one candle has passed its flame to another, or, as is often the case, the candle has flickered out all together. You can live in my physical presence and be a true devotee, even now, and yet were I to die tomorrow, you wouldn't be a true devotee anymore. You would have been living in my Presence without consciously being that Presence. You can live in a state of transformation without being at all aware of what is going on for you. That is the way most so-called communities have been run, and there has been the assumption that true devotees are present, because there are true devotees as long as the master is there. As soon as the master dies, the state of transformation vanishes, and what has always been there anyway, their life of suffering, kicks in again. Only by the understanding of our relationship prior to the mind is permanent awakening established. In the true community, it is no longer the unconscious relationship of the devotee to the guru that is manifested, but the guru-devotee relationship is lived as relationship itself, as existence itself.

Devotee: You mentioned that ego is still there for us, and that mind is still fighting to survive. How do you overcome that resistance to awakening?

Lee: The ego can be tricked. That is the guru's key. The ego can't be reasoned with. You can't sit down with the ego and say, "Don't you see that it's all suffering?" or "Wouldn't you be happier if you realized God?" The ego will simply not respond to reason. Fortunately it can be tricked. Perfect devotees are always tricked into being perfect devotees.

Initially you have to willfully follow the functional requirements of appropriate activity. It is not that you really understand that they are appropriate, or not even that you feel you are going to be healthier or happier if you follow them. It is initially a matter of literally using some kind of will-power, generating the will to make you go through everything, to make you comprehend why you are involved in spiritual life.

So you start following the requirements, you give up meat and cigarettes and so on. You are pretending, acting out appropriate activity. You would really rather eat meat and smoke cigarettes. But it's not such a big deal, so you go along with the guru and do it. After a while, you start to forget that you are acting. You don't miss meat, in fact, you are a dogmatic vegetarian. You're really into it, and it has become second nature to you. You go a little longer, and then you even forget that you ever were acting. It seems as if you were always that way.

The same process goes on in other aspects of your life with the guru. So at first, with devotion and its expressions in prasad and pranam, you are aware that it is just an act, and you do it anyway. When you approach me with your gift, you are very self-conscious and you try to force yourself into a devoted frame of mind, which is, of course, impossible. Later on, it begins to seem very natural for you, and you experience love for the guru. Eventually, you forget that it was ever a pretense, and you really believe that you are devoted.

Most "gurus" stop there, because, to all appearances, you really are devoted. Actually you have become an excellent actor, to the point of losing yourself in the role. That's all. It is not real spiritual life, but a facsimile of it. When you really believe in your devotion, when you have been absorbed into the act, that is when the ego can be tricked. At that point you are very vulnerable, because you are sincerely convinced that you've gotten somewhere. As long as you know that you are acting, the guru can't touch you, because you are in control of it all, you are still the actor, aware of what's going on. As soon as you forget that you are acting, and you think that it is your natural condition, you become very open to the guru. When mind knows that it's in control, the guru doesn't have a chance, since mind will create fresh strategies to avoid the guru at every step. When mind forgets, the guru can slip in and hit you with some genuine devotion. That's when real movement starts, when the wedge starts to be put in.

When people in this vulnerable state start to experience real devotion, they start to contract because they realize that they were never devoted. Then they look at their life and realize that everything they have ever done parallels that. They thought that they were good fathers, and they really weren't. They had forgotten that they dislike children. They start to look at their entire life and they see that they have always forgotten the way it really is, and that it is all an act. When they begin to see that their whole life has been invalid, the strategies of mind do not offer much as alternatives. That is when the argument of the guru becomes very present in their life. Their only resort is the guru. If they are in the community, there is really no choice involved. What is left but the relationship with the guru? That is the first intense and honest turning to me that occurs. Then the movement of Grace starts to present itself more forcefully.

That time when the ego is vulnerable to my trickery is basically later on in the disciple stage, towards the transition to devotee stage. Until then the ego is just too strong to be tricked, especially as observer of the drama, which is characteristic of the disciple stage. Despite the rhetoric of non-attainment, it is perfectly appropriate for the disciple to believe that he or she is getting somewhere. It couldn't be otherwise. If the disciple did not believe that, he or she would be a devotee. Denying or avoiding that is just ignoring what is. People's basic activity is not going to change, not in the disciple stage, anyway.

The process of our relationship involves the undermining of your basic assumptions concerning life. The expression of this relationship that I need to have, can not be exhibited or lived in the context of conventional society. People get offended when the guru tips the cart of separation. So our relationship is one that needs to be applied in an environment which is in large part exclusive of the world. Society can not deal with this kind of process on even the most superficial levels, much less in its full measure.

If we were not exclusive, and we were philosophically directed to serving the world at large, people would take that service without doing anything about it, without conscious participation or understanding. In effect, we would still be allowing mediocrity rather than transforming it. People have to see the true community as unreachable, as a dream. They have to be willing, it would seem, to crawl their way to it, so that it will be meaningful for them. The conventional ways of "serving" the world have only made matters worse. Look around you.

If the community is comforting and open-ended, it will allow the world to continue to be ignorant. If the community is exclusive and rare and valuable, it will serve the world by having it know that the Divine Presence is available and present for it. I recognize that there are few people who will understand. I simply present the possibility of my company, and the people who are ready for that will be drawn to me. And I am not interested in being overly exclusive. It is tempered by the game, by seeing where people are at. If I applied the strict standards of the Divine without tempering them by the game, there would be so few people around that it would be uninteresting for me, and therefore no game at all.

Ideally, the ultimate community would be the world itself. Utopia is when truth becomes so evidently clear that everyone becomes the perfect community. That is a real pipe dream. If there are a hundred people in the community living satsang, that is incredible, fantastic. The world has never seen anything like that. So it's a matter of optimum results, not of utopia.

Devoting one's life to God is not a prospect that is attractive to the vast majority of people in the world. Everyone wants to further their own little cause; it is "me" against "everyone else". How could I exhibit the full force of this relationship in such an environment? The delusion of separation is the very fabric of society.

We went to a play in New York and after we got out, we went to the parking lot and there was a gigantic line of people waiting for their cars. We got in the back of the line, and as people were walking up to the lot, practically every one would complain and moan and bitch, "Oh my God, what a bore! We'll be here forever!" Everyone apparently thought that he should be first. That is all of you! Do you recognize yourself? This is your deluded, stuck image of yourself. You need to know this, for the way of the world, self-destruction, is your way:

It is five-thirty and you are in a traffic jam thinking, "Why does everybody slow down? If everyone would just keep moving at forty miles per hour it would be fine." It is really annoying to be in a traffic jam, because after all, this little ego of yours is the center of the universe. There is nothing even slightly amusing about the ego, because it is really important and significant. And especially this particular one, because it is yours.

Stop and think about whatever you want to be different. Why do you want things to change? What makes you think you deserve it? Is it because life is basically flawed, an endless waiting line or a big joyless traffic jam, and you want to "get" there but you are stuck here?

Someone came to me and said, "I never knew that I was unhappy until you told me." It is interesting how many people think that they are happy, and as soon as they are told that they are not, they start seeing where they really are beneath what they thought to be happiness. They start to consciously recognize their life of separation. They may attribute their unhappiness to the guru, but he only brought to the surface what was there for them anyway. Society will only maintain that life; the guru will destroy it.

I am not here to support you. I am not here to be leaned on. I am not the spiritual counterpart to the great welfare state. I am not here to be argued with, either; I am only here to tell you what to do, not to care for you and provide for you, certainly not to be that figurehead to whom you look for salvation.

Your definition, your agreement as to my identity, is of no concern to me. Lee has learned to become no one. He is not interested in agreement making him someone. It is uncomfortable to be made someone, and our relationship is founded on the fact that I am going to allow you to join me in this place of no one and no thing.

If you look to Lee as the great protector, very much as masses of people have looked to the government as the great provider, disillusionment is bound to occur. Just as people have put their faith in the great welfare state, and been disillusioned when they discovered that it was corrupt to its very core, so you will be disillusioned if you put your faith in your figurehead, your guru-idol, for I will smash your idol.

Even while it was shown that the state was totally corrupt, people allowed themselves to pretend that everything was fine. They are still comfortable, within their disillusionment, to be protected. The guru is not your protector by any means. Neither is he your savior or leader. He is simply your nature. You can't use that as your refuge, excuse, game plan, compensation, ideal, or even your fulfillment. It just is. Period.

If your conception of our relationship is one of being protected at any cost, you will not be happy and humorous in my company. You will be fearful. Your relationship with me is one of joy and the certainty of bright optimism, one of awe for playing the game that allowed you to be present with a player who can be so enjoyable. That's all. Be happy that we are together, be present with me, and you can enjoy it all.

How often I used to go to various teachers! I didn't really care what they said and I never had any questions. I was never much interested in much of the teaching, besides a moderate curiosity. I went only to be with those teachers. That should be your attitude in sadhana. Be happy just because the guru is present and not for any other reason. Your sadhana should be one of simply appreciating the Presence of the guru.

There is only God. All happiness can only be found in true spiritual life. The spiritual masters have held the key throughout the ages, and it is no different today. There is only devotion; there is only service to God. God is none other than what is, inclusive of reality, of all worlds, particularly of this world. The Divine is inclusive of the world of the senses, the world of form and three dimensions, the world of the mind; God is undifferentiated from everything, non-different from the very reality that is.

Real spiritual life has always been the same. There has never been an alteration in it. From the earliest times of recorded history and before, up to today, real spiritual life has always been lived exactly the same way. There is not even the slightest difference, regardless of the different ages, societies and conventions that have applied when the spiritual community has been present. It is the timeless, ancient life that is always new, always ripe. And it is never broken.

The guru's contribution to the world is not in some speculative philosophy or system of belief. It is in his uniqueness, his eccentricity, his selfishness, his commitment, his vision. The fact that what I would have for you are the traditionally sought-after goals of friendship, peace of mind, faith, love, comfort, happiness, and pleasure, does not mean that they are my gifts to the world. My gift to the world is my very Heart, and I am glad in giving it.

The vision of my life-relationship with the community is one of a very basic and simple life: self-sustaining, self-sufficient, natural. It is one of eating simply, playing with family and friends, enjoying reading and studying, enjoying exercise, being Alive and productive, absorbed in the pleasure of the Divine. With laughter resounding at least eighteen hours a day.